JAMES DEAN
AMERICAN ICON

Photo Credits: Page 285

Photo Consultant/Archivist DAVID LOEHR
Text Editor COCO PEKELIS
Book Design by STANLEY STELLAR
Cover by ANDY WARHOL©
Back Cover by KAREN SANDT©
First published in Great Britain in 1984
by Sidgwick and Jackson Limited

Originally published in the United States of America in 1984
by St Martin's Press

First published in softcover in 1985

JAMES DEAN: AMERICAN ICON Copyright © 1984 by
David Dalton and Ron Cayen.

ISBN 0-283-99159-3 hardcover
ISBN 0-283-99160-7 softcover

Printed in Great Britain by
R. J. Acford, Industrial Estate, Chichester, Sussex
for Sidgwick and Jackson Limited
1 Tavistock Chambers, Bloomsbury Way
London WC1A 2SG

JAMES DEAN

AMERICAN ICON

Text by David Dalton   *Photo Editor* Ron Cayen

SIDGWICK & JACKSON • LONDON

CONTENTS

Times Square, New York, 1955.
©DENNIS STOCK/MAGNUM.

INTRODUCTION

JAMES DEAN was the strongest influence of any actor that ever stepped in front of the camera. Ever! And that strength has never really diminished. If anything, it has grown. Young people who weren't even *alive* at the time are still influenced by his work. That's the power of film when it's done that well — which is not very often.

In the mid-fifties, young people really didn't have a voice, they were just null and void. No one dealt with them or took them seriously until James Dean came along. I was just fifteen and living in Ohio at the time Jimmy died, but he left me with the impression that *anything* was possible.

Jimmy dealt in a very special and spiritual way with people. He was in touch with himself and he reached out to anyone who would ever see his work. And it's there for the life of the film. You never thought he was acting. Whether you were awkward or graceful, he made you feel good about being yourself. That's what Jimmy was above all — himself. And that's what an actor's job really is: to be able to do publicly what everyone else does privately. James Dean was able to do that better than anyone else.

Dean was just a genius at a time when one was needed. There were only two people in the fifties: Elvis Presley who changed the music, and James Dean who changed our lives. Nothing really happened again until Bob Dylan came along — and Dylan himself was influenced by Dean. If you can imagine the strength and influence Dylan had in the sixties, that's what Dean was to the fifties.

When I was a young actor in New York, there was a saying that if Marlon Brando changed the way actors acted, James Dean changed the way people lived. I believe that. No one came before him, and there hasn't been anyone since.

MARTIN SHEEN

A-1
FAIRMOUNT,
INDIANA

Why, I am as a long-lost boy that went
At dusk to bring the cattle to the bars,
And was not found again, though Heaven lent
His mother all the stars.
"A Country Pathway," James Whitcomb Riley

Fairmount, Indiana. The town's original name, "A-1," reflecting the surveyor's coordinates, was both a humble "X" on the map and a wry statement of the self-effacing pride of Quakers. Like Jett Rink (the defiant ranch hand portrayed by James Dean in *Giant*), Indiana's Quakers felt "ain't nobody king in this country...no matter what they may be thinkin'." Fairmount is a sleepy country town whose customs, morality, and inventiveness are, like Jimmy, quintessentially American. Fairmount's values—even the land itself—suggest the ingenuity, simplicity, and hidden ironies of all people who live on the frontier. The frontier is the border, the edge of consciousness, and its people filter the old through the new while pushing back the boundaries.

At a high school football game. Age 17,
Fairmount, Indiana.
LOEHR COLLECTION.

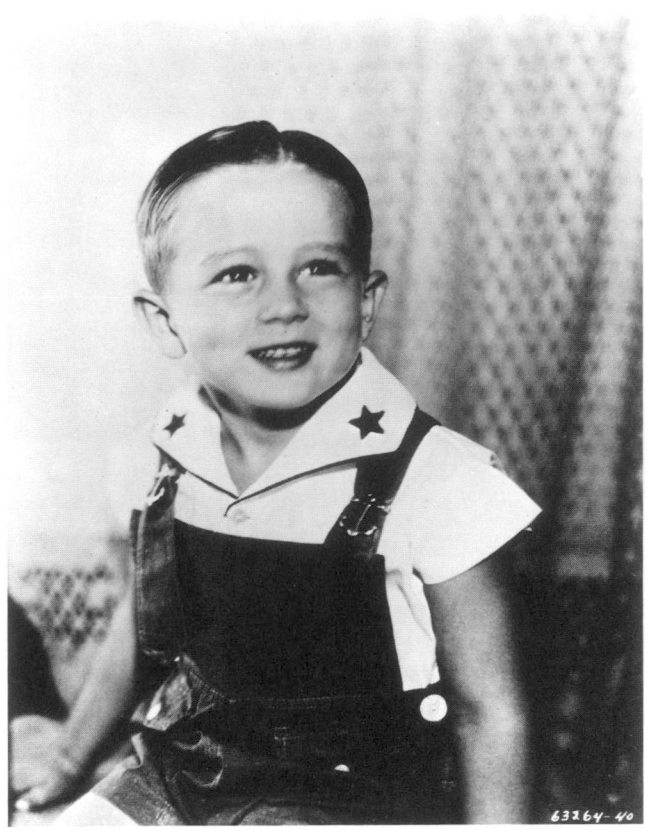

The Oxymoronic Kid himself: awkwardly graceful, withdrawn and self-possessed. Left: Age 4. After the death of his mother, nine-year-old Jimmy went to live on his aunt and uncle's farm in Fairmount, Indiana. Below: Although only five foot eight, he was to break the pole vault record for Grant County by the time he was seventeen.
Right: With cousin, "Markie" Winslow.
LOEHR COLLECTION.

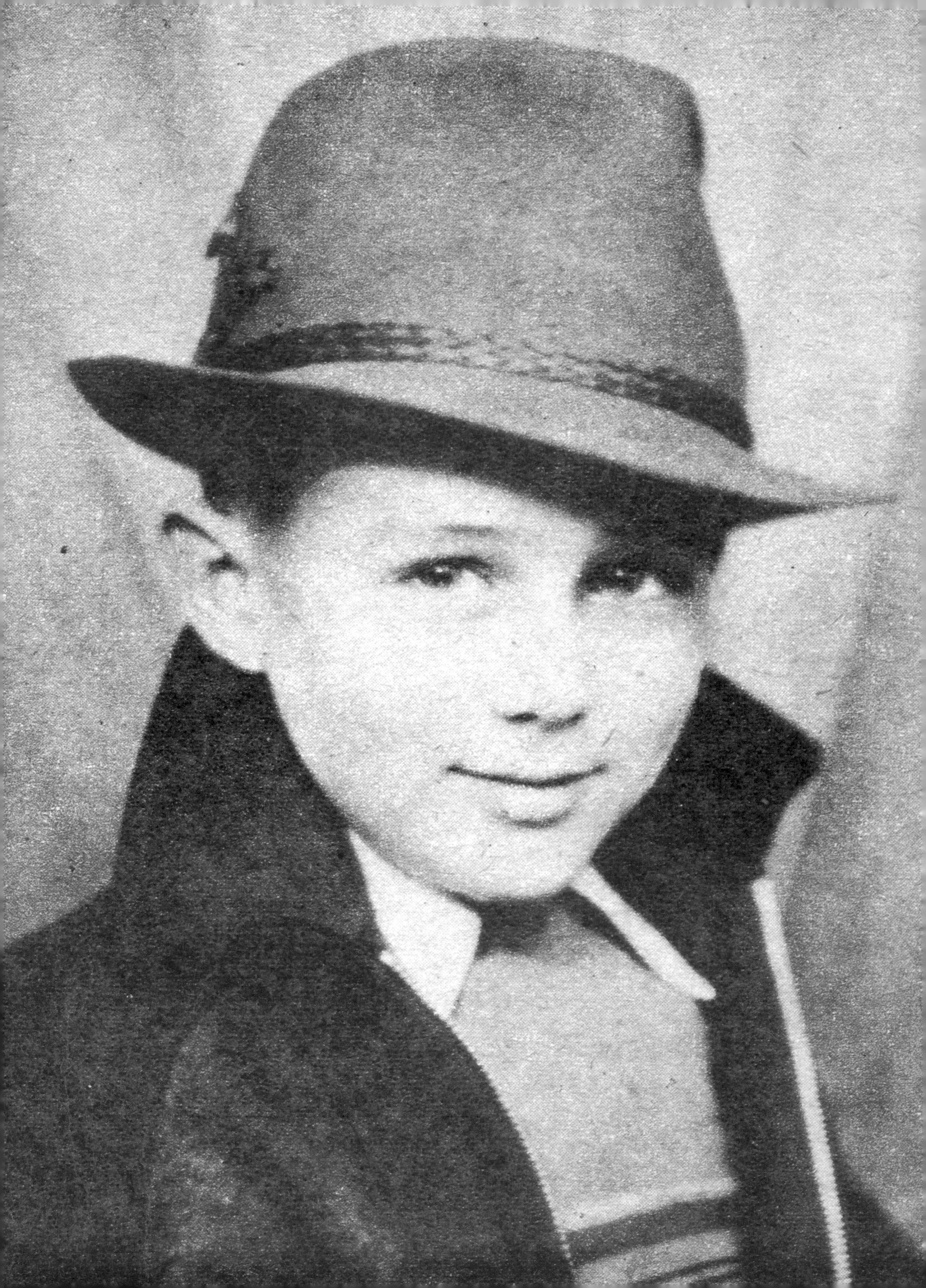

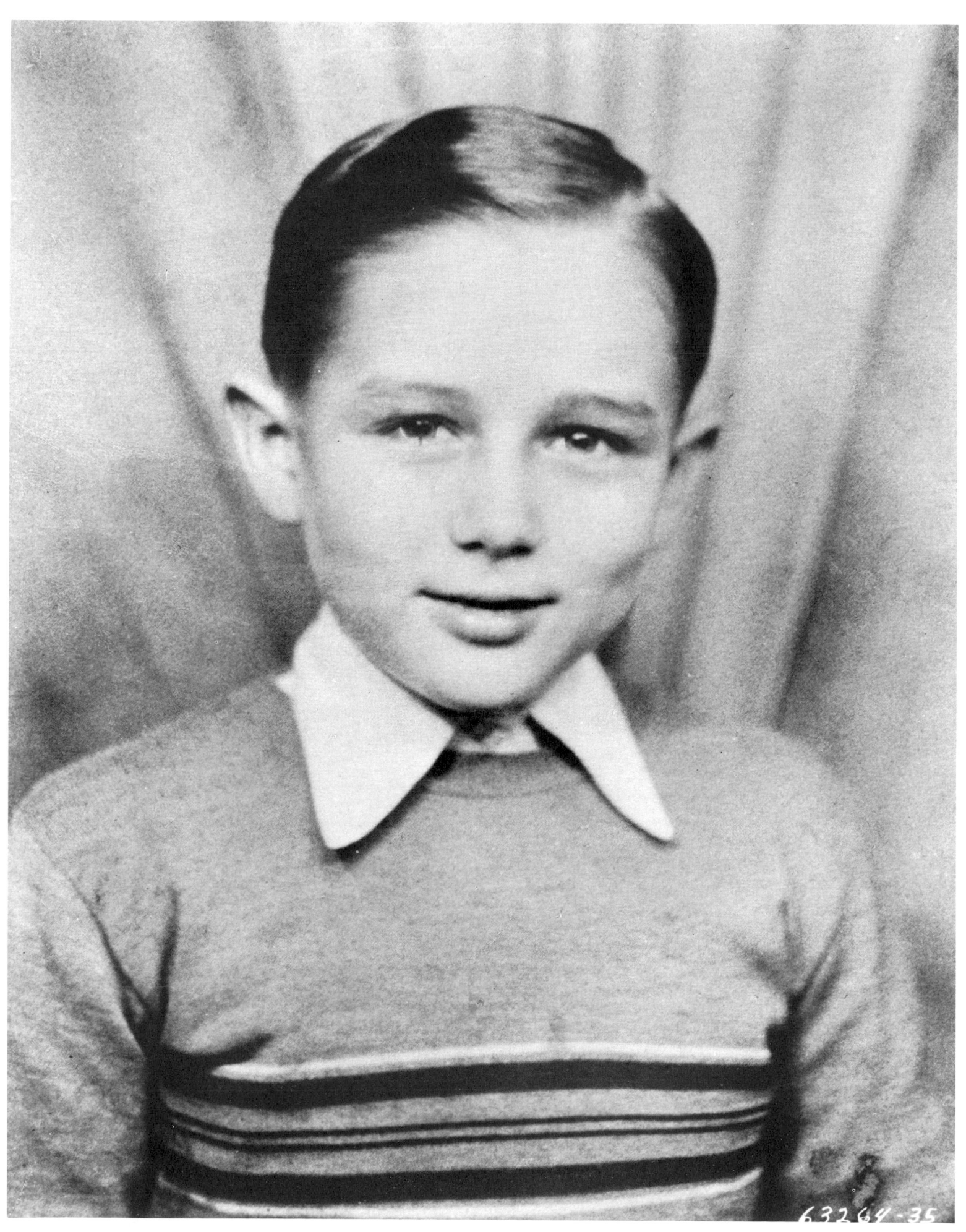

The face that was to become as well known as that of Mickey
Mouse or Mao takes shape. Age 8, Santa Monica, California.
LOEHR COLLECTION.

13

The town itself is so representative in its plainness and generic values that it is almost invisible, an indecipherable repository of lost American frontier values usurped by Hollywood. Indiana is the true West of Johnny Appleseed, Jesse and Frank James, the Dalton Gang and the Wright Brothers. On the border between the wild and the new, it is a zone of transition where America realized itself. And it was in this fertile, nurturing Eden of the old American Adam that James Dean, as the Typical Grant County Boy, came of age. Its mysteries are his mysteries.

The old Palace movie theater is now the local bar, but apart from that, Fairmount hasn't changed much

since Jimmy left. The James Dean Factor has, inevitably, altered our perception of the town. It is now a place of pilgrimage, a numinous site. Dean imbues Fairmount with the aura of origins, and Fairmount substantiates the James Dean legend by binding it to the myth of American evolution.

Fairmount was physically inscribed in him. The first pioneers who settled in Fairmount left their mark on the land's surface just as indelibly as the face of James Dean imprinted itself on the landscape of the imagination. He remains within the range of Fairmount's umbilical eye: it was the home he always returned to and could calculate his distance from, a reservoir of uncoerced images and things he could draw on.

Jimmy mined and undermined his own history; the material for his star would be made out of the plasma of that past. Nothing more eloquently describes his intimate kinship with Fairmount than the pictures Dennis Stock shot of him for *Life* magazine (later published in Stock's *James Dean Revisited*). On a visit immediately following the completion of *East of Eden*, Stock caught Jimmy looking at himself for the last time in the mirror of his origins, contemplating his shadow in a frozen pool.

Dennis Stock: "February is a rough month in the Midwest — not the ideal time to observe anything, much less to probe your past. It is a lean, gray time, and that is the mood, too. But maybe this was part of Jimmy's constantly testing everything: nothing ought to be idyllic. As was so often the case with Jimmy, he seemed to stack the cards against himself."

Jimmy understood the nature of his debt to Fairmount, but he realized the precarious ecology involved in the exploitation of his personal substance. In *East of Eden*, Elia Kazan had forced him into a painful regurgitation of his strained relationship with his father. Jimmy's last pilgrimage to Fairmount reflected the need to resolve the essential dilemma of his success.

Stock: "At this point he was straddling two worlds — the world of his origins in Fairmount, and the early stages of stardom — and he knew instinctively that the two were in conflict. He went back to Fairmount to examine his origins and to preserve what was relevant."

But it was, Stock pointed out, for the last time. "When Jimmy posed in the driveway of his aunt and

uncle's house, he'd already written the caption for the picture: 'You can't go home again.'"

It was the home where Jimmy was never quite at home; the orphan, abandoned by his mother, deserted by his father, and, like Oedipus, brought up by "shepherds." Jimmy was part of Fairmount, but he was also apart from it. His awareness of being different from others began in Fairmount, despite all the love he got from Ortense and Marcus Winslow, the aunt and uncle who brought him up after his mother died; despite all the nurturing from his high school English teacher and drama coach, Adeline Nall; despite all the Hoosier humor and sense of place he got from that great tree of a man, Bing Traster, hometown historian and World Champion Liar; and despite all the curiosity about the great world beyond Fairmount's boundaries he absorbed from the Rev. James de Weerd, who introduced Jimmy to classical music, poetry, and philosophy.

"I was never a farmer," Jimmy said. "I always wanted out of there, but I never ran away, because I never wanted to hurt anyone." This ambivalence is pointed out with humorous irony in the "family portrait" Stock shot of Jimmy, titled "Tintype with Sow."

Stock: "When we speak of a tintype we usually think of a portrait or a family image. And family means where we come from, what we belong to. . . . It soon became clear that the barnyard animals easily accepted Jimmy, and he them. Don't underestimate that tintype with sow! A sow can be ferocious, and doesn't easily lend itself to the mad pose you see here."

If Jimmy's trip with Dennis Stock was a way of paying his last respects to Fairmount, the town has also had to come to terms with him. After all, who would want to leave Fairmount, let alone for anything *better*! And most people's impression of Fairmount is just that: it is a sort of perfect embodiment of hometown Americana as we always imagined it. Or maybe just remembered it from Hollywood movies. Of course, it *was* James Dean's hometown and, far from turning his back on it, he took it with him into the world; it was the subtext lying just beneath the surface in all his movies, his source and resource, his "inheritance incorruptible."

Adeline Nall, *genius loci* of Fairmount, is the pre-siding spirit at what have now become the annual pilgrimages that mark the anniversary of Jimmy's death. She has taught three generations of Fairmounters, and, at a screening of *East of Eden* in the Town Hall, she affectionately attempts to place them: "What's your name? Where are you from? Oh, you're from Fairmount? Were you in my class? What's your father's name? Oh yes, Jim was in my class! . . . He will always be my Jim, you know. One of the many wonderful students I've had."

Effervescent and benign, with a touch of waspish innuendo, Adeline is a genuine Hoosier character, and it's that indomitable Quaker spirit that she sees as the principal quality Fairmount bequeathed to Jimmy: "Character, very strong character; a very determined people. . . well, kinda set in their ways. There's a lot of power coming from that in this town, a lot of power. See, even Marcus's [Winslow] folks came over on the Mayflower and Jimmy was exposed to all of that tradition. Of course, you know, half his life was spent here in Fairmount and he was really a very unsophisticated boy, hadn't travelled or anything. The biggest thing about Jim growing up here is there wasn't a strong hand to guide him. His father wasn't in the picture at all; never has been."

As the oracle of Jimmy's theatrical origins, she has become an object of pilgrimage herself: "When Jim came to Junior High School for his seventh grade, he asked me to coach him in his W.C.T.U. [Women's Christian Temperance Union] reading, 'Bars.' Even then I recognized the talent of this gifted boy. Of course there's always the 'all-the-world's-a-stage' bit, but Jim knew how to *play* people; he could work *me* around his little finger! He was very observing of people and he also knew how to get their attention. 'It's better to be noticed than ignored,' he'd tell me. That's how he got all that publicity in Hollywood, you see. He knew he had to move fast; the army was breathing down his neck."

About the studied indifference to him Jimmy's hometown has affected over the years, Adeline continues to be nonplussed: "Oh, it's special, but it's a catty little town. People still don't want to give Jim the credit due him. At the twenty-fifth reunion of his

At eighteen, on his first bike, a Czech Whizzer. Main Street, Fairmount.
COURTESY NELVA JEAN THOMAS.

17

*Despite the "specs," Jimmy was a star of
the Quakers' high school basketball and
football teams.*
LOEHR COLLECTION.

high school [in 1974] Jim was the only deceased member from his class and can you imagine they wouldn't let in a reporter who wanted to do a little piece on Jim's classmates? Said it was *their* reunion. They think they're just as good as he is and they probably are in the eyes of the Lord, but *good night!* There is still a lot of jealousy about Jim in town, but he's now accepted as an artist and their greatest native son."

James Dean's mother, Mildred, has become Mother of All Morbidity, a psychological House of Usher. The dead woman in a sealed vault — the vault of Jimmy's own head — she prefigured the mother in Jimmy's first Broadway play, *See The Jaguar.* Mrs. Wilkins keeps her son, Wally, a prisoner in an abandoned ice locker.

> I used to ask me Ma:
> Let me out of the ice locker
> So I can see the birds
> And all the green things on the hill.
> And she would say:
> You wouldn't like out there. . .

The fact that there are few photographs of Mildred only added to her ghostly status in Jimmy's life. Her image comes as something of a shock. There are the high cheekbones and the sunken eyes she bequeathed to Jimmy and the Nefertiti hairstyle of another era. Yet she's so robust! Especially next to Winton, with his hermetic, imploded head. Countrified, yes, but hardly "the farm girl mother" in T. T. Thomas's highly fictitious "autobiography,"

Jimmy was headline news in the spring of 1949.

I, James Dean, "who when the years has broken off any real hope for herself, passed on to me the dusty dreaming of her youth."

Over the years, the make-believe theater that Jimmy's mother made for him has become more and more elaborate, a psychological site where Dean archaeologists tirelessly sift his mythic childhood for clues. It was a glass menagerie, a miniature world into which Jimmy, as creator and sole inhabitant, could retreat. Like all gifted actors, Jimmy had a child's unquestioning faith in make-believe and the naive ability to lose himself in his roles. His cardboard theater became more and more palpable until, like the facade of the Benedict's Gothic mansion in *Giant,* it haunted the whole screen.

Going to say goodbye to Jimmy after the last day of shooting on *East of Eden,* Julie Harris found him as inconsolable as a child whose spell has been broken: "I was just about to knock, going up the steps, and I heard this sobbing inside. And the first thought that came to me was, 'Surely he can't be alone.' And I knocked on the door. Nothing happened. So I kept knocking. And he opened the door and he was all red-eyed and crying. And he said, 'It's all over. It's all over.' I said, 'Oh, I didn't know anybody could feel that except myself.' He said, 'It's all over.' He was just like a child."

Nick Ray, who directed Jimmy in *Rebel Without a Cause,* also saw Jimmy as a child — the withdrawn, petulant child who would rather remain in his solitary, selfish reverie than play with the others or share his toys and fantasies with them. Ray: "Between belief and action lay the obstacle of Jimmy's deep obscure uncertainty. Disappointed or unsatisfied, he was the child who goes to his private corner and refuses to speak."

Perhaps, as T.S. Eliot said of Mark Twain, "only the child in him was adult." Of course, there was as much of the childish as the childlike in Jimmy, and Tony Parsons could not resist taunting him in *The New Musical Express:* " 'My mother died on me when I was nine years old. What does she expect me to do? Do it all by myself?' This from a California resident

First headline — state champion in the Indiana Dramatic Speaking Contest for his reading of Dickens's "The Madman." Age 18. COURTESY BOB PULLEY.

The 49ers, Fairmount High's seniors, on a class trip to Washington.
Jimmy, top row, center in 49er sweater with button missing.
COURTESY BOB PULLEY.

*Cool Cat Dean entertains at the High
School Sweetheart Ball, February 14,
1955.*
COURTESY SANDY ENGEL.

"*February is a rough month in the Midwest — not the ideal time to observe anything, much less probe your past,*" wrote photographer Dennis Stock about these pictures for a Life magazine story. Jimmy intended these images, shot on his last trip home, as a documentary re-creation of his roots. *Right: Reading from his favorite poet, James Whitcomb Riley.* ©DENNIS STOCK/MAGNUM

Hamming it up in the barnyard. Above, Jimmy parodies the traditional family portrait. Overleaf: For the last photograph of himself in Fairmount, Jimmy had Dennis Stock set up the shot in the driveway of the Winslow farm with him looking one way and his dog, Tuck, turning away from him. "It was his interpretation of that line, 'You can't never go home again.'" said Stock.
©DENNIS STOCK/MAGNUM

Courtesy Sylvia Bongiovanni

©Dennis Stock/Magnum.

Top: Jimmy's mother, Mildred. Below: Jimmy's grandmother, Emma Dean, in Jimmy's old room, Fairmount.

in his twenties with a big fat Warner Brothers contract to make motion pictures. What did he expect her to do? Rise from the dead every morning and make him breakfast?"

As time went on his dead mother became so much a part of his publicity, inner and outer, that Vampira (Maila Nurmi), who, like many Hollywood witches, reads the trades, found it only too easy to wound Jimmy on their first meeting. She described the encounter to Venable Herndon: "'Where is she?' Psychically, I knew him before I even met him, so I didn't waste words: 'Where is she?' He said, 'Who?' And I said, 'Your mother'; and he made a whooshing sound, reddened, and threw his arms over his head.

"And then immediately, he said, 'I want you to come to my apartment. I want to read a poem to you.' And it was actually a Ray Bradbury short story about a boy who hanged himself, a boy who had a close relationship with his mother.

"I found it disconcerting—his fascination with that story, because I felt it was his own suicide he was talking about. When I asked him, 'Where is she?'— his mother—and he said, 'She cut out.' I tried to get to the bottom of it: 'What do you mean, she cut out?' 'Well,' he said, 'she, you know, left, she died.' I asked, 'She killed herself, or she died?' 'Well,' he said, 'yes, she committed suicide, in a sense.' Intellectually, he knew she had died, but emotionally, he felt that she had abandoned him."

After Jimmy's death, Vampira posed in *Whisper* magazine before an open grave. Her ghoulish proposition appeared in the peculiar headline: "Darling, Come Join Me!"

Somewhat more eerie is the relationship between Jimmy and his mother suggested by this exchange with Dennis Hopper on the set of *Rebel*: "'What are you doing that I don't know?' And Jimmy said, 'Why do you think you became an actor?' I said, 'I hated my mother and my father, and I wanted to show them, when they were in the audience, that I was better.' He said, 'Well, my mother died when I was a kid. I used to cry on her grave and say, *Why did you leave me? Why did you leave me?* And that changed into, *I'm gonna show you! I'm gonna show you!* I'm gonna be great!'"

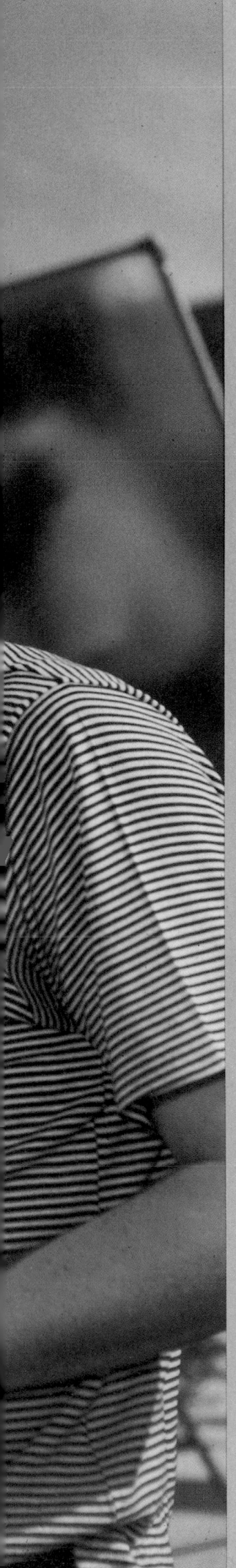

*With Nicholas Ray and Natalie Wood,
on the set of* Rebel, *April, 1955.*
LOEHR COLLECTION.

Shrill lobby cards for Rebel Without a Cause stress middle-class delinquency. Above: A black on black Jimmy Dean looking like a punkoid replicant of himself.

LOOK

15¢ OCTOBER 16, 1956

THE AMERICAN WOMAN:

She's winning the battle of the sexes

JAMES DEAN:

The story of

the strangest legend

since Valentino

*1956: a year after his death, he was
bigger than ever. These pages: Lobby cards
for Robert Altman's* The James Dean
Story *depicting scenes from James Dean's
ongoing life on earth: the existential
loner, adrift on the street of dreams; and
(self-recorded) Beat bongomaniac.*
LOEHR COLLECTION.

: East of Eden opens to the public,
10, 1955 in New York City.

rner-weary James Dean outside his
on location for Giant, *Marfa,*
July 1955. His fatal crash, two
s later, was to make him a world-
symbol.

THE KINGDOM OF CAIN

*Listen well, not to my words but
to the tumult that rages in your body
when you listen to your self.*
A Night of Serious Drinking, René Daumal

James Dean is absolutely hypnotic as he prowls the streets of Monterey in the first moments of *East of Eden*, a riveting physical presence that we track with voyeuristic fascination. It is pointless to debate whether or not he was a great actor; his identification with Cal Trask in *East of Eden* is consummate. It is the nature of the beast — a volatile, ephemeral creature who hints at voracious depths. As in all true fables, it is impossible to believe that the story is anything but the hero's version of it, and our suspension of disbelief makes the feat look easy.

Since Jimmy was always acting in the context of his own life, and, consequently, always unbalancing it, he didn't find it easy to recover from these willed dislocations. Dick Davalos, who played Cal's brother, Aron, observed: "Jimmy didn't know how to take hard criticism. He had no acting persona that could

Theater marquee, 1955, in Jimmy's birthplace, Marion, Indiana.
©WARNER BROS. INC.

These Famous Stars
PAID $50. A SEAT
for the New York Premiere of
'EAST OF EDEN'

PRODUCED BY ELIA KAZAN
John Steinbeck's
'EAST OF EDEN'

starring
Julie Harris · James Dean
Raymond Massey

WarnerColor   CinemaScope   Stereophonic Sound

Presented by
Warner Bros.

Starts SATURDAY APRIL 9th

soak it up and deal with it and not let it get through to him too personally. It just bewildered him. Then he'd have to sort himself out before he could sort out what was wrong in the acting."

Jimmy was, invariably, asked to play himself. John Steinbeck, who wrote *East of Eden* (the film is taken from the last third of his book), was introduced by director Elia Kazan to a then-unknown James Dean. Kazan: "I took Dean up there, and John liked him right away for the part. He said, 'Jesus Christ, he *is* Cal!' which is pretty close to truth—he was."

It is not as Jim Stark, the seductive propagandist of *Rebel Without a Cause*, or as Jett Rink, the sullen scapegoat of *Giant*, but as the complicated farm boy in *East of Eden* that Jimmy achieves his purest and most incandescent self-portrait. In *Rebel*, Jimmy will begin to show signs of a more self-conscious style. But the more intentional and didactic qualities of his acting were what made *Rebel* so universal, a message movie for both Ray and Dean, *the testament of teen.* And although his performance in *Giant* borders on the baroque, this image of Jimmy (slouched in an

antique convertible, legs stretched out, boots on, cowboy hat pulled down over his eyes, the Reata mansion in the background) has become a "household image" in the eighties.

Yet it is in *East of Eden* that we see the quintessential Dean: "All of us felt we were right there with him," said Adeline Nall. "Many of the movements of 'Cal Trask' were characteristic movements of James Dean. His funny little laugh which ripples with the slightest provocation, his quick jerky, springy walks and actions, his sudden change from frivolity to gloom—all were just like Jim used to do."

Elia Kazan knew intuitively what he was doing when he cast Jimmy to play Cal. Nevertheless, despite his prestige as a director and his track record with another unconventional actor, Marlon Brando (in *A Streetcar Named Desire, Viva Zapata,* and *On the Waterfront*), Kazan had to convince the studio heads at Warner Brothers to cast an unknown as the lead in a "major motion picture."

"To them it was like taking a horse from a horse-and-carriage and putting him in the Belmont Stakes," as Kazan put it. To convince them, he shot a series of highly erotic and suggestive black and white tests of Dean with Julie Harris and Dick Davalos at the Gjon Mili Studios in March of 1954. These images of James Dean spoke for themselves. Simultaneously benign, furtive, wholesome, malevolent, arrogant, and angelic, Jimmy's screen presence was disturbing, to say the least. Even threatening. These elusive qualities might have seemed gratuitous—if not actually oxymoronic—in an actor less willing to expose his own contradictions. But in James Dean they became the signs of a new sensibility.

Jimmy is an active principle unknown before him, unavoidable after him. Something new had come into the face of adolescence, into the language of gesture. An image as potent as that of James Dean in *East of Eden* is the prime mover whose radiance projects, suffuses, and transforms. Images are their own value, and if we are to be moved by them we must assume them. Dennis Stock speaks for many who first sat spellbound watching *East of Eden*: "I

The mythic Marilyn alights on earth.
Handing out programs at the New York premiere
of East of Eden, *March 9th, 1955.*
©WARNER BROS. INC.

James Dean's total immersion in Cal is reminiscent of the actor who commits a crime in order to better understand the criminal mind. It is the documentary impulse, the Method becoming its imaginative power. Jimmy's is the innate fear and hostility of the criminal whose crimes are committed in a state of amnesia and ethical confusion. The conspiratorial quality of the scenes between Cal and his mother, played by Jo Van Fleet, makes them especially engrossing. The prevailing atmosphere is one of evil-as-goodness-perverted or, perhaps, misunderstood. Cal perceives his mother as more honest than either his father or his brother or, for that matter, the hypocritical townspeople of Monterey.

"What Cal feels for her is a tolerance for the evil that's in people," says Kazan, "a tolerance of the non-puritanical elements." It is a tolerance for the evil in himself, and the poignancy of Cal's rebellion is that he plays the bad boy who secretly yearns to be "good" but can't play the game. He is cut off from his family not because he hates them but because he loves them more then they can fully grasp. Or take. He is the Prodigal Son who knows that without his waywardness there could be no parable. "I like bad people. . . ." says Cal. "I guess that's because I want to know what makes them bad." James Dean's Cal seems to burn through evil, splitting atoms to find his core, splitting Adam to find Cain.

But Kazan, an incorrigible moralizer, couldn't leave the mystery of evil alone. Rather bizarrely, he later attempted to recant the only original and indispensible element in the film: the paradox of good and evil. "There's some judgement I make in there that goodness is sterile," said Kazan. "I don't agree. I think there are 'good' people who are not sterile, who are not cruel. But I don't know if that's within the scope of this story."

Francois Truffaut, writing in *Cahiers du Cinéma*, believed that it was only through Jimmy's complicity with the malign that the otherwise withered and complacent moral message of the film was redeemed. "*East of Eden*," wrote Truffaut, "is the first film to give us a Baudelarian hero, fascinated by vice and

and the movie audience clearly empathized with Cal as Dean led us masterfully through his plight of alienation and innocence. Capitalizing on the limits of the adolescent's ability to articulate, Dean used his body to the utmost."

According to Dennis Hopper, when Kazan introduced Jimmy to the cast of *East of Eden*, he told them, "You're going to meet a boy, and he's going to be very strange to you and he's gonna be different; no matter what you see or what you think of him, when you see him on the screen he's gonna be pure gold."

Jimmy's strangeness was of an almost otherworldly nature, an eerie charm that fluctuated wildly, shuttling between attraction and repulsion in obedience to some inner compulsion. "The American farm boy with eyes of an injured animal. . .the innocent grace of a captive panther," said Herbert Kretzmer, reviewing *East of Eden* for *The Daily Sketch*. And that force, the electricity we see sheathing his body with static, is the thing that drives him. Behind Cal's troubled fury rises the specter of self-doubt and the moral ambiguity it expresses. Like the werewolf who does not know when the fit of metamorphosis will take him, he gives off a feral apprehension that is viscerally communicated to us.

Jimmy with Julie Harris in some poignant publicity stills for East of Eden.
©WARNER BROS. INC.

48

COSTUME DEPT. PROD. 810
NAME JAMES DEAN
PART CAL TRASK
CHG. # 2 SC. 51-66
EXT. RAILROAD YARDS

be tests for East of Eden, *May*

COSTUME DEPT. PROD. 810
NAME JAMES DEAN
PART CAL TRASK
CHG. #3   SC.157-159
INT. KATE'S BAR
+ OFFICE

contrast, loving the family and hating the family at one and the same time. James Dean, the freshly plucked 'fleur du mal,' James Dean who *is* the cinema, in the same sense as Lillian Gish, Chaplin, Ingrid Bergman. . . .'' Continuing, Truffaut almost seems to invoke human sacrifice: "[Dean's] powers of seduction – one has only to hear an audience react when Raymond Massey refuses the money, which is his love – are such that he can kill father and mother on the screen nightly with the full blessing of both art-house and popular audiences. His character in the film is a synthesis of *Les Enfants Terribles* – a solitary heir to the triple heritage of Elizabeth, Paul, and Dareglos.''

The idea of the actor becoming both scapegoat and monitor, by mirroring the evils he portrays, is as old as the theater itself. In James Dean-as-Cal it again attains its pure moral force. Samuel Foote, the eighteenth-century playwright and actor, defined theater as "an exact representation of the peculiar manner of that people among whom it is performed; a faithful imitation of singular absurdities, particular follies, which are openly produced *as criminals are publicly punished*, for the correction of individuals and as an example to the whole community."

With James Dean the matter becomes more insidious. So great is his understanding of Cal's motivations that he sails dangerously close to absolving evil itself and, unavoidably, carries us along with him. And it is precisely the uncertainty with which he constantly risks stepping across this fine line that makes his performance so suspenseful. It's not so much what Cal says or does that makes him unforgettable but simply what he *is*.

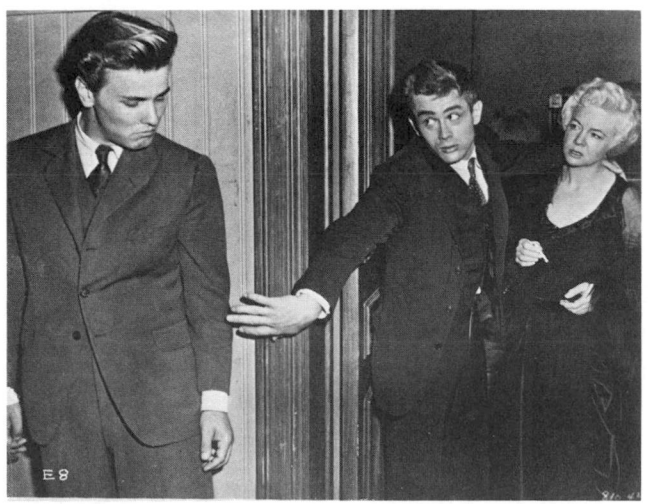

Cal confronts movie brother (Dick Davalos) with their mother, the town madame (Jo Van Fleet).

Jimmy's body is a universe where gravitational pull stems from instability; fascination from asymmetrical shifts and awkward physical contortions formed under internal stress. An athlete of transference, he was a victim of that supreme infection, identification.

Mike Wilmington: "Perhaps part of this power came because he was nearsighted, because, in all his films, he couldn't *see* much of what was happening – and, therefore, fell back on himself; created a universe out of his body, his face and his words that *forced* the other actors to adjust to his rhythm – enter his world. James Dean is the Saint of Narcissism, adolescent confusion, anguish and the struggle to belong. The world of his three major movies is *his* world – and when, as in *Giant*, the emphasis shifts away from him, it almost seems as if the world has been torn from its axis."

To the extent that Jimmy played himself, he was a virtuoso performer. What we call "bad acting" is usually nothing more than *acting* emotions, often out of an inability to find the real ones *at all*, much less call them up at will. Jimmy had the capacity to be himself under imaginary circumstances, something most people find trying under *any* circumstances.

Elia Kazan: "As an actor, Jimmy was tremendously sensitive, what they used to call an instrument. You could see through his feelings. His body was very graphic; it was almost writhing in pain sometimes. He was very twisted, almost like a cripple or a spastic of some kind. He couldn't do anything straight. He even walked like a crab, as if he were cringing all the time."

The constellation of these infirmities was to become, however, the stigmata of his star. He was, like Cain, marked in some way that allowed the secret life of possession to show itself as a second nature at work in its own coilings. An alien personality cleaves Jimmy's spirit, mumbles through his mouth, and tosses him relentlessly in its spooky grip. His performances often seem like a form of exorcism.

Like a marionette, Jimmy's body obeyed an unnatural yet coherent set of physical laws all their own. Alternating contractions and expansions, tautness

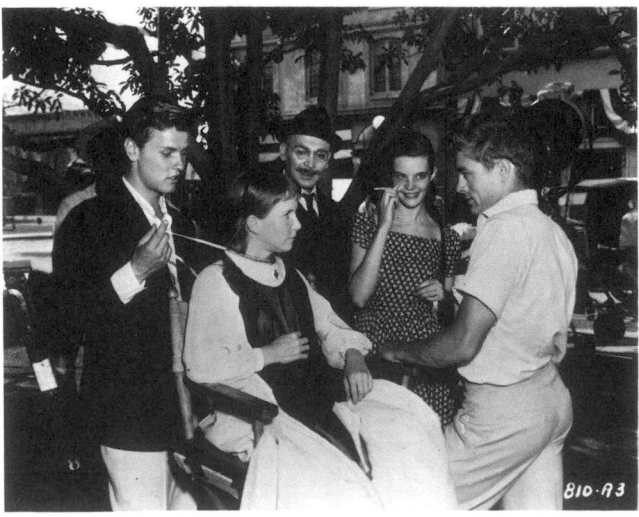

dissolving into jangling looseness, his body seemed to operate on hinged joints held up from a point beneath the nape of the neck, his psychological springs like the shade too tightly wound. And it was on this exquisite tension, as the film critic Georges Beaume noted, that Jimmy played his emotional vibrato: "He acts like a gypsy playing the top string of the violin — a quarter-tone higher, a fraction louder, and it would set the teeth on edge. That judgement is half the pleasure. And James Dean knows very well how far it is possible to go."

For a director who intuitively selected this unknown entity, Kazan seems oddly unable to recognize Jimmy's "defects" as assets: "His face is so desolate and lonely and strange," says Kazan. "And there are moments whey you say, 'Oh, God, he's handsome — what's being lost here! What goodness is being lost here!' "

But it was just this sense of something beautiful, flawed and thrown off balance that intensely suggested vulnerability to his audience. Jimmy's face speaks eloquently of the contradictions surging within him.

Kenneth Kendall, who made the famous bust of James Dean that once sat on a brick plinth in the Fairmount Cemetery, made the amazing observation that Jimmy thought his face was lopsided — which he compensated for by adopting what appears to be an exasperated or contemplative pose in many of his photographs: "You'll notice in many pictures that he's got his left cheek resting in his hand. There seems to be this constant reaching up to his own face, as if one side of it was slipping down or collapsing. . . ."

This imbalance conveyed on the screen a charged insinuation of inner fluctuation. According to William Mellor, Director of Photography on *Giant*, Dean's face was "probably among the most expressive faces in the world from a cinematographer's point of view. When looking through the camera, I see the way a face is put together differently than it appears in normal life. And usually the more difficult it is to key, the more potential it has for expressiveness."

James Dean existed in a state of indomitable uncertainty, his every gesture on its way somewhere

else, darting back and forth as if it has just changed its mind. An image incapable of repose.

If the camera wanted to make love to Marilyn Monroe, the CinemaScope lens was mesmerized by James Dean. Jimmy seemed to be able to see himself as it traced him. A deviant eye following him everywhere, occasionally moving out of sight, just as planets may be obliterated by the blurry curve of one's own cheekbone.

William Mellor describes the filming of a technically difficult scene in which the room is tightly packed with actors, a scene that revolves around the willing of a plot of land to Jett Rink: "In front of the camera [Dean] had an instinct that was nearly uncanny. I don't ever recall working with anyone who

Torrid promotional graphics, like the sketches on this page and opposite, attempt to make Eden *look like a "hot" movie. Opposite, top: Jimmy inscribed this photograph to Barbara Glenn: "You think I have to come down from up here, don't you? I hate all earthlings." Opposite, bottom: With Dick Davalos, Julie Harris, Harold Gordon (Mr. Albrecht, the old German shoemaker), and Lois Smith (the barmaid, Ann).*

*Top: Brando on the set with Julie Harris
and director, Elia Kazan. Right: An
unlikely folk duo featuring Burl Ives on
bagpipes and Jimmy on recorder.
Overleaf: A brooding, sexually charged
outtake of Davalos and Dean.*
LOEHR COLLECTION.

had such a gift. . . . He was in shadow and had to lift his head to the light. We explained how it should go, and he played it exactly right, to the half-inch first time."

Elia Kazan used CinemaScope's panoramic eye to isolate Jimmy in a lush existential landscape. "I think his face was very poetic. I think his face was wonderful and very painful. You really feel so sorry for him when you see him in close-up, but I realized there was great value in his body. Dean had a very vivid body, and I did play a lot with it in long shots. And CinemaScope emphasized Dean's smallness. When he runs in the bean fields, there's a big thing, like that wide, and you see Dean running through it, looking like a little child. I also like the scene under the tree; the tree is a willow, and the branches fall down and are covering Dean and Julie. That's an adolescent dream: to get under and cuddle with a girl, and you're alone in the world."

Dick Davalos, like most actors who worked with Jimmy, could not help but feel threatened by the ominous, oscillating charges he gave off on the set. Davalos described Jimmy's acting style as "dangerous, unpredictable. Just being in a scene with him could be an unnerving experience. He had that instinct to *disturb*." It is the very wariness of his animal presence that Aron and his girlfriend Abra sense uneasily as Cal lurks in the bushes watching them or, concealed in the icehouse, eavesdrops on a moment of intimacy. "He's scary," Abra says with a shiver. "He looks at you like an animal."

Jimmy used his body as the converse of his inarticulateness. And he used a combination of the two to stalk the quintessential imagery of growing up, its furtiveness and fitfulness. Had *East of Eden* been the only movie James Dean ever made, he would nevertheless have created an imperishable portrait of childhood's end. He gave his face the untamed indeterminacy of adolescence which heretofore had been not only invisible, but virtually taboo in Hollywood movies. As Cal Trask, James Dean made teenagers defiantly visible for the first time.

Kazan seems to have had something else in mind. In fact, he often appears somewhat bewildered at the imprint Jimmy's performance left on what he himself had intended the movie to *mean*.

Kazan on Kazan: "This was the first film in which I opened up and allowed myself to experience the emotion of tenderness and lovingness towards other people. . . . You have to forgive your father, finally. You have to say: 'Well, I don't like you for this, and I don't like you for that,' but if you continue to live in that hate, you don't grow up. I've always believed that hate destroys the hater. . . . I have to rid myself of hate. See, I have been psychoanalysed. And one of the things I learned was not to blame other people

for my problems but to look at myself."

Twenty years later, Kazan, after cautioning Derek Marlowe that "I'll talk to you only about Dean as an actor," continued, "I was lucky. I mean, how lucky can you get? He was *it*. He didn't even have to act. . . . He was never more than a limited actor, a highly neurotic young man. But he had a lot of talent, and he worked like hell. He was very completely involved, I'll say that. And he was the perfect boy for the part. He did a swell job, you know."

But then something clicks and Kazan, well, *expresses* himself: "And yet Dean was obviously sick. I don't know what was the matter with him. He got more so. . . . But I'd rather not talk about him. . . .

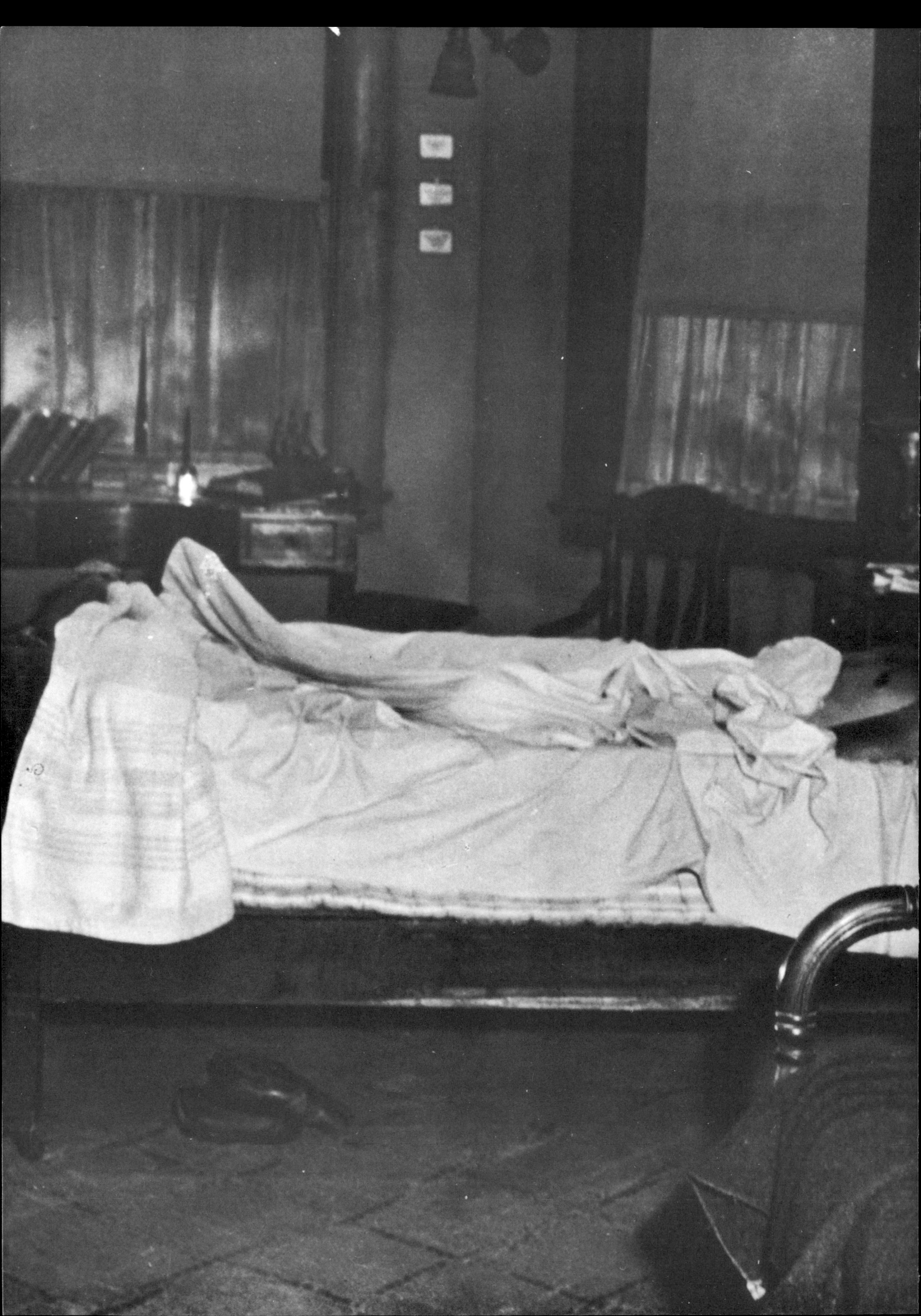

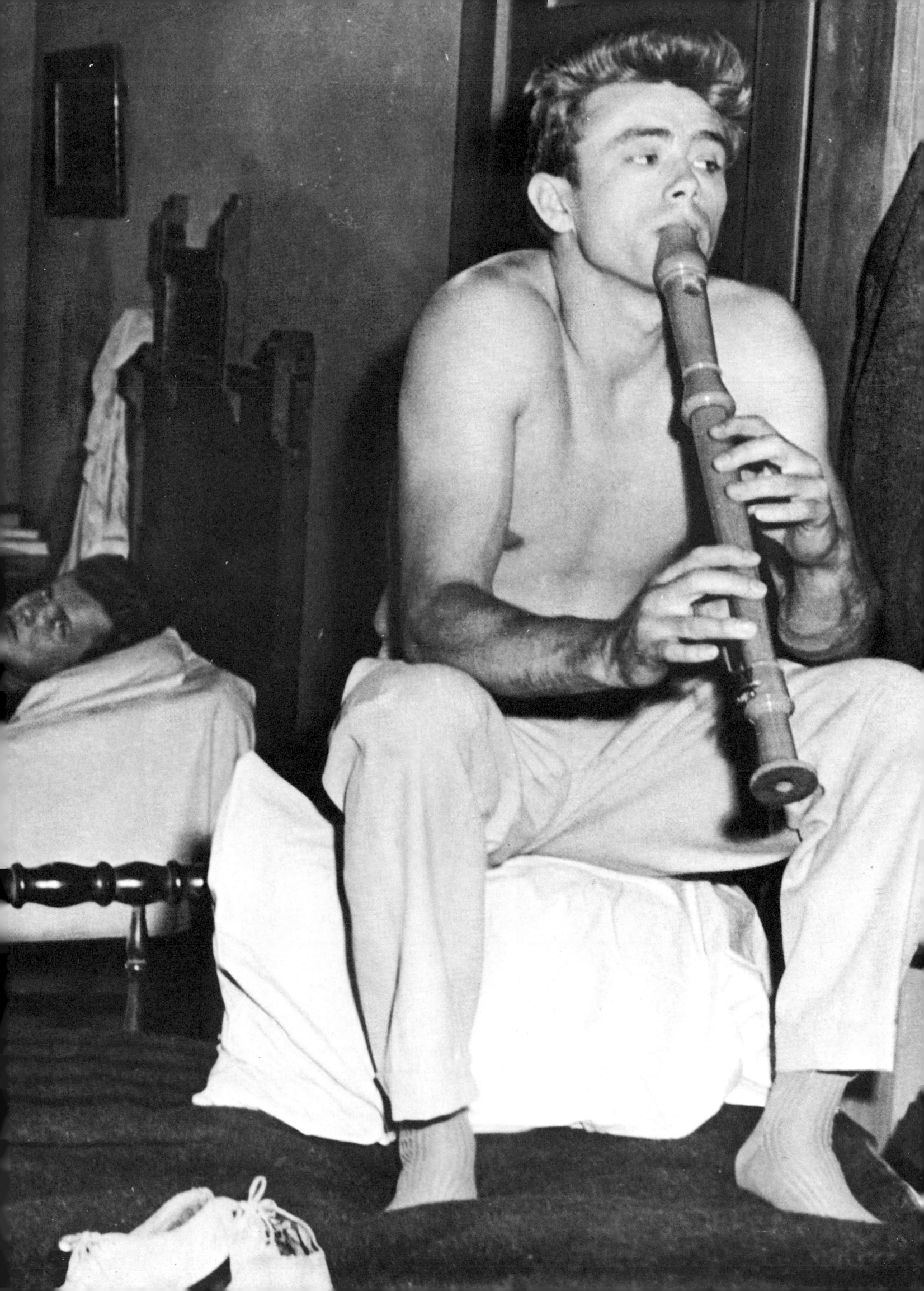

Dean, Davalos and Harris in a series of surrealistically choreographed stills for Eden.

He was not like Brando. Dean was a cripple . . . inside. He was a far, far sicker kid, he was so sick and twisted. And Brando's not sick, he's just troubled."

Something in Jimmy seems to have revolted Kazan, *disturbed* him in some way he couldn't deal with. A disillusioned radical, now consoling himself with kitsch Americana, perhaps Kazan saw himself too vividly in Jimmy. Having informed before the Committee on Un-American Activities, he may have wanted this specter of himself, when he still had his passions and beliefs intact, burnt at the stake.

"What attracted me to *East of Eden* was nothing very mysterious," said Kazan. "The story of a son trying to please his father who disapproved of him was one part of it. Another part of it was an opportunity for me to attack puritanism; the absolute puritanism of 'this is right and this is wrong.' I was trying to show that right and wrong get mixed up and that there are values that have to be looked at more deeply than in that absolute disapproval syndrome of my left friends."

James Dean as Cal reveals Cain as a new, more honest variation of the myth of Adam. Yet Kazan remains profoundly ambivalent about the pubescent pest he unwittingly unleashed on the world (the pest that consumed its host!) and even more jaundiced about the culture it spawned.

"The first manifestation was this one of 'Pity me, I'm too sensitive for the world. Everyone's wrong except me,' " moans Kazan. "It was a fairly universal attitude. That's why James Dean was an idol everywhere. You see all these little boys around the street still looking as if, 'I'm a homosexual because my mother did this to me,' or 'I'm neurotic because this happened to me.' They should shake this off and go on to solve the problem."

Kazan's means of manipulating actors stopped just short of electric shock treatment. Here he describes applying a little bit of the old Pavlovian "boot-and-bone" routine to Jimmy: "Directing James Dean was like directing the faithful Lassie. I either lectured him or terrorized him, flattered him furiously, tapped him on the shoulder or kicked his backside. He was so instinctive and so stupid in so many ways."

Kazan seems never to have forgiven his creature for escaping from the Temple of Method. Yet every creature of myth turns on its creator (look at us!), and it must have galled Kazan, who directed almost every famous star of the last three decades, to find himself in the shadow of his own "creation."

In the French poster for *East of Eden*, for instance, Kazan is relegated to almost a footnote while "JAMES DEAN," stenciled across the top in monumental letters, dwarfs even the title. Not only is Jimmy the only image portrayed, it is Jimmy as Jett Rink in *Giant*! The movie has become a mere pretext. As long as James Dean is in it, it doesn't really matter which film it is. *Or* who directed it.

To the public at large, Kazan's name is known, if at all, *because* of James Dean, a prickly fact that Kazan confronts everywhere he goes. Even among worshipful *cinéastes*, the ghost of James Dean rises up to haunt him. In his "Soliloquy on James Dean's Forty-Fifth Birthday," Derek Marlowe described a typical encounter: "Kazan was invited to lecture at a college in Purchase, New York. The subject was specifically the two films, *A Face in the Crowd* and *Baby Doll*, neither of which starred James Dean. His audience were film enthusiasts who listened attentively, then almost unanimously abandoned the schedule and said, 'Tell us about James Dean.' Before him were not street-corner teenagers of the fifties but mature, sophisticated students of the seventies. And yet it was James Dean that concerned them. And James Dean alone. For a moment Kazan stared at them, then walked slowly to the window, gazed at the snow on the campus, and said quietly: 'You *really* want to know about Jimmy Dean? All right, I'll tell you about him' and for half an hour proceeded to talk on every aspect of Dean, interrupting himself constantly to interject, 'Is *this* what you want? Is this what you want to hear?' The myth hadn't died. Hysteria had simply been replaced by intellectual curiosity, part nostalgia, part reverence."

Kazan's decision to reconcile Cal with his father in the final scene of *East of Eden* all too tidily ties up all the loose ends and diffuses the social potential that the film constantly promises and implies.

Jimmy had an uncanny knack for finding the key light, "that light that shines on you alone."

Despite Kazan's addiction to Oedipal pronouncements ("a son has finally to kill his father"), Cal's apparent acceptance of and by his father in the last scene remains a squirmy effort to make everything seem all right in the end.

The anti-climatic footnote at the end of *East of Eden* appears as a last ditch attempt to dissipate the rebellious message Jimmy's mere presence exudes. In its place, Kazan substitutes this moral: in order to grow up you have to come to terms with your father. Even, apparently, if you have first to kill him, since Cal has been, for all intents and purposes, "the death" of his father.

Raymond Massey lies paralyzed from a stroke as a result of Aron's getting drunk and going off to war, a situation provoked by Cal who, by now, may be feeling guilty about possibly having killed off his brother as well. And let's not forget Mom, while we're on the subject! In any case, Kazan pawns off this patent bit of *bovaryisme* on us with the earnestness of a man wrestling with a leg of mutton. But it's just this sort of hypocritical morality that the movie seems to be questioning!

The literalness of Adam's Calvinist beliefs, epitomized by the rigidity of Raymond Massey's portrayal, is inadvertently duplicated by the movie's slick, sentimental ending. Kazan's simpleminded sophism — growing up is becoming *like* grownups — is underlined by the atmospheric chlorine lighting in Adam's room, as well as the surefire tearjerker of the bedridden parent. Kazan's message of resignation implies, instead, that the adult is the self you finally have to stop fighting and learn to love *as* yourself.

It's not that these themes are not already present in Steinbeck's novel. Steinbeck liked his characters in CinemaScope dimensions even if he had to pump them up with pulpy emotional froth until they were the right size. Adam and Eve! We always wanted to know what happened after they were evicted from Paradise. Apparently, *he* went on to invent frozen food, and she — what else? — took up the world's oldest profession. Abel went into the Army, and Cain ended up on the therapist's couch. As if *Genesis*

Above: Brothel bouncer (played by baseball pitcher Timothy Carey) drags Cal out of his mother's "house."
©WARNER BROS. INC.

J.D.

Jimmy, Julie and Dick pose for snaps
on location in the Salinas Valley.
LOEHR COLLECTION.

weren't enough, Steinbeck, infatuated with the psychoanalytic fetishes rampant in the fifties, made his epic into the *Quest for Freud*!

With the exception of James Dean and Julie Harris and, to a different degree, Dick Davalos, the pneumatic figures in *East of Eden* stride the Salinas Valley as no more than stick figures. As textbook psychological types, what else could be expected of them? They represent an allegorical past in a simplistic problem-to-be-solved. As Adam, Raymond Massey's lack of psychological dimension often makes it seem as if it would be dangerous for him to turn sideways. Dick Davalos, who played a sort of Pat Boone to Jimmy's Elvis, resented bitterly (even at the time) the saccharine namby-pamby portrayal of Aron that was forced on him. This was not lost on reviewers. Bosley Crowther in *The New York Times*: "The stubborn fact is that the people who move about in this film are not sufficiently well-established to give point to the anguish through which they go, and the demonstrations of their torment are perceptibly stylized and grotesque."

Reviewing the film in *Cahiers du Cinéma*, Truffaut concluded that only the direct current of Jimmy's acting could have saved such schematic presentations of character and a plot overfreighted with significance.

Truffaut: "James Dean has succeeded in giving commercial viability to a film which would otherwise scarcely have qualified, in breathing life into an abstraction, in interesting a vast audience in moral problems treated in an unusual way. . . . His shortsighted stare prevents him from smiling, and the smile drawn from him by dint of patient effort constitutes a victory."

In a sort of mental bloodlust, Kazan attempts to compensate for the two-dimensional qualities of his villains by the sheer virulence of their emotions. But the paint is slapped on with such broad strokes that their cartoon-like dimensions are actually emphasized. Both *Waterfront* and *East of Eden* have their share of human furniture through which emblematic Biblical beasts (Brando and Dean) wade, violently raging with animal passion.

Tony Parsons twits Kazan's claim to make folk films: "What Kazan made were films wherein male impersonators like Dean and Brando played what

Kazan hoped were the Christ figures of a rural and urban American fantasia full of mawkish brutality."

Roland Barthes, in "A Sympathetic Worker," sees Kazan as the supreme mystifier. What conceals his fraudulent politics in *Waterfront* is Brando: "As we see, it is the *participational* nature of this scene in *Waterfront* which objectively makes it an episode of mystification. Taught to love Brando from the beginning, we can no longer criticize him at any particular moment or even acknowledge his objective stupidity."

What saves *East of Eden* from being a tidy psychological melodrama is James Dean. Incredibly, Brando and Clift *were* originally cast (in 1952) as Cal and Aron. Clift was interested, but wanted to play Cal, and, when Brando turned down both parts, Kazan shelved the project for a year and a half, finally deciding to use unknowns in the roles.

It's a bit unfair to ask — but we will anyway — what *East of Eden* would have been *without* Dean. Brando's version would have been a sort of psychological safari. With Clift, *East of Eden* would still have been a fake Freudian garden, but with a real neurotic in it! As for Paul Newman, it would have been a sort of Cal U. Without Jimmy, the movie would have sunk irretrievably into its picturesque panoramas. As it is, the whole effect of *East of Eden* has the sketched-in quality of a musical, an impression which Leonard Rosenman's lyrical soundtrack only serves to underline.

Kazan neatly ascribes to CinemaScope framing the quaint proscenium-arch partitioning of the sequences in *East of Eden*: "The face didn't fill the screen so I did a staging that was much more relaxed, more like a stage — more 'across,' more at ease. It was not intentional; I was forced into it by the aesthetics of that shape. I also did something else; I combated the shape; I tried to get inner frames. In other words, I would put something big in the foreground on one side, something black, that you couldn't see through, and put the action on the other side. The next time I'd have the action in a corner over there and have something blacking it here. I tried to make frames within the frame."

But the very set piece quality of the film inadvertantly worked as a foil for the realism of Dean's

performance. And it wasn't only the compartmentalization of space that undermined *East of Eden*'s dynamics. More serious was the literalness of its narrative and its stilted transitions. This, Kazan rather ignobly palms off on screenwriter Paul Osborn: "I got Paul Osborn because I think he's an excellent constructionist and still a very adaptable man. I wanted him to provide a unity of structure that I felt I was not yet able to provide for myself. About five or six years later, I found that it was better to have more of my own statements and my own life and a little less unity, because the unity, I began to find, simplifies things too much. Sometimes it simplifies the life out of things and makes them too clear."

What saves the interminable final scene (ten minutes of screen time) from becoming a maudlin

Father's Day tableau is that the messenger, Jimmy-as-James Dean-as-Cal Trask, *is* the message. Jimmy so infected the movie that the conclusion seems merely the obligatory "happy ending." There's a certain black humor about this reconciliation. After all, Raymond Massey is now at the mercy of the Cain he's raised at his own bosom. James Dean, the Mutant King, just stopping by to see poor old Dad (who's in no position to object anyway) and ask if he can have the keys to the Model-T so he and Abra can go to the chickie run. James Dean on his way to the apocalypse. Just blink your eyes if it's okay with you, Dad.

Cal riding the rails between Monterey and Salinas.

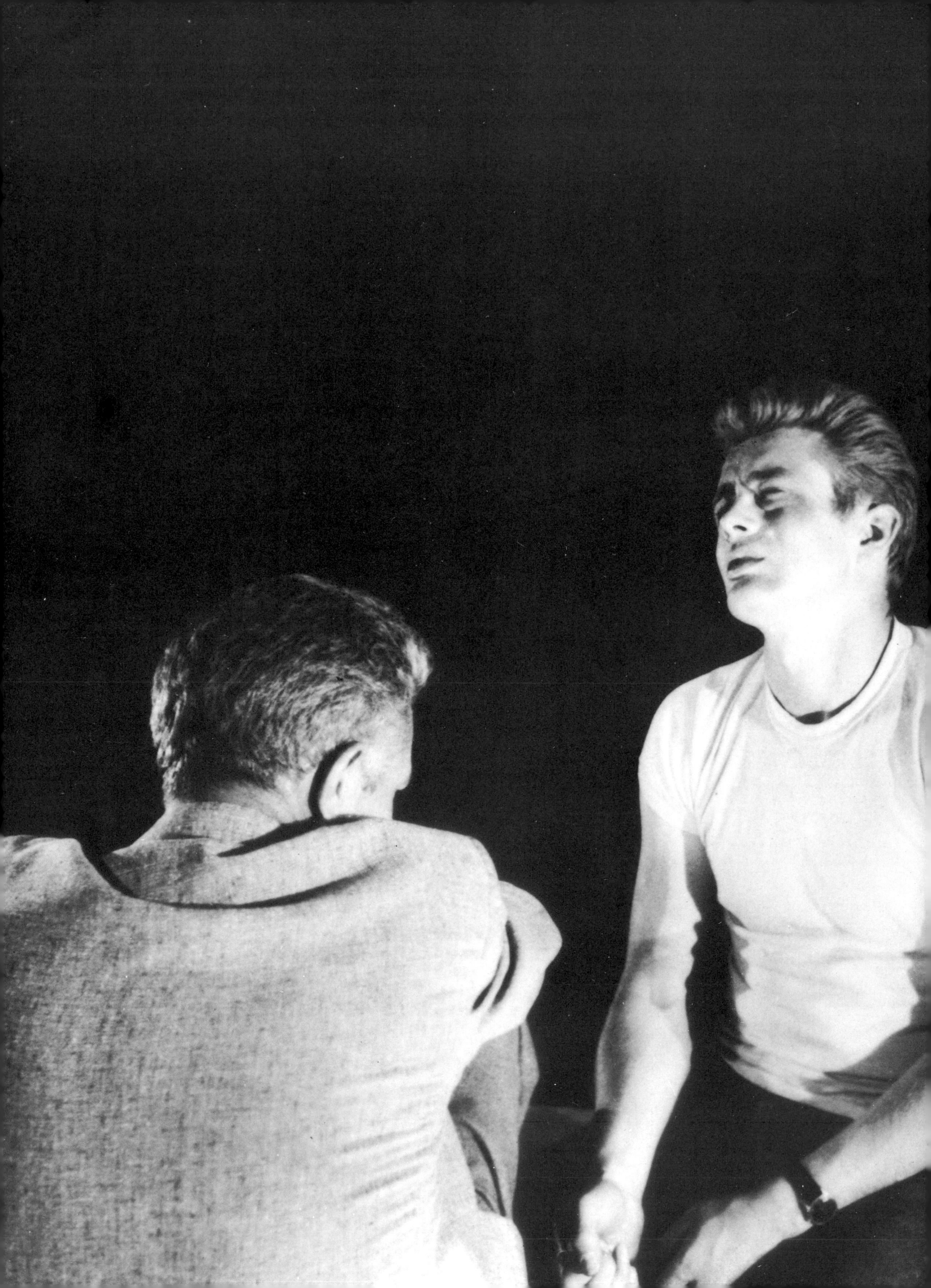

COSMIC RAY

Every movie I ever made I wanted to call
"I'm A Stranger Here Myself."
Nicholas Ray

The quintessential film about adolescence, *Rebel Without a Cause*, made as it was with an adolescent's intolerance and urgency, is almost willfully spasmodic. It kind of *lurches* from one thing to another, as do all the classic films Nicholas Ray directed. His convulsive rhythms, disruptive expositions, distorting angles, and nervous framing draw us into *Rebel*'s teenage turmoil. Nothing in Ray's movies is allowed to remain impersonal; everything is permeated with the same subjective bias. In one especially charged scene in *Rebel*, it's as if the camera—infected by the surge and ebb of the story, the psychological and emotional upheavals of the characters—suddenly loses its balance, upset by what it is recording. When Jim Stark returns from the chickie run to confront his parents, the camera gets almost comically carried away. For a moment, it becomes Jim Stark as he watches his mother descending the stairs (upside down, from his point of view), and then, tilting back to normal in a 180° sweep, sits up to face her, as if startled by her mindless confusion.

Like Baron Frankenstein preparing his Teen Monster, director Nick Ray psyches Jimmy up for his "I-got-the-bullets!" scene in Rebel Without a Cause.
©WARNER BROS. INC.

The whole film *is*, in fact, put together in an unabashedly adenoidal manner. But that's just the point. For instance, those garish colors, those indelible bleeding reds and blues (red jacket and blue jeans) were deliberately oversaturated by Nick Ray *as symbols*, flags in a kind of war game. Ray, at one time, wanted to call the film *Blind Run*, a title which turned out to be a metaphor for the process of making *Rebel*.

Ray is the "master of the brilliantly broken rule," and in *Rebel Without a Cause* he fearlessly faces down that most insidious of aesthetic taboos, the cliché. The sheer audacity of that blatant parade of naked Freudianisms! The corny crescendos! The melodramatic mush! The preposterous plot! The dumb dialogue! The clanking cosmic symbols shoved down our throats!

Ray treats The Big Questions of Life in so utterly breathless a fashion and with such pubescent earnestness it is almost shameless. Some found the whole thing so offensive they reacted with acute embarrassment, as if they had just been mooned by Buzz and the gang. But *Rebel* is actually an adolescent's movie about adolescence, and that's just why some people find it so tacky. Like adolescence. This

had been Ray's plan all along: "It should be kept in mind," he wrote in a production note, "that the youth is always in the foreground and the adults are, for the most part, shown only as kids see them."

It was to be a film about adolescence from within, and it is the continuity of this vision throughout that makes *Rebel* so riveting to those who identify with it and so insufferable to those who don't. Ray was always too much. For many of those who worked with him, Ray always went too far, stretching the improbabilities of the story and the audience's suspension of disbelief to the breaking point. Irving Shulman, who preceeded Stewart Stern as screenwriter on *Rebel*, threw up his hands in despair when Ray insisted that Plato's fatal shooting take place on the steps of the planetarium. This was just *too* cosmic. Coincidence is one thing, this was molesting the improbable.

Then there was the most unlikely coincidence of all: the coming together of Nick Ray, Apostle of Alienation, and James Dean, God of Adolescence. "Where [Ray] sees pertinent truth," wrote John Howlett in his biography of Dean, "he stretches the

The classic James Dean in some Warner Brothers promotion shots on the back lot.
LOEHR COLLECTION.

material, and the audience's imagination, to embrace it. In terms of good drama, he lives dangerously; the timing and nuance have to be perfect. But this was exactly the tightrope atmosphere of Dean's own acting style."

The crucial line in *Rebel* — "I-got-the-bullets!" — has the same shudder of startled immediacy that infused all Jimmy's acting. Ray told me the playwright Clifford Odets had written that line for Jimmy and that its urgency derived from Odets' credo that "every line in a play should be like the fuse burning; I mean, it should be like the first and last time a character would ever say it."

The point is not to learn the lines but to find the moments, as actress Laurette Taylor once said, and Jimmy unerringly homed in on every one of them when allowed the psychic space to do so. His was a sort of existential acting. With both the intellectual wonder of a child and the physical immediacy of an animal, Jimmy had the ability to experience things for the first time every time, and we follow him, alert to the suspense of the moment.

October 1955: A month after Jimmy's death, Rebel *opens in New York.*
©WARNER BROS. INC.

The same qualities that made his style of acting so unique were precisely what suited Jimmy to play Jim Stark, mirroring, as they did, the adolescent state of newness: from macrocosm to microcosm, from planetariums to dating. At any given moment, Jimmy seems as taken unawares by what is happening to him as we are. Jim's first day at Dawson High is almost like the first day of an extraterrestrial on earth; he was "never properly introduced to this world," as Ray said of the adolescents at the beginning of his *Party Girl*. Jim's sense of astonishment is immediate and understandable. He's as new to the situation as we are. Ann Doran, who played Jimmy's mother in the movie, recalled a scene that he prepared for in an almost obstetrical manner: "Jimmy dropped to the floor in the fetal position for the longest time, chin and knees together, holding his legs — still on his feet, but as close to the floor as he could get without lying on it. Finally, came this weak little whistle and he stood up, ready to do the scene, which he'd rehearsed once, in a single take."

And it is with this image of the character newly hatched that *Rebel* begins. James Dean as Jim Stark, lying on the ground in that fetal position, curled around a toy monkey. Due to the film's abbreviated time-scale (everything takes place in 24 hours), Jim Stark's evolution is accelerated through a series of symbolic scenes: ceremonial battle (the knife fight); testing of the hero's courage (the chickie run); winning the girl and constitution of the new order (playing house with Judy and Plato in the abandoned mansion); confrontation of hostile forces (the gang, police, parents); and final reconciliation of all parties in the shadow of the planetarium.

The crucial scene in the metamorphosis of Jim Stark takes place before the chickie run when he sheds his drab wardrobe (brown-flecked jacket and flannel pants) for his battle colors (red jacket and blue jeans), and leaves behind the compromised "Jimbo" for the heroic Jim Stark.

Just as a series of rituals mark the metamorphosis of Jim Stark, the film itself has become a rite in the cult of its ceremonial hero, James Dean, as fans reenact its gestures, lines, and attitudes. By raising everyday turmoil to the level of significance it has for teenagers themselves, *Rebel* evolves towards a social myth that gives form to adolescent doubt and longing.

As Jim Stark in Rebel. *From the top: With father, Jim Backus, at Juvenile Hall; Dennis Hopper and the gang outside; and kicking in Grandma Stark's portrait.*
©WARNER BROS. INC.

In stills from the opening scenes of Rebel, *Jimmy poses as "the bad boy from a good family."*
©WARNER BROS. INC.

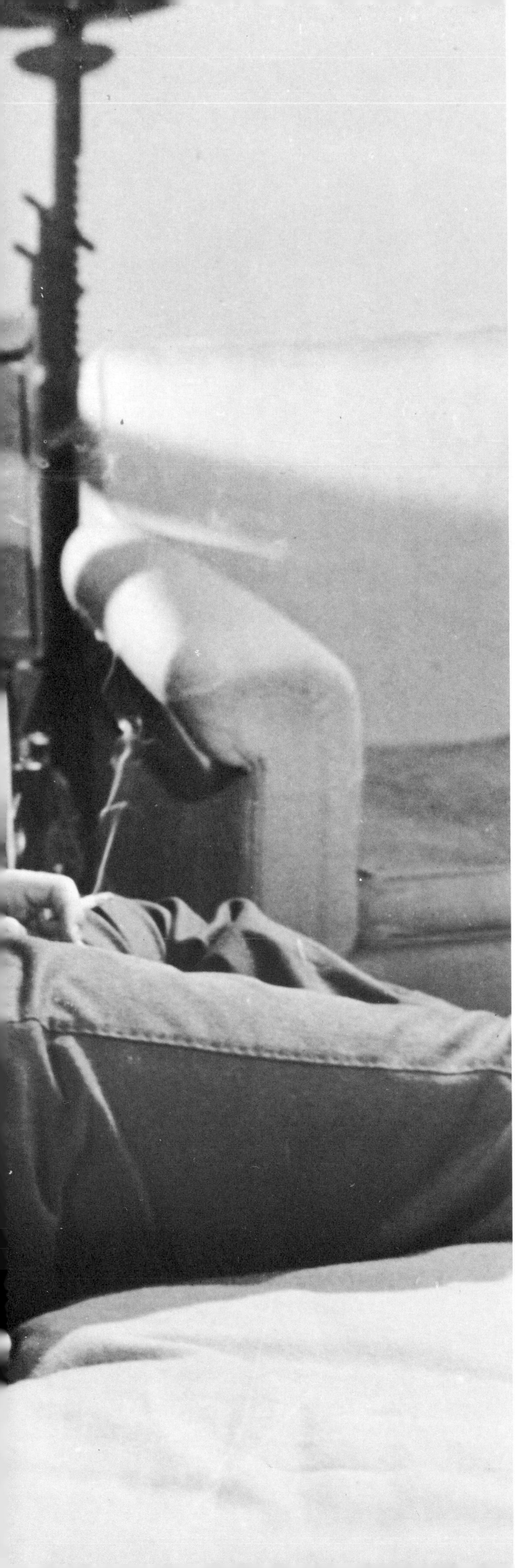

Nick Ray and Jimmy were a couple of desperate characters: Ray, who believed that a moral life could only be lived at the edge, and Jimmy, who threw himself impulsively into every role. The two of them set about their Great Work with relentless zeal, as if their very lives depended on it: *Rebel Without a Cause* was to bestow immortality on both of them, but Ray paid for it with his career, and Jimmy with his life.

As Terry Curtis Fox wrote in the *Village Voice*, "While Ray considered living outside an ideal, he also understood that the tragic component of an outsider's stance comes not from a vengeful society — which one can and must choose to defy — but from an inevitably flawed self. The rebel, Ray told us again and again, is his own victim."

Nick Ray was obsessed with the juncture between his and Jimmy's real lives and the imaginary lives of the film's characters, a transmission of themselves in almost literal fashion into the substance of *Rebel*. Both Nick and Jimmy were ruthless in this self-consuming act. It was to be Ray's masterpiece and James Dean's last immaculate conception. Ray's subsequent movies would pale beside *Rebel*, and, as an actor, the movie literally *used up* Jimmy, who

The Teen Dreamscape quality of Rebel's
*fantasy is caught in these outtakes of Jim
Stark preparing himself for the chickie run.*
LOEHR COLLECTION.

821-402

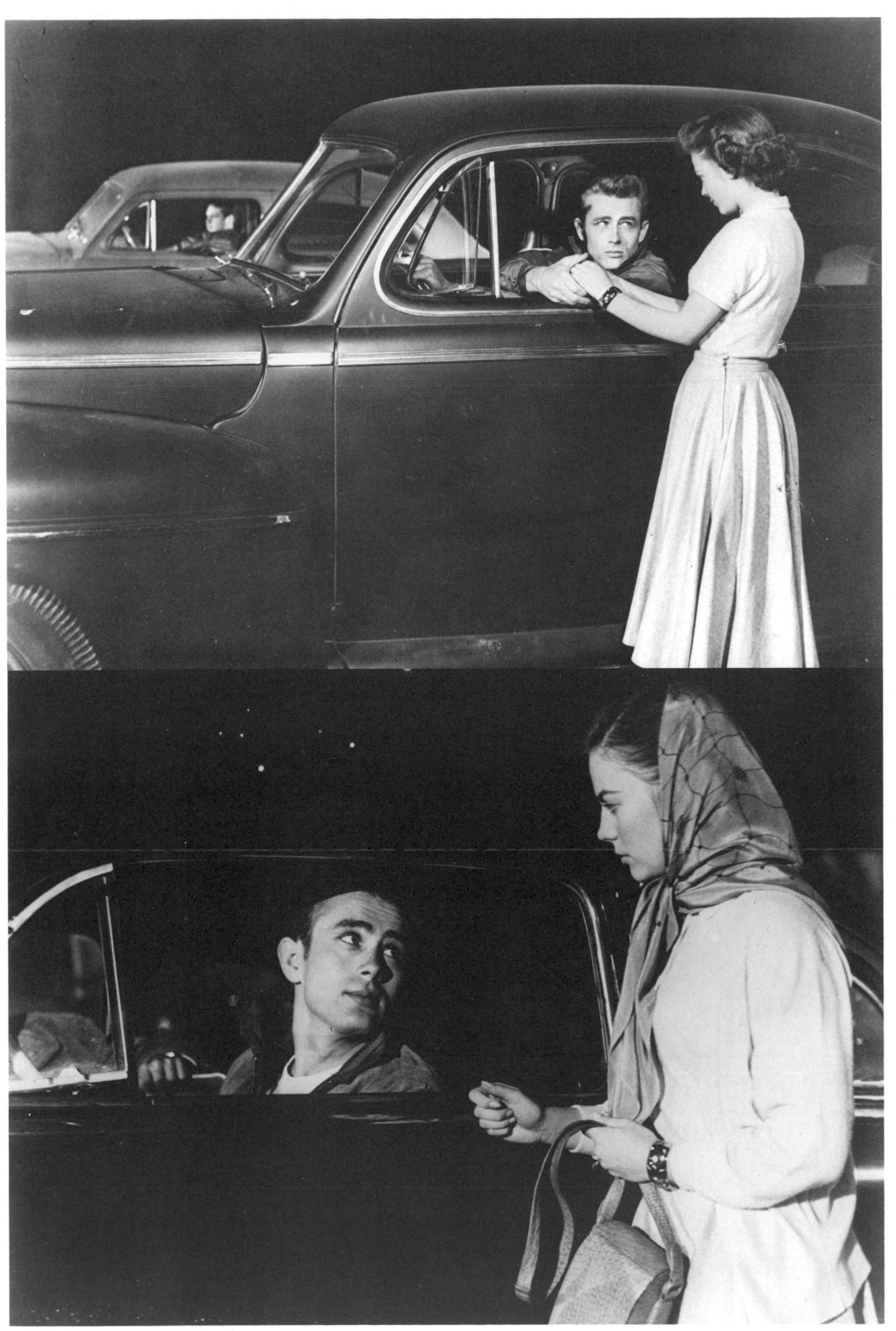

Natalie in her first "adult" role: the gangleader's girl who learns to love the star. Above: Giving Jim some grit before the chickie run.

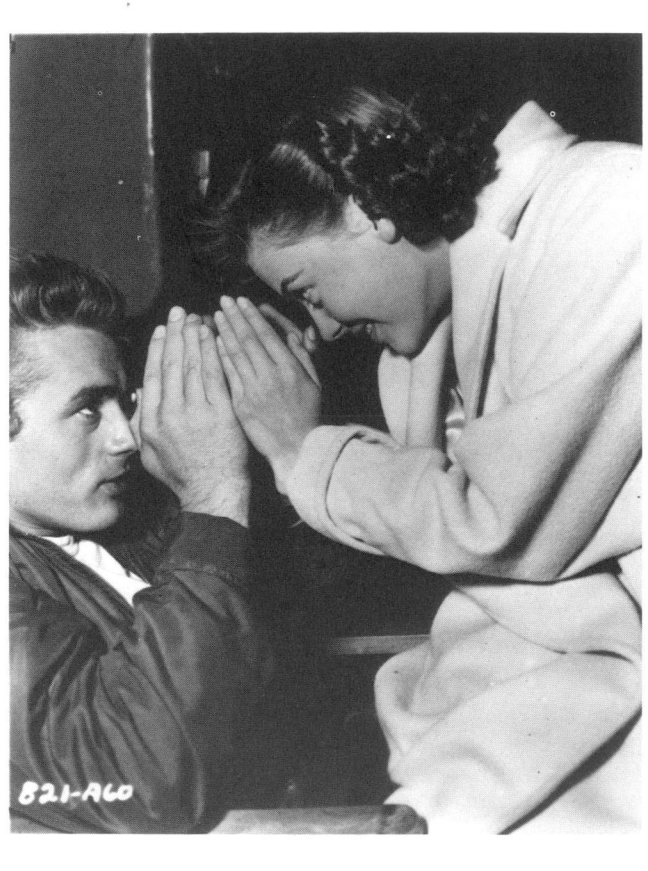

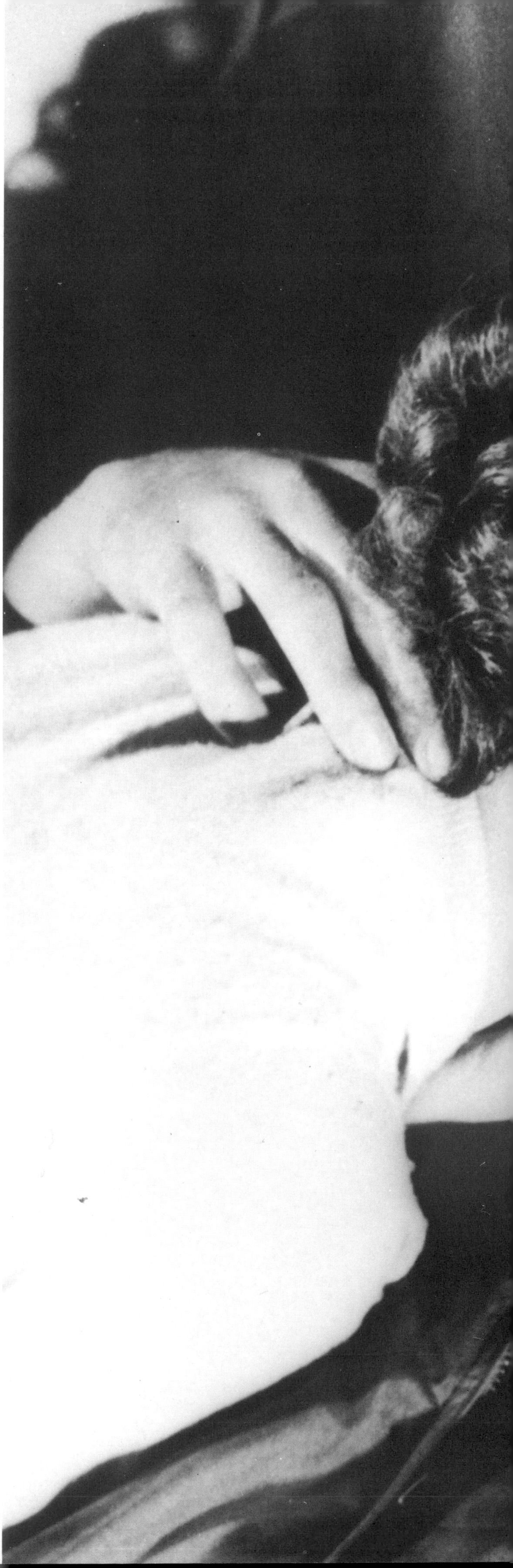

Quintessential Teen Angels James Dean and Natalie Wood. Above: Natalie mimics Jimmy as he frames her in an imaginary lens.
©WARNER BROS. INC.

admitted: "I could never take so much out of myself again." If, for Ray, *Rebel* was "drawn only too directly from personal experience," for Jimmy, it was to be an epitaph.

Ray had the ability to saturate his actors with his own personality, and, inevitably, the protagonist that emerged was a fusion of identities.

In his collusion with James Dean, Nick Ray approached his ultimate synthesis with an actor whose oscillating signals often came close to a fatal confusion of life and art. Speaking of Jimmy, Ray said: "The drama of his life, I thought after seeing him in New York, was the drama of desiring to belong and of fearing to belong (so was Jim Stark's). It was a conflict of violent eagerness and mistrust created very young . . . the intensity of his desires, his fears, could make the search at times arrogant, egocentric; but behind it was such a desperate vulnerability that one was moved, even frightened."

Obsessed with his own role as a father, Ray's films are parables about the endemic American conflict between fathers and sons which he believed hid at the root of all types of social unrest: alienation, violence, drugs, permanent anxiety. Jimmy was the living embodiment of this conflict; he was the malcontent, loner, and prodigal son. Out of their compulsions, Nick and Jimmy took on their roles with an almost alarming literalness: Ray actually played Jim's father while rehearsing crucial scenes. They improvised, using Ray's bungalow in the Chateau Marmont. At one point, Jimmy let himself in through the kitchen door and, in a now classic gesture, rolled a cold bottle of milk over his forehead, preparing himself to tell his father about Buzz's death in the chickie run. Ray, the sleeping father, secretly watched all of this reflected on a blank TV screen! Ray's voyeurism and Jimmy's mimed anguish as he wrestles with his dilemma and finally flops down on the couch are as much about James Dean and Nick Ray as they are about Jim Stark and his father. To transfer this primal scene to film intact, Ray had his living room recreated on the set of *Rebel*.

One has to remember that James Dean had a tremendous hand in the way *Rebel* was shaped. It was built *around* him. Jimmy was given both the encouragement to improvise on the set and the responsibility of collaboration in developing the

Preceding page: Sal Mineo, as Plato, tries to help out his buddy, Jim, outside the planetarium. Top: Corey Allen (as gangleader, Buzz), taking a break on the chickie run location. Center: Jim Stark gets conflicting directions to Dawson High from Buzz and the gang. Bottom: Plato and locker room pin-up of Alan Ladd.
©WARNER BROS. INC.

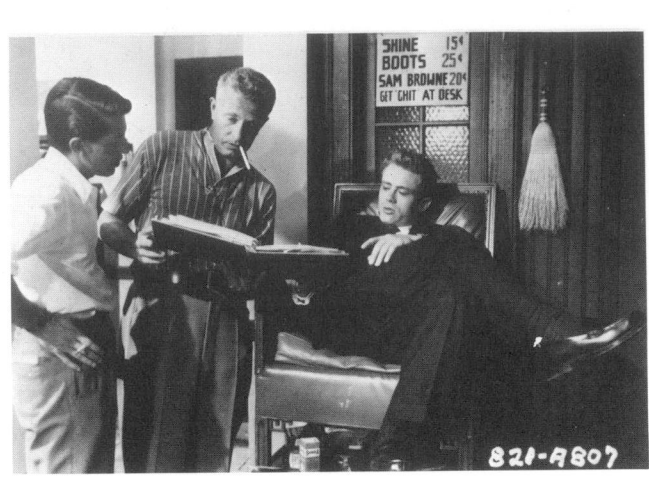

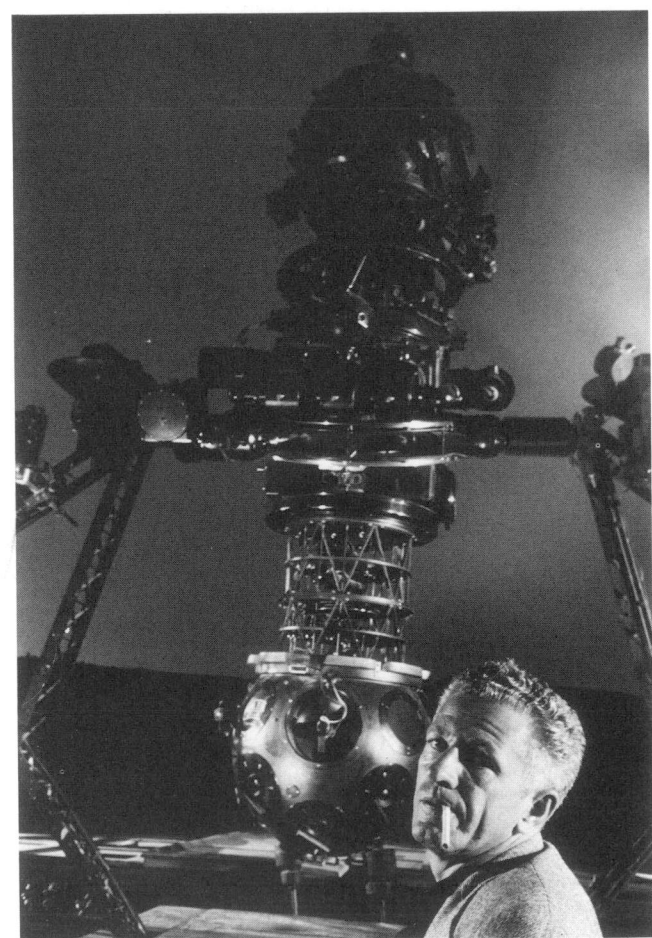

*Clockwise, from right: Jimmy rehearsing
shoot—out at planetarium; Nick, Natalie
and Beverly Long; Cosmic Ray with
his central metaphor, the planetarium
projector; photographer Dennis Stock,
as dialogue coach, goes over lines with
Nick Ray. Opposite: Judy leers as Buzz
prepares to stick the whitewall of Jim's
'49 Merc.*

821-300

89

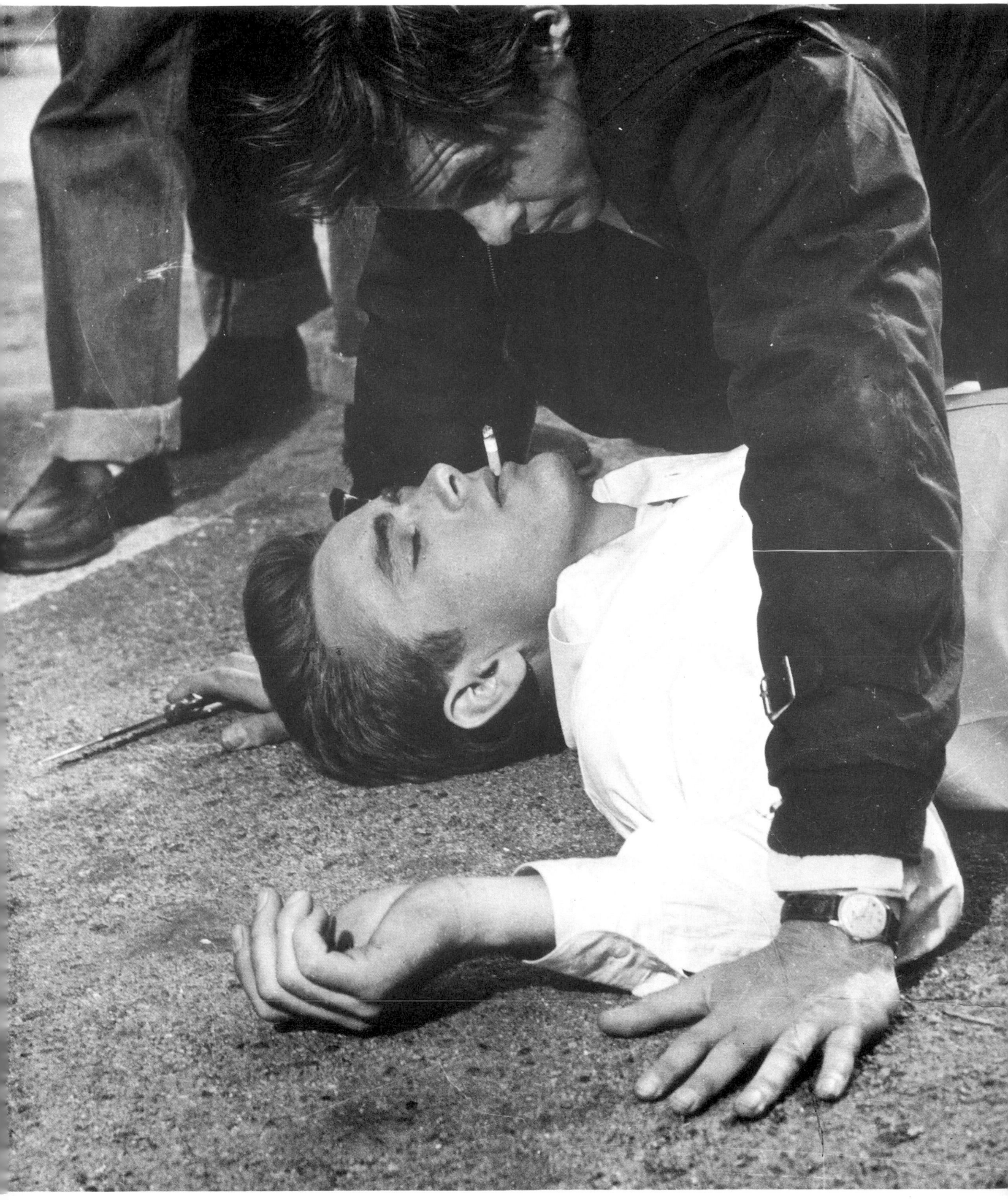

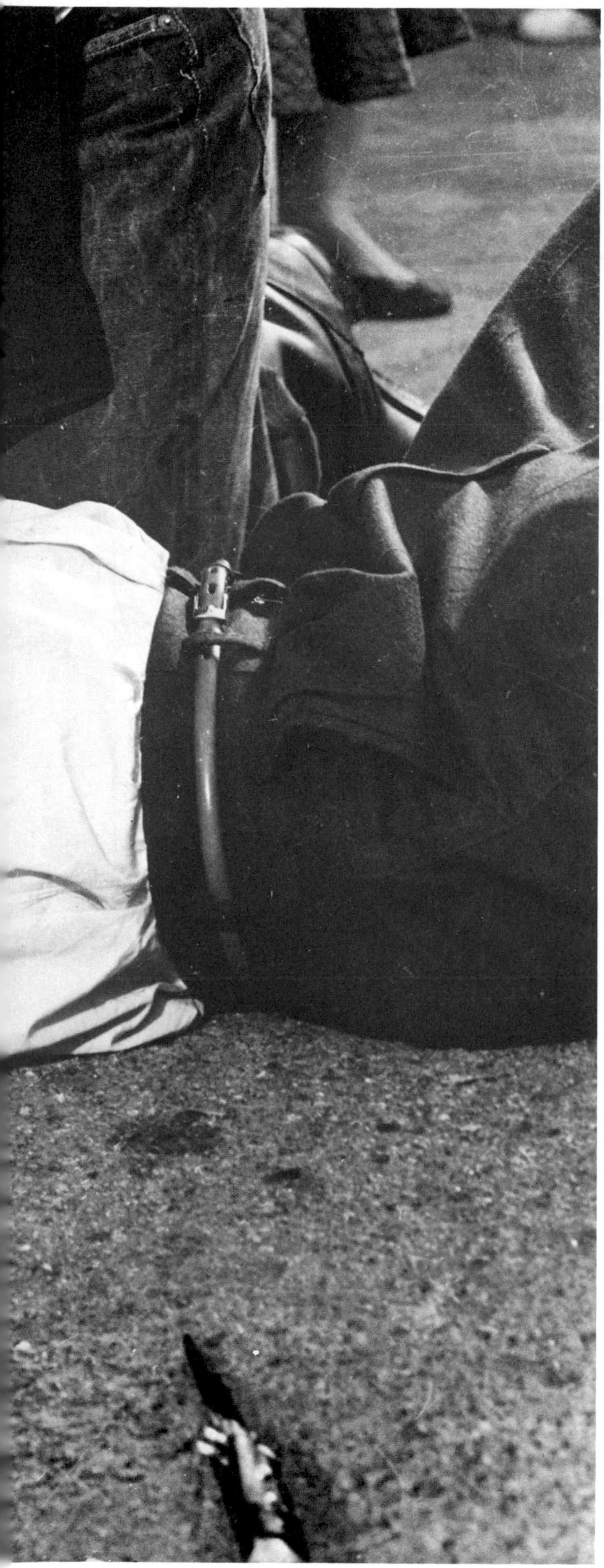

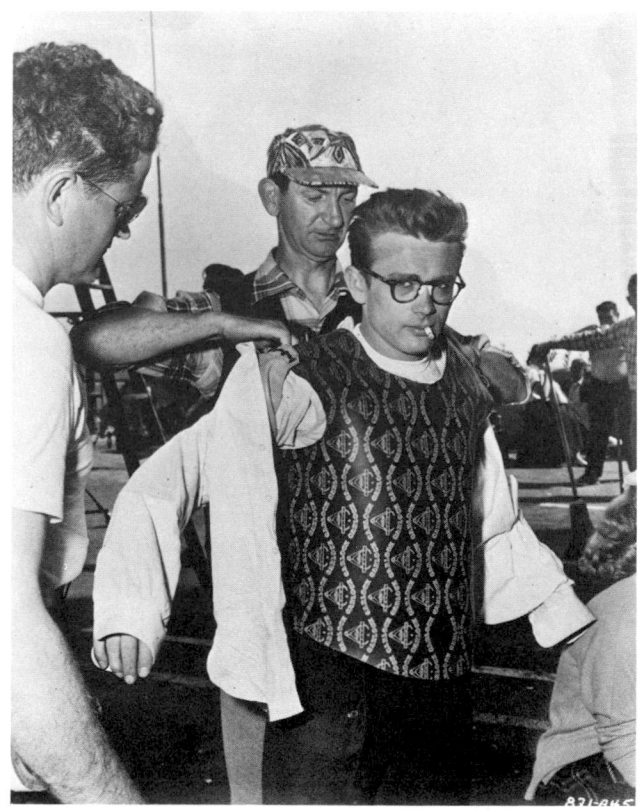

Rehearsing knife fight sequence with
coach; getting into protective vest.
©WARNER BROS. INC.

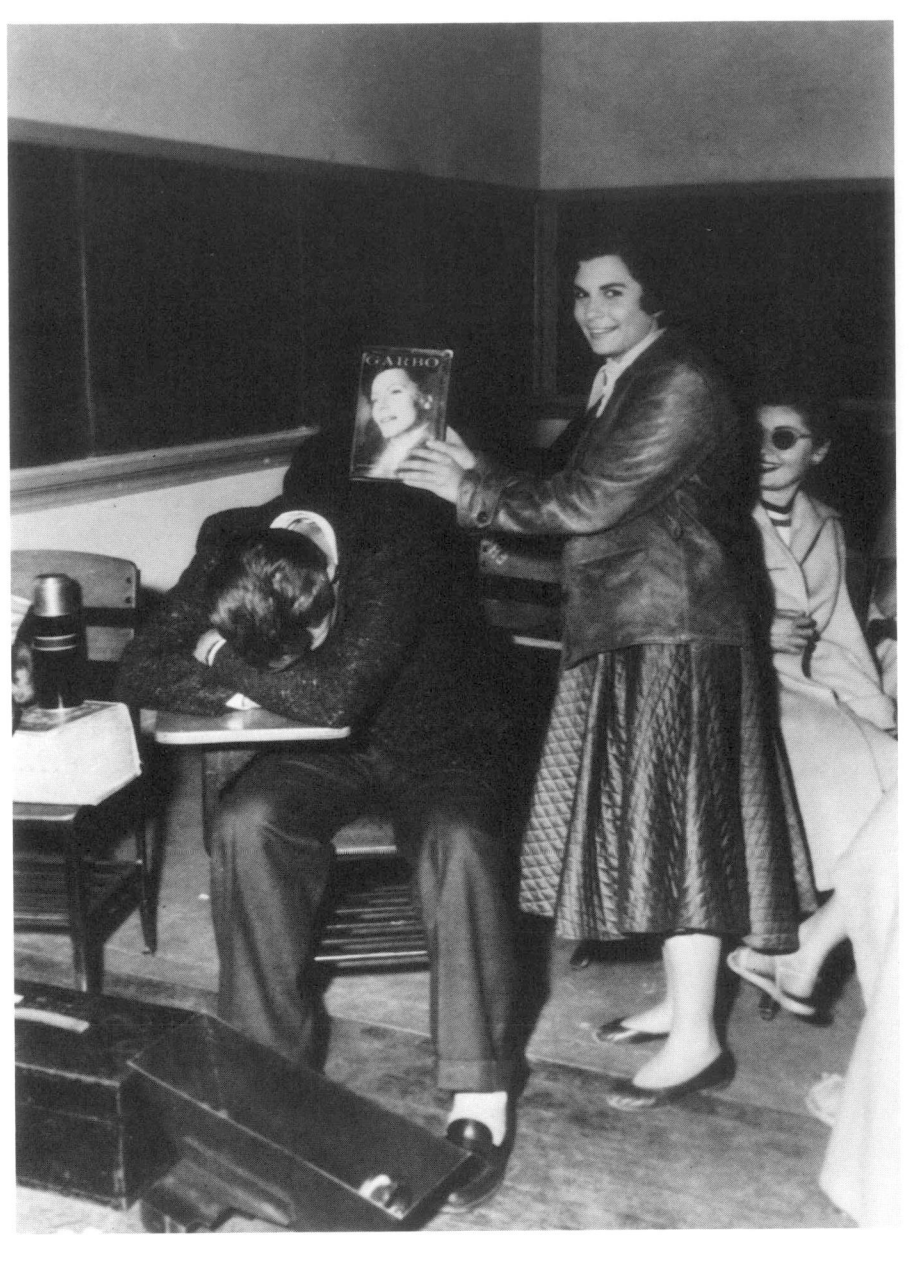

*Jimmy and fan, above, play on his
reputation for being reclusive.*
LOEHR COLLECTION.

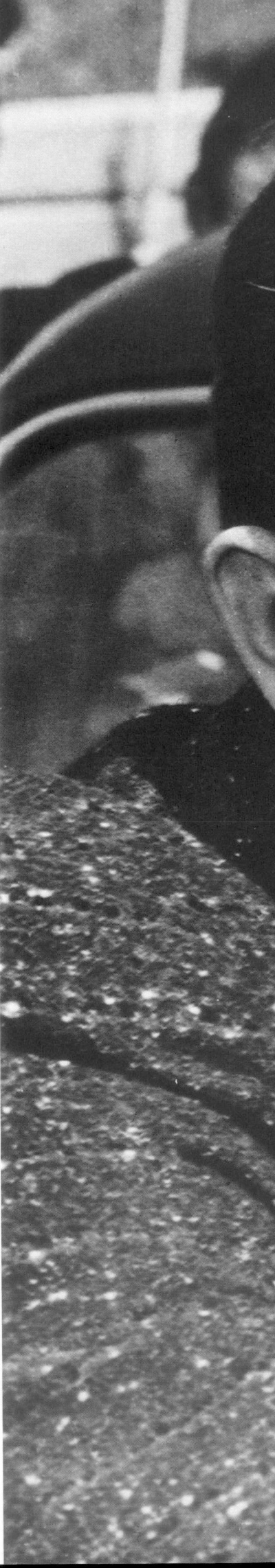

The many moods of Jimmy Dean.
Above: With fellow actors, Perry Lopez
and Natalie Wood.
©WARNER BROS. INC.

character of Jim Stark. According to Nick Ray, "On one side the difficulty was personal since, beginning to know him a little, I realized that, for a successful collaboration, he needed a special kind of climate. He needed reassurance, tolerance, understanding. An important way of creating this was to involve him at every stage in the development of the picture."

According to Maila Nurmi, even the character of Plato was taken from a relationship in James Dean's own life—his friend, Jack Simmons. "They wrote that part about Jack. I don't know if they admit it. I had the impression that Sal Mineo in that picture was Jack Simmons as I knew him at that time." Simmons actually auditioned, but, apparently unable to play himself convincingly enough, was turned down. His performance, it was decided, was too "mannered."

Jimmy's uncanny improvisations and his almost supernatural sense of timing create the unexpected quirky moments that give *Rebel* depth. His instinctive grasp of the biology of gesture creates a subtle subliminal counterpoint to *Rebel*'s blatant histrionics.

James Dean is a moving target (as Jim Stark and as an actor), dodging clichés like bullets. Part of the suspense of the film comes from watching Jimmy weave through the labyrinth of stereotypes that—as in some carnival game—are thrown in his path. Stewart Stern, who as scriptwriter was responsible (along with Ray) for creating these phantom traps, watched this inner plot develop: "He was trying to get out of the role he felt he was being shoved into, whether as a son or a bad boy. Whatever it was, he wanted to be *himself*."

"James Dean," said Dennis Hopper, "was the first guerrilla artist ever to work in movies." As generational propaganda in the combat story between teenagers and adults, *Rebel* was loaded with messages by screenwriter Stern, who actually believed a movie could have the power to make parents "understand."

"After him came a new world," wrote William Zavatsky. "The civil rights movement, Black Power, women's liberation, gay rights. All of them, at least for me, had something to do with the struggle for identity depicted in *Rebel Without a Cause*. I had to think about the movie again when, instead of working things out with our real fathers, my generation

The cosmic and comic faces of Jimmy Dean. Left: "The boy inside"
at the planetarium. Right: Beatnik at a Hollywood party.
©WARNER BROS. INC.

For crew, actors and director, Rebel became a family affair, off the set and on. Opposite: With Nick Ray, Natalie and screen mother, Ann Doran. LOEHR COLLECTION.

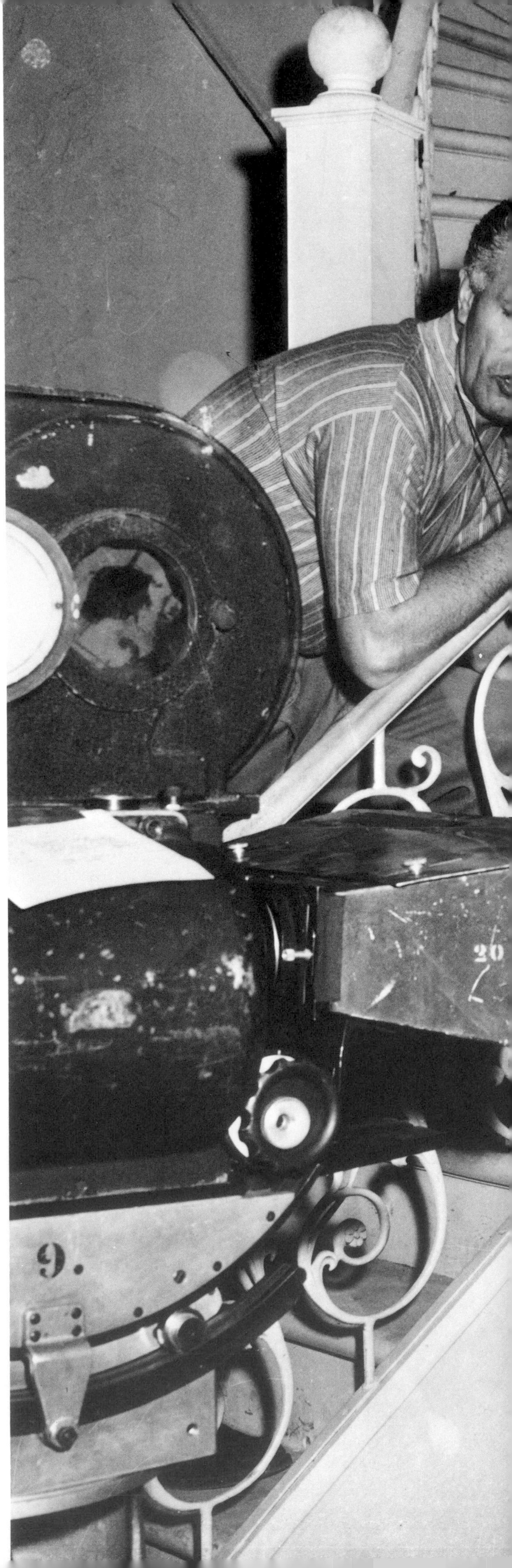

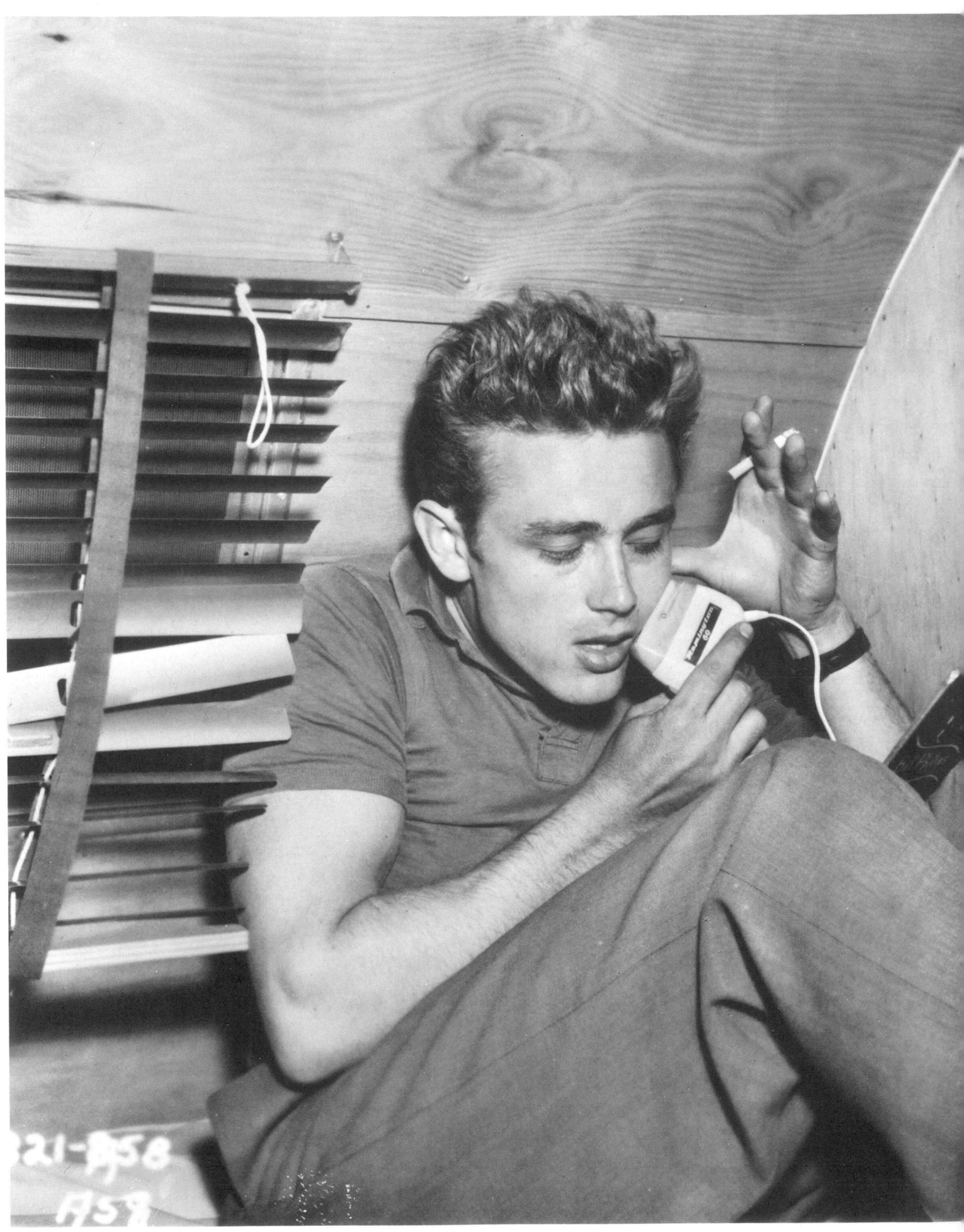

Above: On the set with Tab Hunter and composer Leonard Rosenman. Opposite: with Nick Adams, Natalie and Perry Lopez. LOEHR COLLECTION.

chose to bang heads with substitute ones — the police and the Selective Service."

Stewart Stern's script for *Rebel* took a popular theme from fifties theater — lack of communication — and applied it to the misunderstandings between parents and children. But the caricatures that passed for mothers and fathers in *Rebel* did little to bridge the gap. The very quality of these parents, like people from Edwin A. Abbott's geometric fantasy, *Flatland,* make them seem culpable on the grounds of insubstantiality alone. Their schematic quality and lack of depth suggests that they exist only as Jim Stark's projections, stock characterizations from an adolescent's allegorical imagination in which the most believable scenes are the dream sequences. A Teen Dream account of the world.

Although Cal is more obviously like the farm boy James Dean seemed to be, he is also someone who has a problem with his identity — with his father, with his mother, his brother, his brother's girlfriend — whereas Jim Stark is someone whose problems are relative; it is everyone *else* who has problems (the quintessential teen conceit). Jimmy's subtlety as an actor came from his ability to magnetize his characters, to give them a sort of multiple personality that extended into and absorbed the other characters. Jim Stark in *Rebel* identifies with all the other factions: he sympathizes with Plato's weakness, relates to Buzz and the other gang members, and, instead of abandoning his parents, tries to engage them. Like Jimmy, Jim Stark is an extremely empathetic character; he seems to be personally involved with everyone in the story.

The surrogate family of scarred teenagers — Jim, Judy, and Plato — extended to Jimmy, Natalie, and Sal outside the movie, as if a breach had been made in the line between fantasy and reality, as if this fantasy was, in fact, a model for a future reality.

Natalie Wood: "He was so inspiring, always so patient and kind. He didn't act as though he were a star at all. We all gave each other suggestions and he was very critical of himself, never satisfied with his work, worried about how every scene would turn out. He was so great when he played a scene, he had the ability to make everyone else look great too. He used to come on the set and watch the scenes, even when he wasn't in them. He was that interested in the whole picutre and not just his part."

In a 1974 television special devoted to James Dean, Peter Lawford (standing on the steps of the planetarium where the knife fight in *Rebel* takes place) spoke with Sal Mineo. "This place is full of spirits for me," said Sal. "Not only Jimmy's spirit but my spirit and everyone involved in that picture because it was an incredible experience. Something happened during the making of that picture for

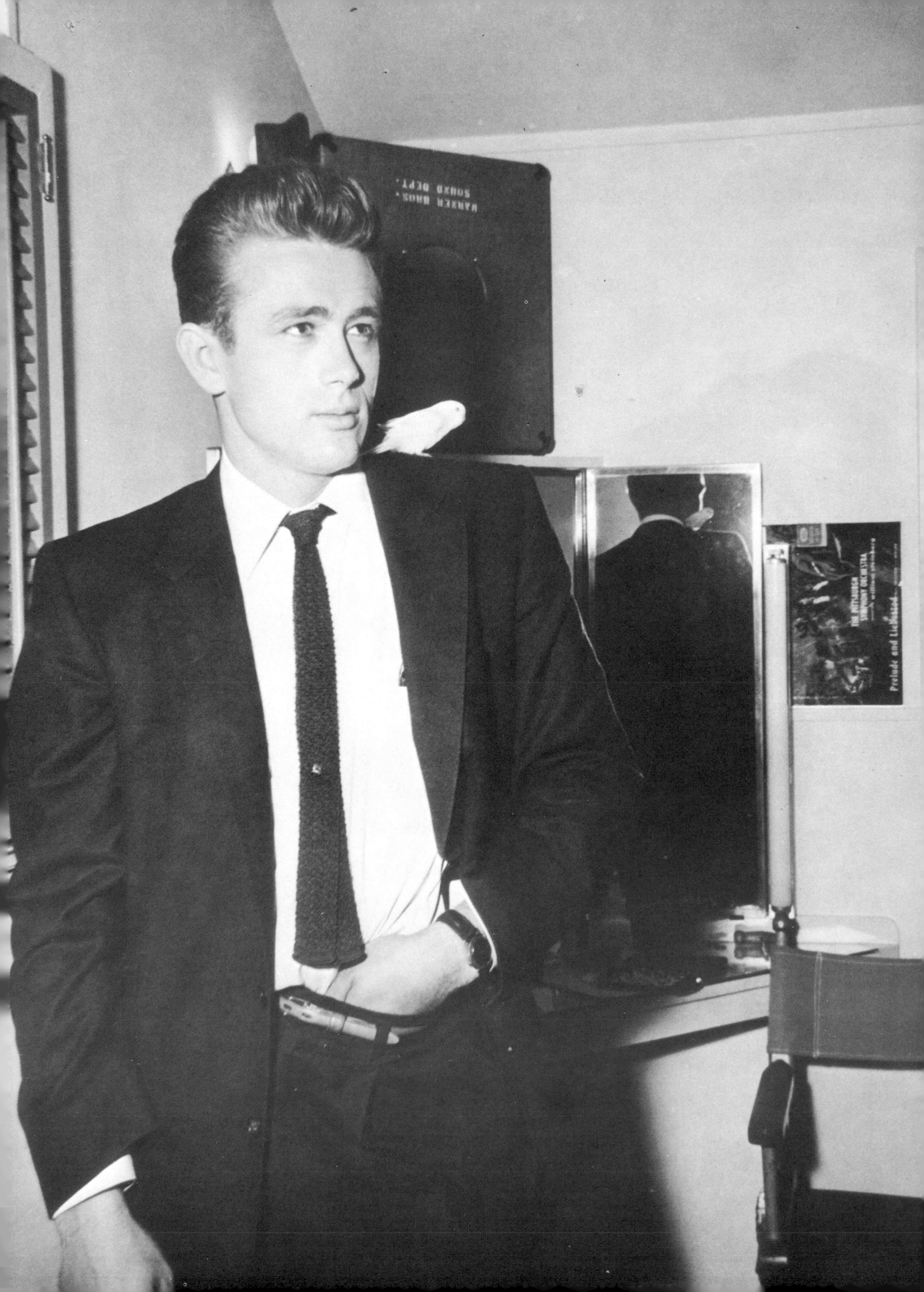

Opposite: In Rebel's make-up department with feathered friend. Above: Lunch with Jim Backus.
LOEHR COLLECTION.

everybody. It wasn't just making a movie. It was as close to a spiritual experience as you can get. And Jimmy was the focus, the center of it all. It all happened because of him."

Cars, clothes and codes of behavior are already magical emblems for teenagers, and Ray gave them a Larger Than Life meaning by clustering the central action of the movie around the granddaddy of cosmic metaphors, the planetarium, on whose temple-like steps the final ceremony takes place. The planetarium and its earthly counterpart, the deserted mansion, are symbolic spaces, metaphors for cosmos and community where, through Ray's magic realism, the teenage worlds of ritual and dream intertwine.

With Existential aplomb, Ray sets up a symmetry between inner states and outer space through the device of the planetarium projector. Most of the major scenes were shot at night with the peripheral field of vision bathed in shadow so that the actors, like the constellated images in the planetarium, appear to us as clusters of light in a hallucinated parenthesis of darkness.

"A star will appear, increasingly bright, increasingly near," the lecturer intones at the very moment the new student gives his name, "Jim Stark," to the woman taking attendance.

There is a sense of complete rightness about James Dean in *Rebel*. He's at the center of its planetary structure, and as long as that center holds, the whole film works, revolving and evolving around Jimmy's Jim Stark. His performance takes on the quality of gravity, attracting and holding all the other stars together as if he had projected them, as if they were psychic entities drifting through his fitful head.

Like other classic movies of youth and rebellion (René Clair's *Zero for Conduct*, Luis Buñuel's *Los Olvidados* and Francois Truffaut's *The Four Hundred Blows*), *Rebel* tells its story as the dreamscape of "the boy inside." It is a reverie of adolescence, a fairy tale told by "children" to their parents.

James Dean charms us in the magical sense of the word: his hypnotic focus becomes the "I" of the audience, a collective self whose intimate immensity, like that of the planetarium, turns the world outside in and ascribes our widescreen daydreams to the space that induces them.

In an eerie outtake, Jim Stark as a stranger in a strange land.
©WARNER BROS. INC.

THE EXISTENTIAL COWBOY

"Bury me under the X in Texas."
Red Steagill

Quest, horizon, retribution. These are the ineluctable terms of the Western, and *Giant*, although more of a family sage saga, nevertheless uses the Western's cowpoke paraphernalia and minimal, loaded landscape to stage the showdown. This symbolic encounter always takes place in the presence of an audience who, like the cowering townspeople present at the shoot-out, let other people get their kicks for them.

Hero and villain are interchangeable. If Jimmy "was" Cal Trask in *East of Eden*, Jett Rink is what became of Jimmy as James Dean after his well came in.

In the first half of *Giant* we identify totally and uncritically with Jimmy and we participate unreservedly in his story. We see ourselves darkly, the consequence of our identification with this classic American hero in a haunted folk tale of a West bewitched by its own corrupt wishes. It is the other side of the American dream, and no one could have better conveyed our future and own fatal attraction for this dream than James Dean, who saw himself so unflinchingly in his role that we glimpse the horror of what will, in the end, become his own nightmare.

On location for Giant, *Jimmy prepares for his last great role, as the rags-to-riches oil baron, Jett Rink — Marfa, Texas, July 1955.*
©SID AVERY.

We suddenly perceive the self-generating causes of the misfortunes that befall not only our fictional heroes, but the real idols whom we elect to portray them. Success, *the* American tragedy, is not so much a social problem as an obsessive hero worship that reduces everything to plot and personality by the nature of the ritual drama re-enacted. The price we pay for idolatry is self-absolving and self-generating delusions.

Jett Rink is a self-absorbed, selfish giant, mindlessly contemplating his own hugeness. Rock Hudson's Bick Benedict is merely the constant against which the true tragedy and corruption of America is played, a facade as wooden as the great Reata mansion itself. He is a symbol for the powers that be, sort of like General Motors if it were a family man who decided to settle in Texas rather than Detroit.

Hog-tying Liz Taylor and chronic lariat-twirling were among the diversions Jimmy amused himself with on location in Texas.
©SANFORD ROTH.

When Jett Rink's well comes in, oil enters the picture as both power and disease, the blackness of his own heart raining down on him as he dances in a ritual of exultation, the ecstatic and ominous moment on which the movie pivots. Both blessing and curse, oil is the magic equivocal substance of America with which he would wreak vengeance on the Benedicts and bring on his own destruction. But the suppressed energy releasing the Thing beneath the earth also releases something else: the monstrous consequences of the wish come true.

We witness the bullying, bigotry, ruthlessness and pathetic triumph of Jett Rink as *Giant* grinds on as endlessly as the prairie landscape itself. An episodic family album, it finally attains the stunning pointlessness of monotony. We feel like a captive audience watching a homemade movie on a six-million-dollar budget. *Giant* seems to end at least five times. Contrived melodramas and moral pieties that are strangely obligatory yet instantly dismissable; a plodding on of detail and personal accounting as witless and exhaustive as an Annual Report. Its final message seems to have the boggling massiveness of a dinosaur designed by committee: mindless, senseless, out of proportion and out of control. It is an unconscious parody of Hollywood itself, unwieldy and corrupt, almost an extinct institution.

James Dean conceived Jett Rink as a commentary on a petulant malignancy only hinted at in *Rebel*

d Avery.

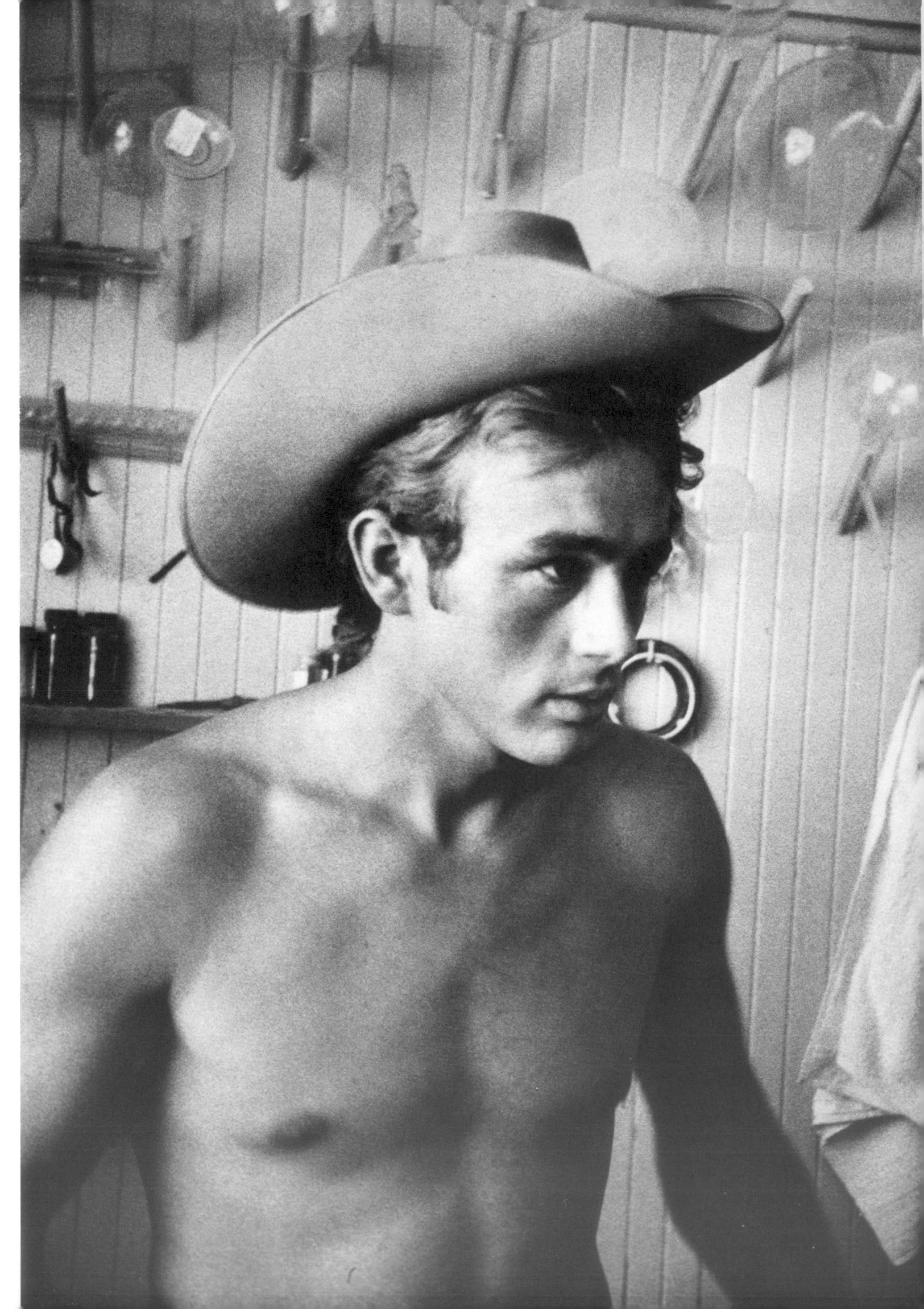

Throwing horseshoes with his father,
Winton Dean, Marfa, Texas.
©PHOTO RESEARCHERS.

and *Eden*. In *Giant* it is a self-condemning, self-destructive tendency that threatens to erupt into a truly hideous realization. Jett evolves into a victim of his own uncontrollable vengeance, revealing the generic perversions of human nature. The things that oppress and humiliate Jett are inherent to the American anti-hero whose retribution is violence and whose reward is isolation.

The hero's rebellion against abstract agents of evil, defines and involves him simply by his own collusion. His motives are deceptively hidden, subsumed in a final sacrificial act. The outsider who is a catalyst for change is also an agent of evil — the disruption and chaos momentarily resolved by the mere force of climax.

Rink is an embodiment of the dark forces that have been foisted upon him. His capacity for ambivalence suggests the sensuous, enticing hero/villain whose seductive surface ripples with undefined menace, something we admit into ourselves at our own peril. Dean seduces the audience and then, layer by layer, begins to peel away Jett's illusions and our own along with them. Exposing the potential corruption inherent in all obsessive dreams, Jett is ultimately a repulsive character at the bottom of the American myth. As Tony Parsons remarks: "Dean was so good as Rink because the part allowed him to give his considerable self-loathing full rein."

Jett defines the ontological drifter, the malcontent who inadvertently seeks his own destruction by attempting to bring down the powers that be. Jimmy's idea of the part would have made Stevens's Gargantuan film an anti-Western, confounding the terms of classic confrontation between good and evil by subsuming hero and villain in the same character. In Jett Rink, Jimmy fused together the qualities of both Alan Ladd's Sir Galahad and Jack Palance's gunfighter, overlapping them and revealing their identical nature: the demoniac hero absolved of everything and the villain loaded with the sins of circumstance. Sheriff and gunslinger, they are both vaudeville hucksters who ritually play out our fantasies of right and wrong and then move on to the next town.

Jimmy's stylized Still Lifes in Giant *congeal the action of the movie into fragments. Opposite: The "crucifixion" still, with Elizabeth Taylor. Above: This classic image made James Dean the first star you could, literally, put on.*
©WARNER BROS. INC.

Ever since he'd first heard of the project while working on *East of Eden*, Jimmy had been nurturing his own image of Jett Rink, using Jett to express the conflicting elements in his own nature: rebel, loner, and anti-hero. Although on the surface physically unsuited to play a surly, proletarian role that might have been more appropriate for Brando, Jimmy nevertheless managed to convince George Stevens. In making his decision, Stevens passed over both Richard Burton and Alan Ladd. (Ladd had starred in *Shane*, the revisionist Western for which Stevens won an Academy Award in 1951.) Stevens cast two other veterans of *Rebel* in *Giant*: Dennis Hopper, who serves as a sort of liberal counterpart to Dean's Rink, and Sal Mineo, who gets to die, again. Taking a chance in casting Dean, Stevens evidently chose him as much for the volatile elements he would inject into this epic of American life in transition as he did because Jimmy was a rising star who would reflect that transition.

Edna Ferber's Jett Rink is a stereotype of the rootless redneck, a stock character in Krantzian-glitz potboilers. Jimmy aimed to remake the central casting cipher of Edna Ferber's novel, *Giant,* into an anti-matter force that would detonate on contact with the other characters in the movie. He stretched out the character beyond anything Ferber ever meant or wished, insidiously enclosing in Jett Rink the paradoxical persona of James Dean, with all its exclusion and resentment. In Ferber's novel, Jett Rink is no more than a conventional ranch hand ready-made: a rough, rags-to-riches roustabout who, by exposing the barrenness of his soul, reveals the vulgarity and futility of the American Dream.

When Stevens chose Dean, he shifted the axis of *Giant*. This change in emphasis was reflected not only in the characterization of Jett Rink as (initially) a more complex and sympathetic role, but in the implications this would have on the plot.

Stressing the bitterness of this orphaned runt adopted by the matriarchal Luz Benedict and then excluded by her brother Bick, Stevens posited Jett as the same ruthless outsider portrayed by Monty Clift in *A Place in the Sun*. Stevens thus set in motion a conflict of American types — a clash of irreconcilable values that he was subsequently to back away from. By failing to carry out this implicit theme and, as he later admitted, by distrusting Jimmy's instincts about Jett, Stevens undermined the one thing that could have pulled his movie together: Jimmy's concentric interpretation of the role.

Throughout the making of *Giant*, Jimmy complained endlessly about Stevens's abuse of his talents. According to Eartha Kitt, "He felt he was being sacrificed for Taylor and Rock Hudson, and he was not pleased about it. He blamed everything on the director. He said the picture was going too big in an artificial way. He wanted the interpretation of him as an old man to be quite different from what it was turning out to be."

As it is, James Dean overshadows everything in *Giant* and belies its colossal timidity. Frustrated at not being able to fully realize and materialize his own construction of Jett Rink, Dean poured the fury of a demon on George Stevens. But how unreasonable! Didn't Stevens realize this film was part of a trilogy in which James Dean as prodigal son/rebel/victim would act out his immaculate conception of the American tragedy?

Although it's tempting to condemn Stevens's lack of vision, one can hardly blame him for not having had the foresight to acquiesce to Jimmy's inner compulsion to star in his own ongoing cinematic myth: the sanctification of James Dean. Stevens, in any case, had already made *An American Tragedy*

At the turning point in the movie, Jett Rink's well comes in and James Dean begins to fade out.
©WARNER BROS. INC.

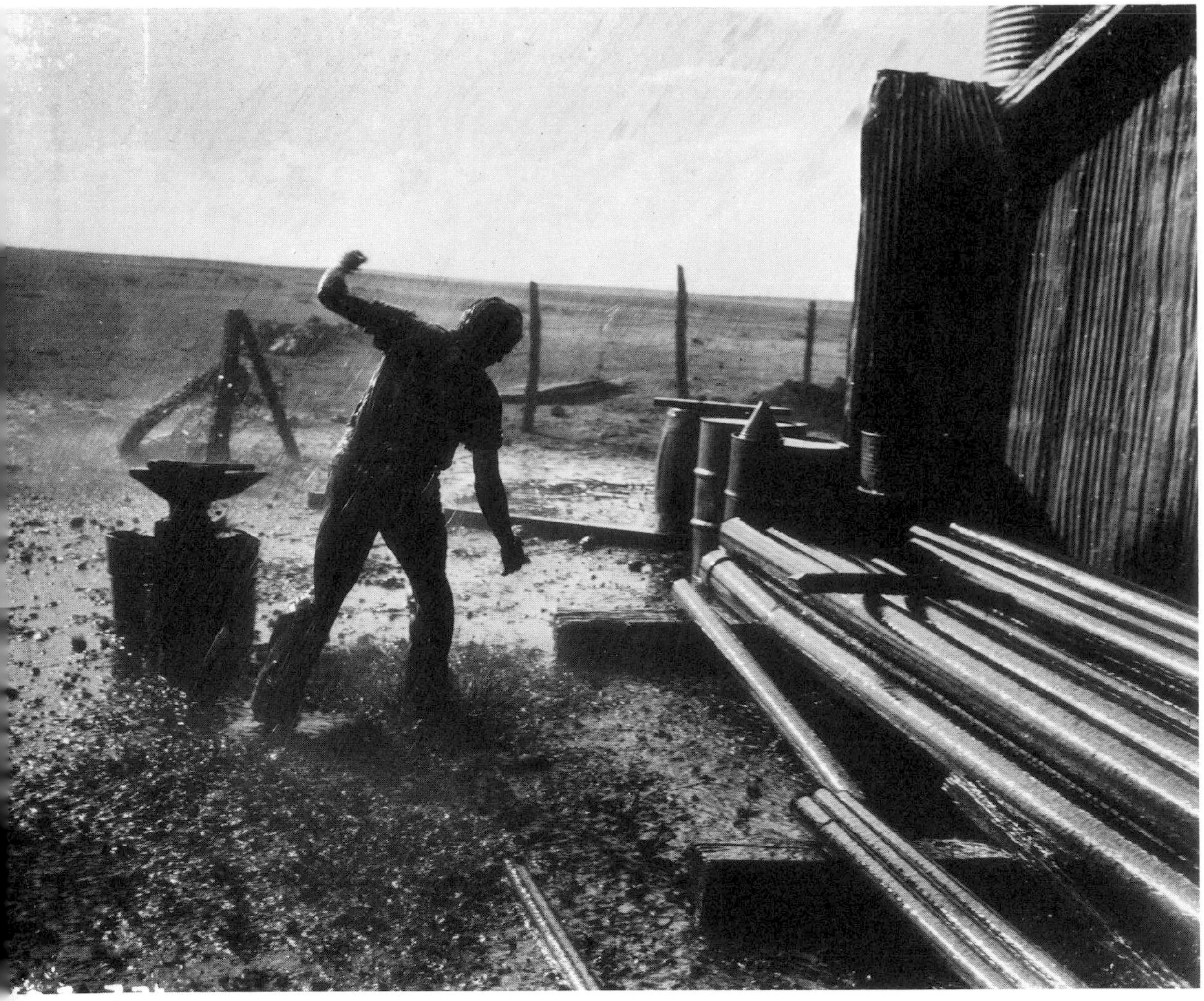

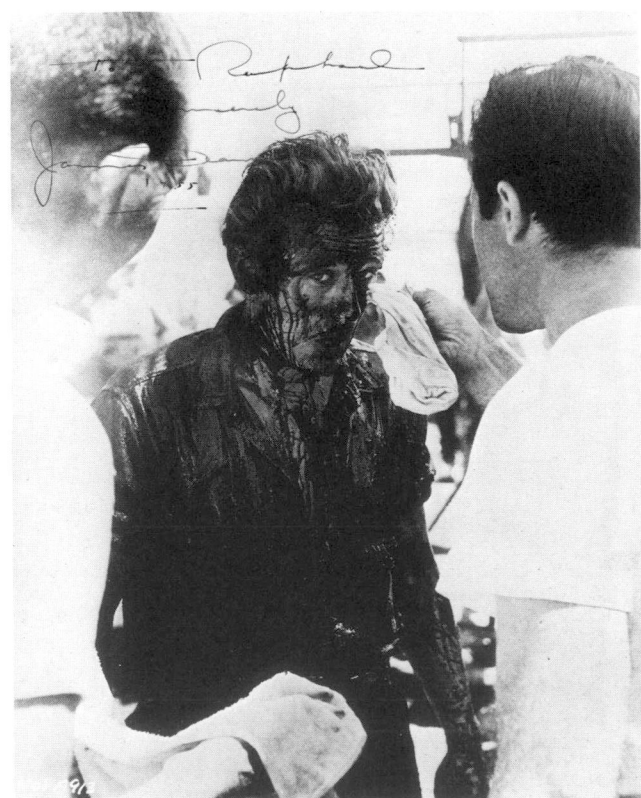

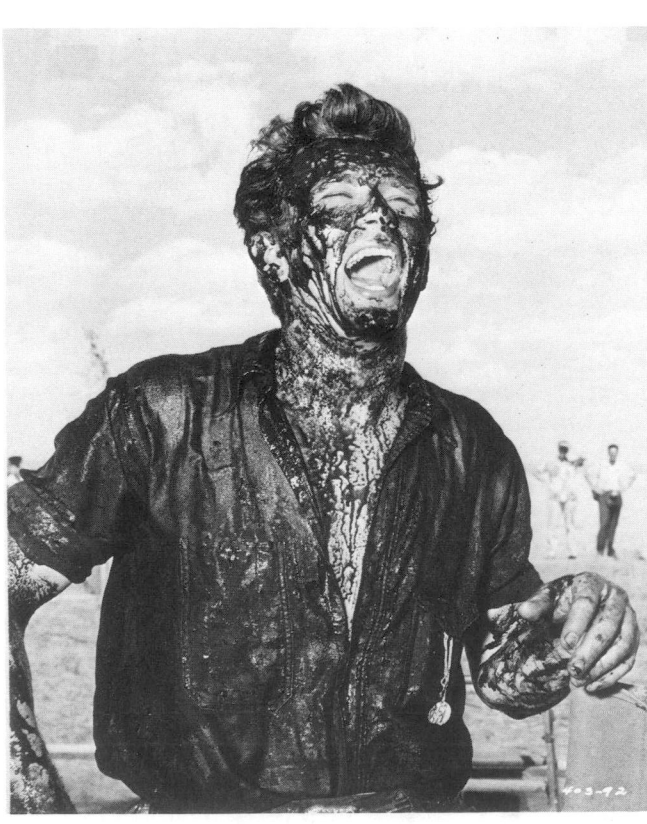

Jett celebrates his fateful strike.
©WARNER BROS. INC.

Courtesy Ron Ianitello

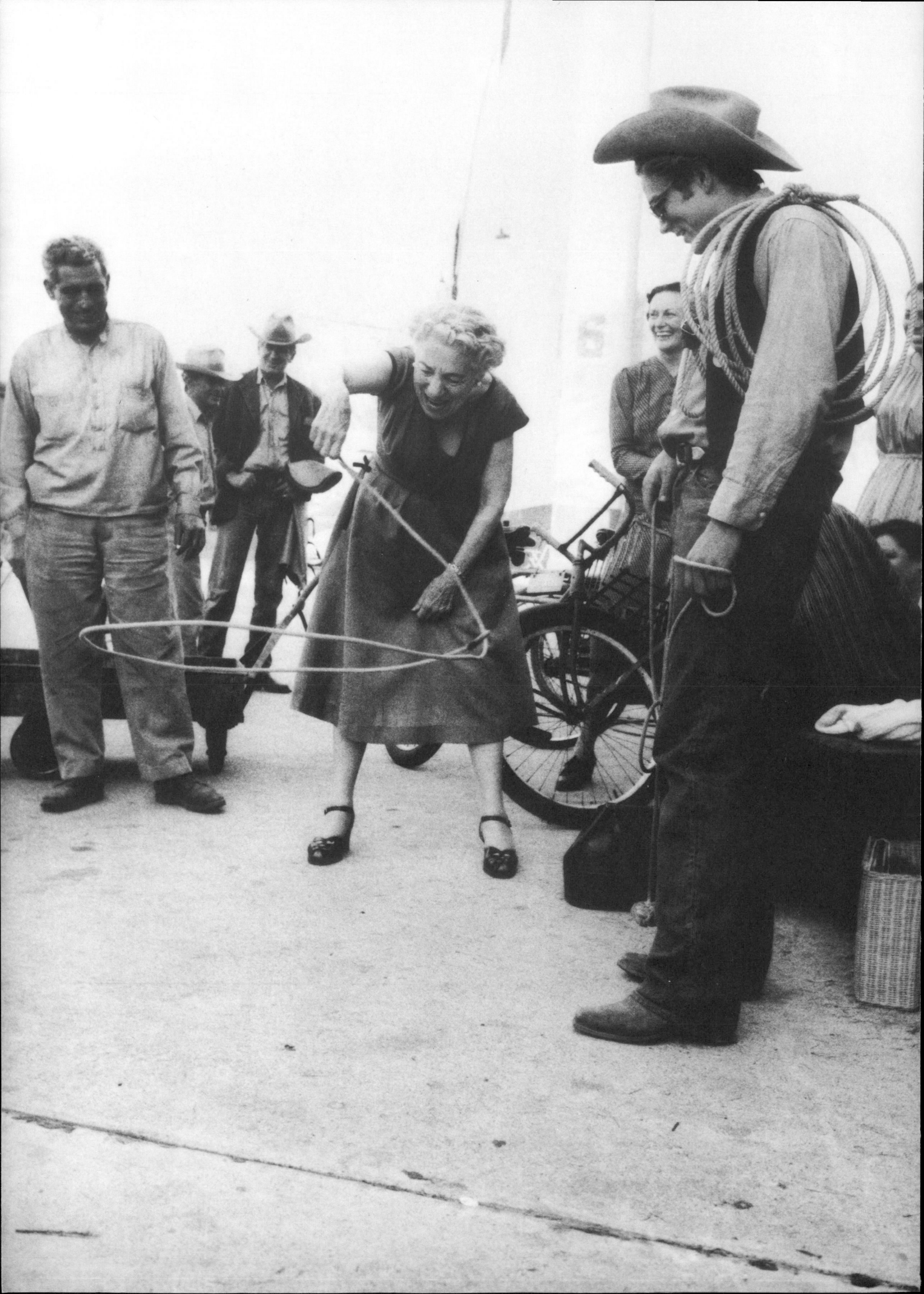

(the novel by Theodore Dreiser on which *A Place in the Sun* is based) with Monty Clift.

George Stevens: "Jimmy never understood that Jett Rink was only *part* of that film, he was never, and Edna Ferber in the book never intended Jett Rink to be, the central figure; he was only one character in all of those upheavals. He was a casualty of them. Perhaps Jett Rink's character should have been more developed, but Jimmy was so into that character he could only see it through Jett's eyes. He was as inflexible and as insensitive as Jett Rink as a performer. Jett Rink was meant to be a collective portrait of America in transition. I didn't want to focus on one character. *Giant* was a different kind of story altogether from *A Place in the Sun*. I was trying to paint a broader picture. To make Jett Rink the central character would have totally unblanced the film. Jett Rink is a pathetic figure. To concentrate on him would have made the whole movie very negative; it's about people who have adapted and changed, and I wanted to show that in a positive light."

But Dean's success in *Rebel* and *Eden* had depended on an absolute refusal to allow his inner demon to be betrayed. The turmoil of Cal Trask and Jim Stark was a willingly encoded message; they were avatars of James Dean. He was hardly prepared to "strut and fret his hour upon the stage" like the hired hand he had been hired to play in *Giant*.

Jimmy's identity confounded, he was caught in a trap not too different from Jett's. His close friend, Eartha Kitt, described his dilemma: "How to handle an individual, that's what Hollywood is all about. If you're run-of-the-mill, if you can sing so that the housewives think they can sing in the bathtub as well as you can, then you're in. But if you're looking for that individual inside of yourself in order to act at all, if you're very different—then there's frustration. What they need is a stuffed doll. I think that's all that Hollywood can handle. During *Giant*, Jimmy was being set up to play Rocky Graziano in *Somebody Up There Likes Me*, and that *Left Handed Gun* picture. . . . Just the same old commerical grind. That sort of frustration is real heavy to carry."

Above, top: Edna Ferber, author of Giant, *explains her own brand of dialect to the Existential Cowboy. Opposite: Showing Edna the ropes.*
©SANFORD ROTH.

©Sanford Roth.

Jimmy was beside himself, eclipsed by his most consummate creation: a seductive, vengeful Jett Rink. Sublimated alive! Stevens had exiled him, doomed his disembodied spirit to wander the wasteland of Marfa for eternity.

"That's not me! That's not where I want to go!" he'd said in a hysterical outburst to Eartha Kitt. Like a character from a folktale, Jimmy had used up his three wishes, and no spell could release him from his final transformation. It was in the form of this impish crone that Sal Mineo saw him for the last time: "Just outside the commissary, a little old man with a mustache passed by. I didn't know him, but, as he passed, I caught him smiling. That grin gave him away. It was Jimmy—with a mustache, hair pushed back, shoulders hunched, still in the part of an old man."

Jimmy's chameleonlike characterizations of Jett Rink are a litany of Hollywood Western postures and a tribute to its great stars, from Gary Cooper to Clark Gable. Significantly, Brando, in his interpretation of Don Corleone in *The Godfather*, used Jimmy's power-crazed oil baron as the basis for *his* characterization, even incorporating cosmetic details like Jett Rink's pencil moustache and hair in his make-up.

East of Eden and *Rebel* were not made the way movies had traditionally been produced. Hollywood was a system of assembly-line production that depended on professionals, and Jimmy was not a professional.

George Stevens, considerably older than Ray and Kazan, was more in the tradition of Hollywood directors in the classic mold — John Ford, Howard Hawks — around whom the writers for the French film journal, *Cahiers du Cinéma*, developed their *auteur* theory. The *auteur* theory, in essence, says that a director's body of work, his *oeuvre*, reflects an inherent personality, just as the writers of books are authors (or *auteurs*) of their collected works. Yet it may be that the collected works of these auteur-itarian directors, works which French intellectuals took as representing the intention of a specific personality, were actually a reflection of the Hollywood studio system. Underestimated under the reign of such pharaohs as Louis B. Mayer, Jack Warner and David O. Selznick, these esoteric codes of cinematic structure were revealed to us by the writers of *Cahiers du Cinéma*. But, like the great stars of Hollywood, directors were often merely glorified workers on the pyramids. If anyone was the *auteur*, it was the studio mogul who decided what kind of movie was to be made by whom and with whom. Directors were the foremen of this production line, and actors, of whatever magnitude, remained unequivocally creatures of the seven-year contract.

Steven's method of directing was to cover each scene from a number of angles, shooting a wide pattern of close-ups, two-shots, pans, and so on. To most filmmakers today, such a tangential process would seem an infamous waste of film. More than 600,000 feet of film were shot on *Giant*, only 25,000 feet of

In this outtake, where Jimmy gets to punch out Rock Hudson yet again, the two stars battle it out over their favorite bands.
LOEHR COLLECTION.

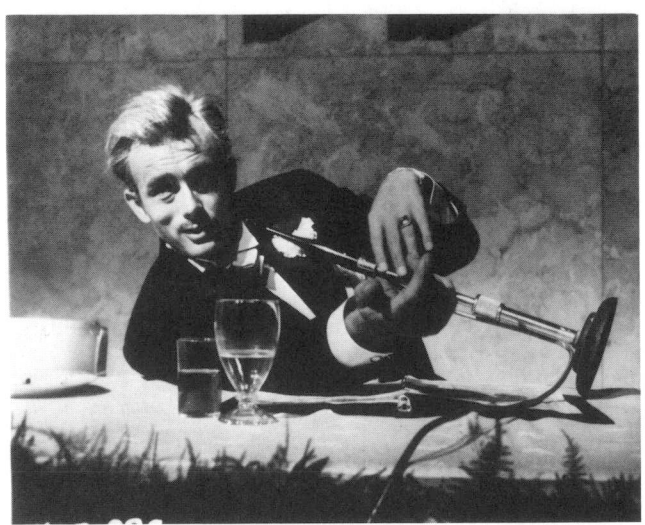

which would be used in the final edit. A ratio of twenty-four to one was — even at that time and even for Hollywood — astonishingly high. Jimmy was contemptuous: "They show up at the beginning of a day's shooting without any real plan. Somehow they sort of muddle through. Stevens has a method I call the 'round the clock' system. He takes all that film and shoots every scene from every possibe angle — all round the scene, up, down, here, there — and when he's through he gets himself the best editor in town. Then they spend a year selecting from miles and miles of film the best shots and the best scenes. They figure the whole thing out like a jigsaw puzzle. And when they're through, surprise! — another masterpiece. How can he go wrong?"

Judging from his description of Jimmy's acting exercises on the set, Rock Hudson's first reaction must have been to shout, "Nurse!": "Before coming on the set he used to warm up like a fighter before a contest. He never stepped into camera range without first jumping into the air with his knees up under his chin, or running at full speed around the set shrieking like a bird of prey."

It's easy enough to see Jimmy as a sort of Che Guevara of cinema and Stevens as a metaphor for the bureaucracy of Hollywood, but *we* didn't have to edit the rushes or even watch them for that matter: thousands and thousands of feet of out-of-sync James Dean, mismatched room tone, discontinuous dialogue. The nightclub scene with Carroll Baker needed thirty different takes alone, and three days of Jimmy's "psyche-up" preparations would be enough to make anyone lose control.

Combined with Stevens's method of directing, Jimmy's acting style was, well. . .talk about pouring salt on a wound! In any case, it was all a bit too suspenseful for Stevens: "Sometimes Dean broke a scene down into so many bits and pieces that I couldn't see the scene for the trees, so to speak, I must admit that I sometimes underestimated him; and sometimes he overestimated the effects he thought he was getting. Then he might change his approach, do it quick, and, if that didn't work, we'd

As the aging oil tycoon, Jimmy didn't even get the last word in Giant. *The "last supper" speech, above, had to be dubbed in by Nick Adams after Jimmy's death.*
©WARNER BROS. INC.

©Sanford Roth.

For James Dean getting old was strictly a cosmetic condition.
Above: In the Warner Brothers make-up department.
Opposite: With the gray scale, used to calibrate skin tones.
©SANFORD ROTH.

403-A471

effect a compromise. All in all, it was a hell of a headache to work with him. He was always pulling and hauling, and he had developed this cultivated, designed, irresponsibility. It's tough on you, he'd seem to imply, but I've just got to do it this way. From the director's angle that isn't the most delightful sort of fellow to work with."

It's as if Jimmy now saw Stevens the same way that Jett Rink saw Bick Benedict. Perhaps he wanted

way twice, based his method of spontaneous combustion on its *unpredictability*.

Perhaps Stevens, having spotted Jimmy as a *Potential Trouble Source*, began to truncate Jett Rink's central role in the plot. But the abrasive quality of Dean's presence in *Giant* eventually divorces Jett from the movie altogether. In his attempt to co-opt *Giant*, Dean becomes a cameo performer, a "supporting role" in the movie he hoped to

©Sanford Roth.

to sabotage *Giant* for the same reason Jett had wanted to bring down the Benedicts — out of sheer bloody-mindedness.

It should be noted that even Liz felt left out: "I found out on *Giant* that Stevens tends to like having a patsy or two on a film. Jimmy Dean was one and I was another. But I'll say this for George — he usually picks people who can answer back."

It was a collision course: the Method meets the System! Stevens's system allowed for as few surprises as possible. Every scene involved a minimum of three camera angles and was meticulously worked out with the actors and crew before rolling the film. Jimmy, who never played the same scene the same

manipulate into the vehicle of his own crusade.

He unquestionably *stands out* against the seamless texture of Stevens's epic, as the French critic, Louis Marcorelles (or anybody else, for that matter) can hardly fail to notice: "James Dean, curiously enough, injects some false notes into the all-too-well-arranged concerto of images and feelings. His style of acting is the very antithesis of the discreet and well-tamed style of the other actors in the film."

James Dean's stylized Still Lifes congeal the action of the movie into fragments: the classic "crucifixion" pose (rifle threaded like a cross through his arms, Liz Taylor kneeling at his feet) is practically

Opposite: With Liz Taylor and Mike Todd, Jr. Above: Rehearsing the banquet scene with director, George Stevens.
©WARNER BROS. INC.

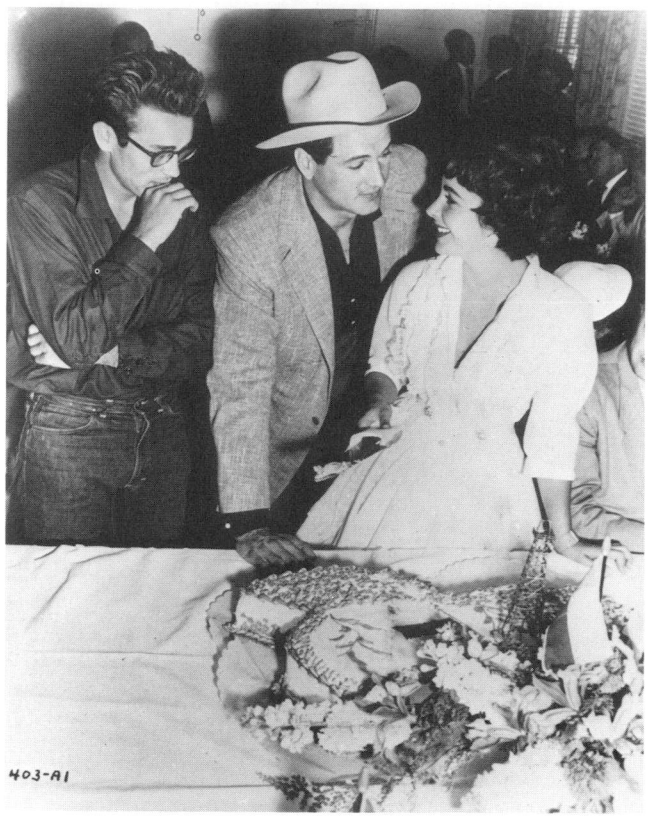

403-A1

Suitable For Framing. A set of anaphoric gestures accompany these images (head hanging, lariat kneading, hip-locked weight shifting), the most equivocal of which, the sign-off hand signal, crops up throughout the movie with subtle variations like a refrain: "count me out," "see ya later," "I quit," "we're quits." Dean's ready-mades of attitude are parenthetical pauses that shift the center of gravity from the flow of the movie to the freeze frame, which, like a quotation, implies that it is from another source.

Jimmy's quite literally outstanding performance makes him a sort of time traveler, in the same way a New Guinea tribesman cast as Caliban in *The Tempest* might be. But this only serves to nurture the image of *James Dean*. His intended self-portrait as Jett Rink creates an uneasy hall-of-mirrors effect as he worshipfully eyes his own reflection. A mannered self-parody that often verges on Camp, it's hardly surprising that this image became the basis for a Levi's commercial in the eighties. It is a pose, an isolated, disconnected image that has become the trademark of James Dean.

Stevens was a Romantic who painted portraits of America in terms of darkness and light falling on an indecipherable hieroglyphic of place. He shared with Jimmy a common American value that appears all the more awesome because of their combined inability to encompass it. Spiritually, they both inhabited the same mythological American landscape for which Texas is only one metaphor, a state of mind so vast that they never seem to be able to find each other in it.

Extravaganzas like *Giant* become their own *auteur.* Too much of nothing is quite a statement in itself! Stevens wanted his epic to be a collective picture of Americans, but "Americans" is such a colossal generalization that it seems to evaporate when applied to a people dwarfed by "virtually uninhabited" territory.

The most maddening thing about *Giant* is its attempt to be almost as big, geographically, as America itself — or at least Texas. And America *is* an idea, its size elusive even to cartographic, never mind cinematic, significance.

"It's fifty miles to coffee," as Bick Benedict puts it. America's vastness is the enigma, an unaccountable paradox that, the more we attempt to circumscribe it, the more evident becomes our dilemma. The vastness of it all swamps everything in *Giant,* so that the themes of racial prejudice, the quarrels of generations and the aspirations of a people are all somehow diminished. A piece of legal stationary with blanks where the parties and special circumstances are left to be filled in, Texas-as-America in *Giant* is so overwhelming that in the end only the artificial grandeur of the landscape seems real.

403-X15

Wardrobe tests for Giant. *Opposite and overleaf:* Giant *opens in L.A., November, 1956.*

By choosing to stage the Death Rites of the Hollywood Epic in the oil fields of Texas, Stevens anticipated the virtually endless allegory of money, power, corruption and sex that would become the nightly fare of television in the eighties. As he dismantled the plot of *Giant* into episodes, it became less a movie than a pilot for a TV series about a dynasty. Is it just coincidence that the malign oil tycoon in *Dallas* is named "J.R.," the same colossal initials we see emblazoned on the wall in the banquet scene in *Giant*? George Stevens had stumbled into the Land of the Prime Time Soap Opera 25 years too soon.

The parallels drawn betwen Jett Rink and James Dean, based on everything from psychology to astrology, range from the narrowly literal to the whimsically speculative. "Jett Rink, gently rebuffed by the young Luz Benedict, brings to mind James Dean's painful rejection by Pier Angeli," writes film theorist Robert Benayoun.

But according to John Gilmore, "Jimmy's tension had to do with the search and acceptance by the Father [capital supplied] in his life . . . . The Father had, in the end, not accepted him." *Totem and Taboo* in Texas!

Semiologists, on the other hand, see embedded in James Dean's Jett a gesture signifying an existential send off. Jean Queval in *Téléciné:* "The right hand held out open, palm up, and insolently swung to the side — the gesture that says: 'count me out'; that indicates withdrawal. And the gesture is emphasized by blue eyes which mock rather than challenge; the gesture of one who is retreating deep into himself, misunderstood, arrogant, and invulnerable."

By the time the unit returned to Hollywood in July to shoot interior sequences on the Warner Brothers lot, Jimmy had become a shadow of himself. During these last weeks of filming, Eartha Kitt greeted him at a friend's house and sensed with a shudder the eeriness of his disembodiment: "He hugged me and kissed me as he always did, but I couldn't *feel* him . . . . It was the strangest sensation. I said, 'What's the matter with you? I don't feel you.' And he said, 'Kitt, you're being a witch again.' "

Jett Rink becomes corrupt while trying to remake the world in his own image, and *Giant*, inevitably,

changed Jimmy into *Hollywood's* image of James Dean. Perhaps Jimmy felt that only an extreme solution would do and tried to write his own exit on the highway. As it turned out, however, Jimmy didn't even get the last word in *Giant*. The sound track for Jett's drunken monologue was too inaudible to be used and had to be dubbed in by Nick Adams after Jimmy's death. It's almost as if Jimmy, lost in the labyrinth of *Giant*, could never get out again, *his* giant entombed in Steven's insipid fade-out, com-promised by the system he'd vowed to subvert, with even his *voice* taken from him.

In the narrative of the hero's itinerary, he is forced with each new resolution to return in exile to the zero in himself. Would Odysseus, after *two* epics, have become involved in yet another one? As Goethe, who should know about selling your soul to yourself, said: "We are our own demon, we expel ourselves from Paradise."

143

DEANABILIA

When one has left many things undone in life,
sometimes it is not easy to find rest.
Mexican proverb quoted in *Whisper* magazine

"Now it can be told: JIMMY DEAN WAS NEVER KILLED! Based on information from authoritative sources, the editors of PRIVATE LIVES believe that Jimmy is really secretly hiding somewhere in NEW YORK CITY. A reward of $50,000 is offered for information leading to the actual person of Jimmy Dean! Informed sources, whose names we cannot disclose, say that Jimmy was horribly mangled by that 'fatal' accident last year. He is said to be afraid for the world to see his now-marred face. So to you, Jimmy, we write this open letter: Come out of hiding. Your fans love you — will always love you — **no matter what you look like!**"

"Serving as a pie target wasn't getting him anywhere." From the comic book biography, The Triumph and Tragedy of James Dean.
JERRY FAGNANI COLLECTION.

*Department store displays featuring
promotional material and James Dean
"tribute albums."*
©WARNER BROS. INC.

This groundbreaking offer, made in the June 1957 issue of *Private Lives*, came with such helpful hints as, "remember the face doesn't make the man," and, to prove it, supplied two of the least flattering photographs of James Dean you'll ever see. One showed a middle-aged man in fedora and black raincoat getting into a cab at Columbus Circle. The other — by far the less enlightening picture of the two — pinpointed an ectoplasmic citizen suffering from advanced airbrushing on a crowded New York street.

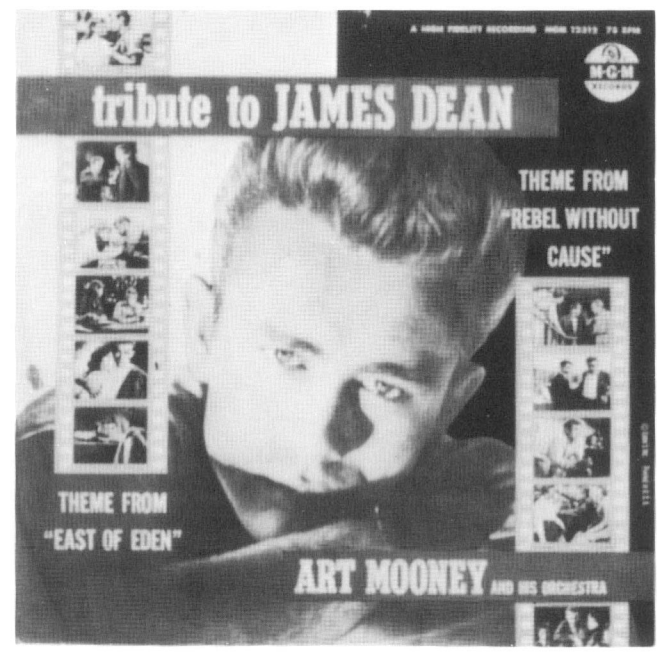

"Death," for James Dean, came in quotes. *Rebel* and *Giant* were released *after* his death, but even the most literal minded could hardly deny that "James Dean lives." To his fans, for whom Jimmy was never entirely mortal, his death was a mere formality.

Death removed Dean from the ranks of another species of teen idol (Tab Hunter, Robert Wagner and John Saxon), and endowed him with the sort of divinity that attached to the stars of Hollywood's classic era. Death also spared him the usual gamut of movie magazine trivia ("Jimmy Dean's Dating Dos and Don'ts"), although he could hardly be expected

to be exempt from the foolish and endless quest for his replacement – also known as, "THE SEARCH FOR MR. X."

"Elvis, Should He?" "Tony Perkins, Could Be!" "Paul Newman, Definitely!" "Cliff Robertson, Possibly," "Don Murray, We'll See," "Sal Mineo, Can He?" Dennis Hopper sensibly opted out, "Don't Call Me Another James Dean!"

Death, of course, did not preclude true love. Far from it. Jimmy – as David Browne assures us – was not only "on cordial speaking terms with death," he actually had "A DATE WITH DEATH!" Even in the hereafter, Jimmy retained the one attribute that every teen idol must have: he was eternally eligible (if still notoriously "altar-shy").

In the afterlife, true romance seems to have been the only thing to totally revive Jimmy, as he himself admitted: "How I found a new life beyond death in one girl's love . . . ." And when he wasn't carrying on his own affairs of the spirit, he meddled in other peoples: "James Dean's Ghost Wrecked My Two Marriages," "The Romance James Dean Couldn't Kill," "Tragic Love Jinx," etc.

It's not that Jimmy didn't have his share of romances before he died. A number of former girl-friends came forward after it was "safe to tell": "You Haven't Heard the Half About James Dean" (Natalie Wood); "The Girl He Left Behind" (Christine White); "Jimmy's Happiest Moments" (Ursula Andress); "In Memory of Jimmy" (Dizzy Sheridan); and Lynne Carter (shown wrapped in a bathtowel, brushing her teeth) confessed: "I learned about LOVE from Jimmy Dean." Jimmy's style was pretty unorthodox: "He bluntly told me I was infantile and recommended that I read several books." Some however, just didn't buy it.

"The article that was in your January issue is an outrage," wrote Maria C. of Philly. "This girl, Lynne Carter, should try doing some work to earn her living instead of lying to get her money." In any case, "this girl" was soon to be outdone by Beverly Willis in

Life-size cut-outs made up by Warner Brothers meant he could now be in more places than ever. Above, left: A winner in a James Dean radio contest (see page 197 for rules). Below, left: Longtime Dean fans welcome a new member to the club. Overleaf: Giant *opens in Tokyo.* ©WARNER BROS. INC.

Modern Screen: "I Almost Married James Dean. Who Am I?" (Which happens to be that freak of movie magazine confessions, a legitimate story.) Unfortunately, the biggest revelation of 1957 – "I was James Dean's Wife" – turned out to be a question of light housekeeping.

The movie magazines that flooded the stands in 1956 with James Dean cover stories confirm that, more than anything else, his was a posthumous cult. While alive Jimmy made barely a dozen appearances in the pages of *Photoplay, Modern Screen* and *Coronet* – for the most part in "mood" pieces: "Demon Dean," "Lone Wolf," "An Actor in Search of Himself." The only entry that could be considered a legitimate teen topic – Lori Nelson's "The Dean I've Dated" – appeared in *Motion Picture* the month of his death: "He's dynamic, deliberate, devilish and direct, but he's not eccentric." Otherwise, Jimmy shows up primarily in columnists' tidbits, like this snippet from Dorothy Kilgallen: "James Dean and his landlady aren't seeing eye-to-eye over the actor's hobby of repairing his motorcycle. He does it in the

ELVIS AND JIMMY

25¢

PDC

HOW IT FEELS TO BE ELVIS

Told for the first time

THE TRAGEDY & TRIUMPH OF JIMMY DEAN

A picture drama of Jimmy's life

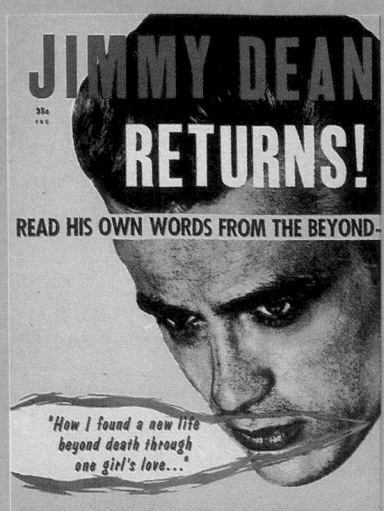

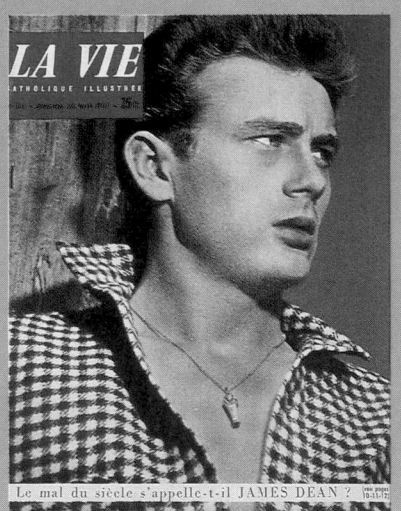

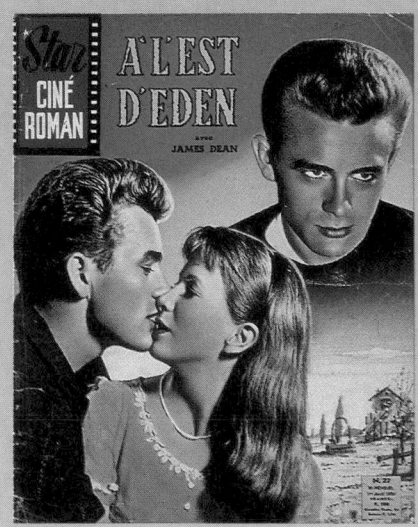

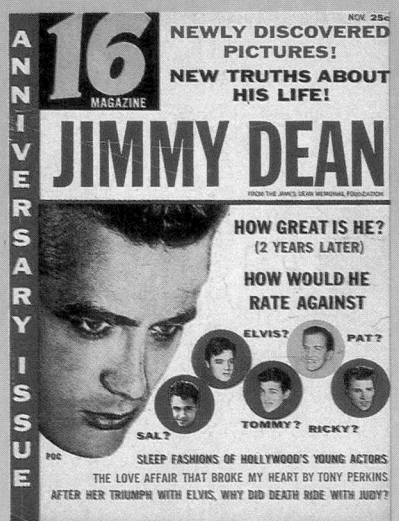

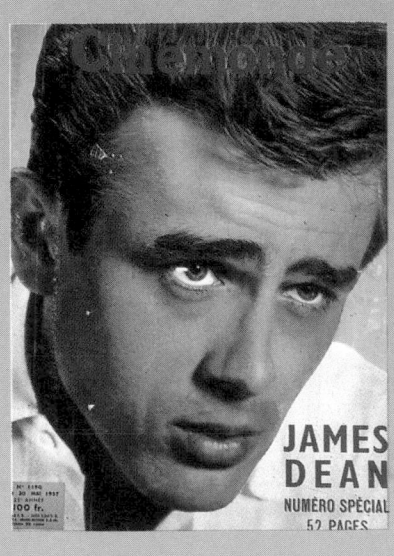

Above: Cover stories from 1956-57 and sheet music.
LOEHR COLLECTION.

THE BALLAD OF JAMES DEAN

Words and Music by JACK HAMMER

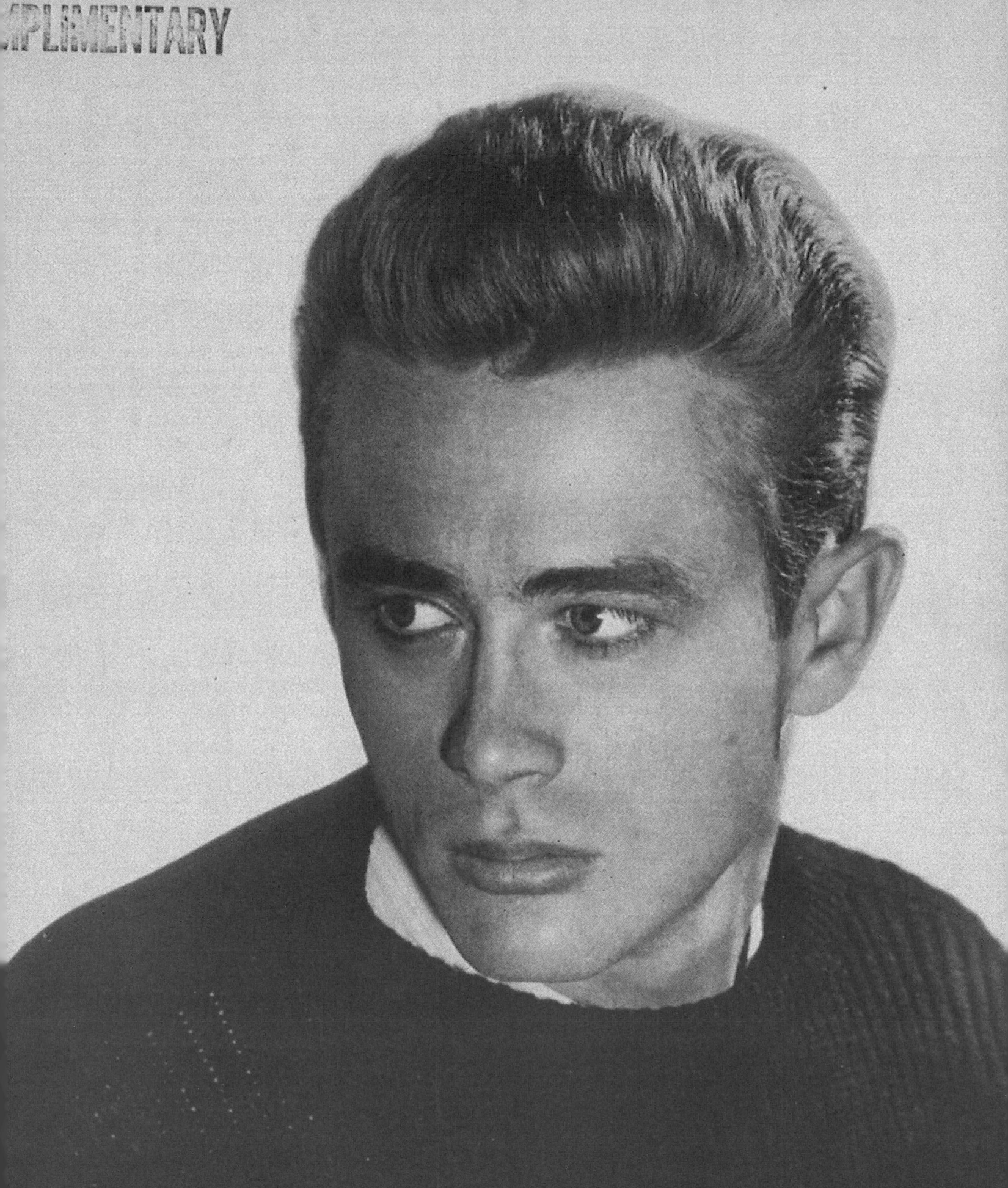

Jimmy as Comedy and Tragedy
on the sound stage for Guys and Dolls, *1955.*

©PHIL STERN.

With a switch-blade knife, symbol of teenage turbulence, in his name-plate, Dean is shown shortly before his smash-up.

storm when he made his first attempt upon ing UCLA. After two years, when he returned a citation as the most promising new actor he year for his Broadway part in "The Im-alist," he set out to even the score in movie-. He was often moody at the studio and ile to anyone who approached him for a r or pried for information. As people tried nterview him or befriend him, it amused him it calmly and stare unflinchingly, just to see t they would do. As Vivian Coleman says:

"He didn't go back with a chip on his shoulder— it was a boulder!"

Jimmy took great delight in surprising people —friends and public alike. He once went to a very fashionable party in a sweat shirt and dungarees and sat all evening alone in the library beating on his bongo drums, which caused rival Marlon Brando to remark: "Humph, last year's publicity."

So little was ever really known about Jimmy, that many of the stories concerning him were almost made up, or at best pieced together from

sketchy accounts. His publicity, both before and after his death, is mostly a repeat of the same basic facts.

He didn't live long enough to satisfy all his impetuous desires and to carry out his unending stream of plans, but he lived long enough and hard enough to create a lasting memory. It is one of the strangest stories ever to come out of Hollywood, this saga of the "rebel," who was almost unknown in life and is now worshipped in death.

SUNDAY MIRROR MAGAZINE, August 26, 1956. King Features Syndicate, Inc.

5

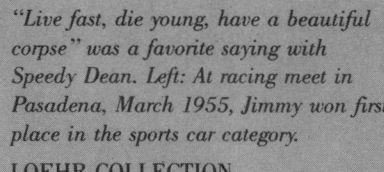

"Live fast, die young, have a beautiful corpse" was a favorite saying with Speedy Dean. Left: At racing meet in Pasadena, March 1955, Jimmy won first place in the sports car category.
LOEHR COLLECTION.

JAMES DEAN—
The Ghost Driver
Of Polonio Pass

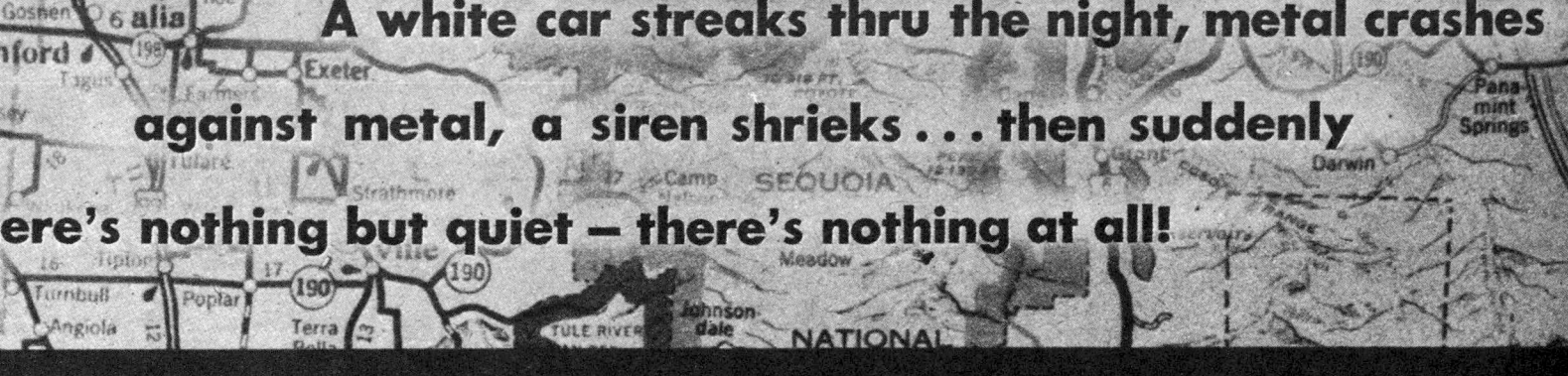

A white car streaks thru the night, metal crashes against metal, a siren shrieks... then suddenly here's nothing but quiet — there's nothing at all!

SAM SCHAEFFER

When one has left many things undone in life, sometimes it is not easy for the spirit to find rest.
— **Mexican proverb**

I THOUGHT A LOT about James Dean as I stood on a desolate stretch of highway just outside Cholame, California, a few weeks back. But mostly I thought about a magic night only a little over two years ago, when Jim and I were standing on Broadway together, the first time he ever saw his name up in lights on the Great White Way.

Manhattan was a city of a thousand-and-one kicks that night, a Bagdad-on-the-Subway for both of us...

And now, in mid-1957, I was thinking about that night again. Thinking about it because here, at the junction of Highways 41 and 466, I was looking upon another sort of marquee dedicated to James Dean.

But this was a macabre marquee, a shrine to a dead hero. And looking at it brought no kicks.

It brought a chill.

For it was on this spot that James Dean had met violent death in his speeding Porsche on the night of September 30, 1955.

Notes of Love

On the shoulder of the road there were flowers. Some were planted, others looked as if they'd been hurriedly tossed from passing cars, perhaps by teenage girls who still remembered the slouched, handsome figure of the boy who'd become loved all over the world as the *Rebel Without A Cause*.

Beyond the road's shoulder, on a small white fence, were thumbtacked some gilded crosses and small pieces of paper. The papers were notes written to James Dean, and I felt as though I were eavesdropping on another world as I read:

To Jimmy — now only in death shall we meet.

Jimmy, you'll always be remembered, you were the greatest, the absolute greatest.

Why did you leave us, Jimmy — why were you in such a hurry?

There were more—different words, different handwriting, but all just about the same. All tributes to a dead idol.

And as I stood there in that weird place of worship, I couldn't help remembering the satisfied grin that had crossed Jim's lips when he first saw his name up in lights.

And I wondered — what would he think of all this?

But it wasn't this eerie altar that had brought me all the way across the country to California. It was other things — whispers.

Whispers of unexplainable things — like a blurred, white sports car that raced thru the night; like the noise of screeching brakes and a shattering, ear-splitting collision where there were no cars; like a phantom ambulance that came careening out of nowhere and, siren screaming, disappeared back into nowhere.

Followed Same Route

I'd heard these whispers second-hand, in letters from Dean fans, or from the lips of people who had met other people who had told them they knew someone who had seen or heard these things.

So I decided to come to California myself. If a phantom Porsche could be seen racing thru the night on the road to Paso Robles, I wanted to see it myself. Or, failing that, I wanted to hear the stories first-hand from people who'd seen with their own eyes.

Then and only then could I come to some conclusion as to whether the whispers were fact or fiction — or something beyond either...

The best way to get at the truth, I decided when I arrived in Bakersfield — where James Dean had begun the last leg of his last journey on this earth — was to leave my rented car and hitchhike over the same route Jim had driven.

This way, I figured, I might meet some motorist who regularly made the trip and had heard or seen something of the "Ghost Driver of Polonio Pass" — as one letter-writer had called the apparition he claimed to have seen.

Polonio Pass is the section of Highway 466 just before it joins Highway 41. On the night of the fatal accident, Dean had been on his way from Bakersfield

TURN THE PAGE

Bums Win, 8-3; Larsen, Erskine Pitch Today

Los Angeles Examiner

CHARACTER QUALITY — AMERICA FIRST! — ENTERPRISE ACCURACY

AN AMERICAN PAPER FOR THE AMERICAN PEOPLE — THE GREAT NEWSPAPER OF THE GREAT SOUTHWEST

Examiner Building, 1111 S. Broadway, Zone 54 — Examiner Telephone Richmond 8-1212

VOL. LII—NO. 294 — LOS ANGELES, SATURDAY, OCTOBER 1, 1955 — CCC — Two Sections—Section 1—TEN CENTS

OFFICIAL WEATHER

Los Angeles and Vicinity: Hazy sunshine Saturday and Sunday but night and early morning low clouds and fog. High Saturday near 77. Slightly cooler Sunday.

Friday Temperatures

	H.	L.		H.	L.
Los Angeles	75	57	Atlanta	81	66
Bakersfield	87	53	Boston	68	51
Burbank	84	56	Chicago	62	55
San Diego	70	58	Detroit	70	66
Santa Ana	78	56	Kansas City	69	55
S. Francisco	66	57	New York	72	60
Seattle	63	54	Washington	73	64

(Complete Tables on Page 9, Section II)

JAMES DEAN, BOBBY SOX IDOL, KILLED IN $7000 CAR

Maywood Claims 'Big 5' Trash Plot

TELLS TOWN'S TROUBLES—Maywood Mayor Ben Lang is shown telling State Assembly Rubbish Investigating Committee the difficulties his city encountered last year in pickup of garbage and rubbish.
—Los Angeles Examiner photo.

City Forced to 85 Mi. Garbage Haul

Maywood Mayor Ben Lang charged yesterday that the "Big Five" garbage monopoly, in which he identified Andrew B. Hohn as a key figure, has barred the city of more than 14,000 residents from dumping its garbage anywhere in Los Angeles County.

For the past year, "since we encountered the wrath of the Big Five," Lang told the Assembly Rubbish Investigating Committee at the State Building, the city's garbage has been hauled 85 miles to a hog farm near Hemet in Riverside County.

HOG RAISER——

Hohn, wealthy South Gate refuse collector and hog raiser, assertedly gave George T. Turner, garbage chief field deputy, a $10,000 bribe to influence board award of rubbish and garbage disposal contracts valued at nearly $850,000.

Lang, spicing his testimony with salty language, injected Hohn's name into the hearing for the first time in relating his city's troubles last year in the pickup of garbage and rubbish.

In August, 1954, he said, the city asked for bids on the service after receiving notice of
(Continued on Page 3, Col. 5)

FRANK COONES
Unable to identify . . .
—Los Angeles Examiner photo.

PODRES, 23, BEATS YANKS ON BIRTHDAY

Strikes Out 6, Yields 7 Hits; Four N. Y. Pitchers Blasted

By Vincent X. Flaherty
Los Angeles Examiner Staff Correspondent

BROOKLYN, Sept. 30.—Johnny Podres celebrated his 23th birthday at the expense of the New York Yankees here this afternoon and, for him, it was a strictly champagne and caviar affair.

The slim Brooklyn lefthander, with the freckled face and rust-colored hair, pitched the Brooklyn Dodgers to an 8 to 3 victory over the Yankees in the third game of the Wold Series, thus pulling them back from the brink of a black chasm which loomed before them as of 1 p. m. today.

FLUTTER BALL——

With the Yankees still gripping a 2-1 Series lead, Manager Casey Stengel will deal fastballing Don Larsen (9-2) at the aroused Bums tomorrow afternoon in the Flatbush park. Curve-balling Carl Erskine, a righthander who set the Series strikeout record of 14 for one game in 1953, will be Manager Walter Alston's hill choice. Erskine has an 11-8 record.

A congregation of 34,209 baseball experts who, of course, knew more about the game than either Casey Stengel or Walter Alston yesterday, fluttered up to the plate like a lazy butterfly, Podres today held the Yanks to seven hits while striking out six and spreading consternation in general among the gray-flanneled men from the Bronx.

As the late innings wore on,
(Cont. on 1st Sports Page)

Ike COULD Run, Doctor Explains

Earlier Statement 'Twisted,' He Says

BOSTON, Sept. 30.—(AP)—Dr. Paul Dudley White, famous heart specialist who attended President Eisenhower, said tonight "I would have no objection whatsoever to his running again."

Dr. White issued the statement here because of "possible misinterpretation" of a statement he made today on a television show.

During that program, Dr. White said if he were Eisenhower he "wouldn't want to run" for a second term.

In a statement tonight, Dr. White said:

"I would like to respond, in answer to many questions coming today, concerning the possible misinterpretation of a recent comment of mine.

ANSWER——

"This was in response to the ever-recurring query as to whether I think or would recommend that the President could undertake to run for a second term.

"This impels me to make a full explanation of a remark that has been quoted (somewhat out of context).

"I indicated that I, personally, as Paul D. White, would have no great desire to undertake such a strain as that imposed upon a President of the United States of America.

"This remark could, and probably already has been, interpreted as meaning that I would give such advice to the President.

"Far from it.

"If the President has a good recovery, as he seems to be on the way to establishing, and if he desires to continue his present career — which would be, of course, to the great benefit of this country and the world at large — I
(Continued on Page 2, Col. 3)

Smog Alert on 1 Hr., 20 Min.

Another Alarm Due in L. A. Today

Smog ozone levels hit a record for the Pasadena area yesterday of 0.65 parts of ozone per 1,000,000 parts of air, triggering a countywide "first alert" at 12:28 p. m. which lasted an hour and 20 minutes.

"SMOG RED" (no burning, probable alert) was the forecast for today.

Yesterday's was the season's 10th alert, and the usual noburning, "keep auto use at a minimum" requests were made.

Pasadena's previous ozone record was 0.60 parts on August 29.

Levels at 434 South San Pedro street, smog control headquarters, hit 0.44 parts at 11:12 a.m.—six points below the alert stage. This station recorded the record level for the county of 0.90 parts on September 13—just 0.10 short of a "second alert."

A "second alert" — health warning hazard—may result in industrial shutdowns and traffic curtailment if smog officials consider these necessary to prevent further dangerous air contamination.

Nixon to Announce Speech Schedule

WASHINGTON, Sept. 30.—(INS)—Vice President Richard M. Nixon will announce Monday how many of 15 scheduled speeches he will deliver during October.

His office said Nixon also will make his decision on whether to go through with a scheduled trip to the mid-East in November.

ACTOR ON WAY TO DRIVE IN ROAD RACES

Young Player Rocketed to Fame on 'East of Eden' Role

By Henry Sutherland

Death overtook speed-loving James Dean, 24-year-old film star and newest idol of the bobby soxers, at a highway intersection 28 miles east of Paso Robles last night.

A 150-mile-per-hour Porsche sport car for which Dean paid $7000 a few days ago collided with a college student's automobile at the junction of Highways 41 and 466 near Cholame.

When he reached Paso Robles' War Memorial Hospital, the boyish, crew-cut Dean was dead. His passenger, Rolf Wuetherich, 28, film stunt man, of 1219 North Vine street was injured gravely.

MINOR HURTS——

But California Highway Patrolmen said that the driver of the other car, Donald D. Turnupseede, 23, of 1001 Academy street, Tulare, escaped with minor injuries.

A Warner Brothers Studio spokesman said that Dean, forbidden to indulge his passion for sport car racing while working, finished a starring role in Edna Ferber's Texas epic, "Giant," early this week.

The young star and Wuetherich were on their way to Salinas, where Dean was to compete in road races this weekend. Patrolmen Ernie Tripke and Ron Nelson said the tear-drop Porsche was traveling west on Highway 466, a cutoff from Bakersfield to Paso Robles, at the time of the crash.

Turnupsede, a student at the San Luis Obispo California Polytechnic College, bound east on Highway 466, left-turned at the intersection to take Highway 41 toward Tulare, the officers said.

AT PASO ROBLES——

The star's body was taken to the Kuehl Funeral Home in Paso Robles.

Dean, once a University of California at Los Angeles drama student, rocketed to fame and teen-age adulation last winter on the strength of a single picture, "East of Eden," the only one so far released of the three he has made.

His instant success brought consternation, as well as excitement, to film producers, for Dean's first act, when he could afford it, was to plunge head over heels into sport car racing.

"This is a dangerous condition that cannot be permitted to continue without posing a serious threat to an important part of the water supply for the people of Los Angeles."

Providing himself with a horsepower - packed German-built racer, the young fellow blitzed the neck or nothing field of road racers as completely as he had the motion picture industry.

After a few days' practice along Mulholland drive, Dean turned up at the Palm Springs Road Races last March 26 and won the under 1500cc race for
(Continued on Page 3, Cols. 2-3)

CAREER ENDED—Actor James Dean, who won stardom in movie "East of Eden," died in an automobile collision near city of Paso Robles yesterday evening.
—Photo by Nat Dallinger, Copyright, 1955, King Features Syndicate, Inc.

Peron Seeks to Take Girl, 15, into Exile

Notes Reveal Romance, Sweetheart Showered with Jewels

BUENOS AIRES, Sept. 30. — Argentine police revealed tonight that Juan D. Peron wants to take into exile with him his 15-year-old sweetheart, six dogs and four motor scooters.

The ousted dictator made this clear in a series of penciled notes to sloe-eyed Nelida (Nelly) Rivas, a janitor's daughter on whom he showered handfuls of jewels, a plush apartment and a new Cadillac.

The notes, intercepted by the police, stressed Peron's affection for Nelida and the dogs, and constantly reminded her not to forget the scooters—on which they would take lonely rides together.

14 LOVE NESTS——

Nelida, described as "extremely precocious" and appealing, told police, who asked her if she was unhappy at Peron's departure:

"No, I wasn't his only sweetheart."

The officers strongly suspect Nelida is correct—14 of Peron's love nests already have been uncovered—but they have little doubt that she was his favorite sweetheart.

Federal investigators said to-

night that Nelida's parents were given a brand-new home by Peron in a good residential suburb of Buenos Aires, although they did not know who the gift was from, regarding Nelida's friend only as a wealthy man.

Nelida herself, who was introduced at times by Peron as his adopted daughter, lived in a luxurious apartment which she left only for week ends at the dictator's summer residence.

NEW CADILLAC——

When police went to Nelida's apartment they found a new Cadillac parked in the garage, close to $150,000 in jewels that belonged to Eva Peron before her death, and about $20,000 in cash.

Nelida met Peron more than a year ago while attending activities at Peron's home, (Continued on Page 2, Cols. 5-6)

L. A. Sues to Close 3 Cities' Wells

Cutting off of the present major water source of Glendale, Burbank and San Fernando was sought yesterday when the City of Los Angeles filed suit in Superior Court to enjoin pumping of water from the Los Angeles River Basin.

Los Angeles owns all rights to this water, it was contended by the Department of Water and Power, and the city intends to stop the pumping by other communities. The Glendale-Burbank phase of the case is returnable October 17 in Department 34 of Superior Court.

The water rights are 174 years old and were granted as "pueblo rights" to the then

new City of Los Angeles by King Carlos III of Spain in 1781. These rights are irrevocable, it was stated. This stand by Los Angeles has been upheld by the courts for more than 50 years, it was pointed out.

MWD SUPPLY——

"We have no desire to cut off these cities from water sources," a Water and Power spokesman said. "Water from the Metropolitan Water District, which brings water from the Colorado River, is still available to them."

It was pointed out, however, that the Colorado River water would cost the municipalities approximately three times what

it costs to pump their present water from local wells.

"More than 20 per cent of Los Angeles' water comes from this source, and pumping by the defendants is creating a large overdraft on the local basin," said City Attorney Roger Arnebergh.

A second action filed by the city involves San Fernando, more than 100 private operators of wells who use water either for agriculture or to supply subdivisions.

Above: Ike considers a second term but Teens, Argentinian and American, grab the headlines.

Natalie Wood's dressing table becomes a shrine in this movie magazine tableau.
©WARNER BROS. INC.

IT'S A BIRD-BATH, BUT WE'RE TURNING IT INTO A SKATING RINK THIS WINTER!

bathroom of his one-room apartment over her garage!''

After his death, however, Jimmy became prime teen idol material. No longer around to complicate matters, he became an infinitely malleable star substance, especially vulnerable to the autodevotional fantasies of his fans and ideally suited to the purposes of fan magazine writers and editors. Anything was possible. He was still alive, but, concerned about his complexion, had become withdrawn. He was dead, but kept in touch. You could never tell what that Jimmy would be up to next!

For someone as closed-mouthed as Jimmy while still alive, posthumously he got positively garrulous, giving us vivid, if fleeting, glimpses of his last moments on earth and his Awakening in the Beyond.

Apparently Jimmy had a lot of time on his hands (and a lot to tell), because he managed to dictate at least twenty full-length versions of his life to evangelists as diverse as T. T. Thomas *(I, James Dean)* and Joe Archer ("Here Is the Real Story of My Life – By James Dean as I Might Have Told It to Joe Archer"). He even made a recorded message, "At Last the Voice of Jimmy," on flexidisc for *Hear Hollywood* ("The World's First Talking Magazine!"). And as late as 1975 he was still talking to Vampira (in *Interview* magazine, no less). No hard feelings, it seems, about that story in *Whisper* back in February 1957 in which Vampira admitted she'd engineered Jimmy's death through black magic.

Probably out of abject boredom from reading all these dumb stories about himself, he turned, periodically, to a life of crime: "Suspicious Cops Nab Ghost"; " 'James Dean Killed Sal Mineo' – Says Author of New Book."

His athletic afterlife went into production almost immediately. According to the sermon delivered by the Rev. Xen Harvey at Jimmy's funeral ("The Life of James Dean – A Drama in Three Acts"): "The career of James Dean has not ended. It has just begun. And remember, God himself is directing the production." With behind the camera credits like this, his upcoming performances had better be incredible.

The pseudonymous Joan Collins, in *JAMES DEAN RETURNS!* ("Read His Own Words From the Beyond"), did not disappoint us:

> The crash itself was nothing. I felt no shock. No hurt. I could see myself lying there, looking down on that other person who was Jimmy Dean and yet wasn't. . . . I watched with amazement and wonder, and the realization gradually sank over me – this was what we called death. But it wasn't 'Death'. . . . The other body that lay down there was only a shell. I, the real I who had inhabited it, was still alive. . .

The spiritualist slant was a natural considering Jimmy's ghoulish pranks, his hocus-pocus Voodoo with Vampira, and – need we add? – his fatalistic outlook on life. A trait, we're told, he shared with the Aztecs as well as *Modern Screen*. In any case, you have to admit there *is* an irresistible fascination about this stuff. Who, on spying such headlines as "Six Unsolved Mysteries of Jimmy's Death" or "James

Hoosiers flock to see their homegrown hero in his first "major motion picture" and sign up for official fan club. Right: Theater manager points out notice meant to deter insatiable collectors of Deanabilia: "WARNING: This billboard is protected by detective agency."
©WARNER BROS. INC.

McDougald Homers, Puts Brooks on Spot (See Sports Section)

Conservatives Far Ahead in England
See Virgil Pinkley, Page 2

Mirror News
YOUR INDEPENDENT NEWSPAPER
FINAL CITY
Vol. VII—No. 306 ★ In Three Parts PART I SATURDAY, OCTOBER 1, 1955 4★ MA 5-2311—145 S. Spring, Los Angeles 53—TEN CENTS

FILM STAR KILLED IN CRASH

France Orders U.N. Delegation Home

—AP WIREPHOTO

SULTAN FLIES INTO EXILE

Mohammed ben Moulay of French Morocco left palace at Rabat today, yielding to French pressure. He did not abdicate but left cousin in charge. (Story, Page 2.)

Action Taken After Rebuff Over Algeria

UNITED NATIONS, N.Y., Oct. 1 (AP)—The French delegation to the U.N. Assembly was ordered home today and the permanent French representative in the U.N. planned to follow in 48 hours, a delegation spokesman announced.

He could not make clear on the basis of present information whether the withdrawal would be permanent, he said. The French delegation walked out of the U.N. yesterday after a one-vote margin ordered France's rule over Algeria taken up in Assembly debate.

But the spokesman said it was impossible to say whether France is quitting the U.N.

One high French delegate said "we might" quit the U.N. altogether.

French Foreign Minister Antoine Pinay and the party which came with him to attend the opening of the 10th Assembly session were packing their bags for a flight back to Paris tonight.

Herve Alphand, France's new permanent representative in the Security Council, will go back for consultation.

There was no definite information whether the withdrawal order included Jules Moch, French disarmament envoy now engaged in U.N. disarmament subcommittee talks here.

The French delegation stalked out of the Assembly hall last night after the 60-nation group voted 28-27, with five abstentions, to upset the steering committee ruling to skip debate on the issue of Algerian independence.

Pinay told the Assembly France would consider null

Turn to Page 4

FILM STAR JAMES DEAN KILLED IN COLLISION OF SPORTS CAR
En route to race at Salinas, young actor made prediction come true.

James Dean Is Victim as Cars Hit Head On

PASO ROBLES, Oct. 1 (AP)—Actor James Dean, the surly, brooding Caleb of the movie "East of Eden," was killed last night in the head-on highway crash of his brand new sports car near here.

The 24-year-old actor, often compared to Marlon Brando, was driving to a road race in Salinas, the location site for the movie which catapulted him to stardom.

Dean, an enthusiastic amateur sports car racer, was the second young Hollywood leading man killed recently. Robert Francis, the "Willie Keith" of "The Caine Mutiny," died July 31 in a plane crash at Burbank.

The California Highway Patrol said a car driven by Donald Turnupseed, 23, of 1001 Academy St., Tulare, turned left off Highway 466 onto Highway 41 and collided almost head-on with Dean's Porsche Spyder. Turnupseed, a student at California Polytechnic College at San Luis Obispo, suffered minor injuries.

The collision occurred near the rural community of Cholane, 28 miles east of here. Dean was headed west in his $7000 car and the student turned off 466 onto 41 which leads to Tulare.

Ambulance Driver Paul Moreno said the Indiana-born actor was still alive when taken from the wreckage but died en route to the War Memorial Hospital in Paso Robles. Dean suffered multiple fractures of both arms and internal injuries.

Dean's mechanic, Rolph Wuetherich, 27, of 1219 N Vine St., Hollywood, was seriously injured.

Warner Brothers had forbidden their young star to drive the car while working on a movie. He had finished "Giant," the movie version of Edna Ferber's novel only this week.

"Dean was the hottest property we had," a studio spokesman said. "We had big plans for him."

George Stevens, who directed "Giant," said the actor's death was "a great tragedy—he had extraordinary talent."

Dean, like Marlon Brando, developed a naturalistic delivery. He and Brando were reported to have feuded because of the similarity of their acting styles.

Dean, a bachelor, leaves his father, Winton, a dental technician at the VA Hospital in West Los Angeles.

MOODY STAR

'Crazy Kid' Death Was Feared

BY DICK WILLIAMS
Mirror-News Entertainment Editor

A Warner Brothers Studio executive who used to watch James Dean zoom out of the studio in his fast foreign racing car often shook his head and declared:

"That crazy kid is going to kill himself."

Last night his prophecy came true as one of the most brilliant newcomers I've discovered on the Hollywood scene was killed in his white Porsche in a highway accident near Paso Robles.

I don't think you'd find anyone, whether business associate, girl friend or buddy, who wouldn't agree that James Dean was a strange, moody, sensitive boy. He was unpredictable and eccentric in his social behavior. He was tough to understand, this one. But likable, too.

The 24-year-old young man from Marion, Indiana, proved his mettle in his screen debut in John Steinbeck's "East of Eden," released last year. It was a first performance, unrivaled perhaps since Marlon

Turn to Page 4

Doctors Determine Pace for President

DENVER, Oct. 1 (AP)—The signing of two official documents restored President Eisenhower to the helm of his administration today but the temporary White House said that doctor's orders will determine how fast the Chief Executive can resume additional duties.

The President's assistant, Sherman Adams, set up shop here to pave the way for his chief to undertake gradually a greater degree of control of affairs of state. A medical bulletin said Eisenhower had

Doctors keep close watch on Mamie—See Page 4.

"a good night's sleep" and was "relaxed and comfortable this morning."

Adams arrived here last night, conferred with Eisenhower's doctors, and headed into more discussions this morning.

White House Press Secretary James C. Hagerty said that Adams is trying to determine how rapidly the Presi-

Turn to Page 4

Dr. White Clarifies Ike Stand

BOSTON, Oct. 1 (AP) — Dr. Paul Dudley White, eminent heart specialist who was called to Denver after President Eisenhower's heart attack, last night said "I would have no objection whatsoever to his running again."

Dr. White's statement was issued in Boston because of "possible misinterpretation" of a statement he made earlier yesterday.

Dr. White had said that if he were Eisenhower he "wouldn't want to run" for a second term.

Last night he said:

"I indicated that I, personally, as Paul D. White, would have no great desire to undertake such a strain as that imposed upon a President of the United States of America.

"This remark could, and probably already has been, interpreted as meaning that I would give such advice to the President. Far from it.

"If the President has a good recovery, as he seems to be on the way to establishing, and if he desires to continue his present career — which would be, of course, to the great benefit of this country and the world at large — I would have no objection whatsoever to his running again.

"But that remains still for the future to decide."

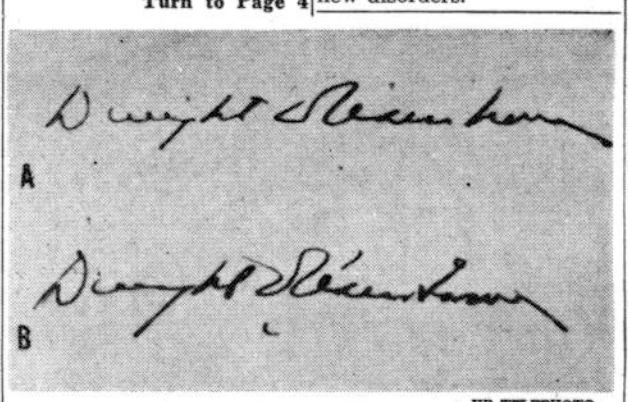

—UP TELEPHOTO

HOW IKE SIGNED BEFORE, AFTER

Signature A, before the President's heart attack, was made in June, 1954. Signature B was affixed yesterday in Denver to the measure raising diplomats' pay.

Algerian Rebel Clash Kills 12

ALGIERS, Algeria, Oct. 1 (AP)—At least a dozen French soldiers and Nationalists were killed in Algeria yesterday in scattered clashes.

The outbursts of violence came as the United Nations in New York voted to take up the question of self-determination for Algeria.

There was no immediate indication whether the U.N. vote would help bring a temporary quiet to the rebel-infested areas of Algeria or whether the vote would spark new disorders.

FIRST ADDAMS CARTOON TODAY

Charles Addams, the famous New Yorker cartoonist, finds humor in the unlikeliest places.

Addams pokes fun at humans, witches, trolls and all kinds of monsters.

Starting today, his cartoons will appear in the Mirror-News each Saturday.

Look for today's Charles Addams cartoon on the editorial page.

First-Stage Smog Alert Shaping Up

A first-stage smog alert was forecast as probable today by the Air Pollution Control District.

Yesterday the ozone concentration reached .65 parts in 1,000,000, and caused an 80-minute first-stage alert beginning at 12:28 p.m.

Yesterday's ozone concentration set a record for the Pasadena area. The previous high was .60 on Aug. 29.

China Reds March in Birthday Fete

TOKYO, Oct. 1 (AP)—Thousands of Red troops and 500,000 Chinese civilians paraded through Peiping today, celebrating the sixth anniversary of the founding of the Communist regime, Peiping radio reported.

Red China's top officialdom — including Mao Tse-tung, chairman of the People's Republic; Vice-Chairman Chu Teh and Premier Chou En-lai — reviewed the parade.

WEATHER BY POGO

SAME DEAL
Generally clear today and tomorrow. Night and morning low clouds. High today about 80 deg.

See Pogo Today on Page 6, Part I

MOTORIST SLUGGED, 3 MARINES QUIZZED

Three Camp Pendleton Marines were picked up for questioning today when a motorist complained they slugged him and took his car after he gave them a lift.

Taken into custody after a chase on the Santa Ana Freeway were Larry Harston, 18, of Houston; Jim Ercanbrack, 18, of Dallas, and Bill Sharp, 20, of San Francisco. East Los Angeles Sheriff's deputies said they were driving a car belonging to James R. Neely, 32, of 13871 LaPat St., Westminster.

Neely, in Orange County Hospital with a bump on his head, said he and his Doberman Pinscher dog were forced out of the car north of Buena Park after having picked up the youths near Oceanside.

The Marines told conflicting stories of the incident, investigators said.

—MIRROR-NEWS Photo

3 MARINES ACCUSED IN SLUGGING OF DRIVER
Officer W. A. Lynch (stooping) and Sheriff's Deputy Bill Dikeman put handcuffs on Larry Harston, 18.

Oil Tycoon Buys Balboa Bay Club

Texas Oil Multimillionaire Clint Murchison now owns 90% of the exclusive Balboa Bay Club at Newport.

Kenneth T. Kendall, retiring president-director of the club, announced yesterday that he has sold his interest to Murchison. The price was not disclosed.

Lake Arrowhead Forest Flames Under Control

Fire fighters reported that the blaze sweeping through the rugged mountains northeast of Lake Arrowhead was virtually under control this morning.

Seven hundred men manned the fire lines on the 11-mile perimeter. At its peak, the blaze reached within four miles of estates around Lake Arrowhead.

In four days, the fire burned over almost 3000 acres.

Sub-freezing temperatures, with a low of 28 degrees, hampered fire-fighting crews Thursday and Friday nights.

Salk to Test Stronger Polio Serum

PITTSBURGH, Oct. 1 (AP)—Dr. Jonas E. Salk, discoverer of the polio vaccine, today disclosed plans for testing a more potent vaccine within a few weeks.

He said the tests will be made in Pittsburgh schools on children enrolled in kindergarden or the first three grades.

Dr. Salk wants to obtain information on antibody status in all children who were inoculated one or more times.

He said blood will be drawn from the finger tip to determine the presence or absence of antibody for each type (of polio strain).

Children who possess no demonstrable antibody for any of the three types will receive the vaccines under test.

He said these will be administered in two doses, and at the time of each inoculation blood will be drawn, by vein, for the quantitative measurement of antibody level that requires a serum sample.

In this way, said Dr. Salk, relative potency of different batches of vaccine can be ascertained.

MIRROR-NEWS INDEX

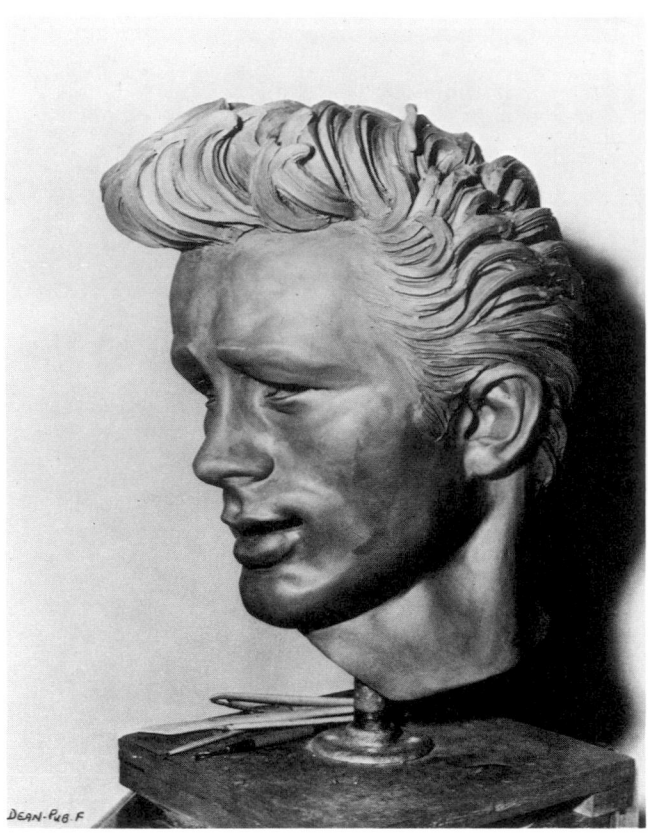

Dean's Black Madonna," could resist flipping to see what sinister secrets might lurk within.

My personal favorite in the Spooky James Dean Story variety is "The Ghost Rider of Polonio Pass," by Sam Shaeffer in *Whisper* magazine, December 1957. Here's the gist of it:

> The story the driver told me was as weird as any I've heard.... It seems that on the night of December 30, 1955 – which was three months to the day, after Dean's death – he was driving south on Route 41, headed for Paso Robles when... he thought he heard a car coming from the direction of Bakersfield.... The noise got louder and louder...
>
> Then suddenly a blurred white streak whizzed by. A second later there was a screech of brakes, followed by the sickening crash of metal ripping metal and glass shattering into a million pieces. The sound was loud, the truck driver said, trying carefully to be precise, yet in a way it wasn't loud either. It was almost "like the echo of a sound." Then silence.
>
> The crash brought him back to his senses. He hurried to the intersection, feeling sure that he would see a truly sickening sight. He saw nothing. No tire marks. No wreckage. No shattered glass....
>
> In Paso Robles we stopped at a one-arm diner for coffee.... When he finished don't you think one of the other truck drivers in the diner didn't cross himself too. "It's very bad!" this other one said. "That was Señor Dean in that car. He drives that road every night between sundown and sunrise. It's as though he is looking for something or someone."
>
> "Or as if he is a lost spirit, looking for a place to rest."

Whisper ran a light industry in this creepy line for a couple of years, but gradually lost ground to an even more portentious genre: the In-Depth Dean Analysis (Psycho and Auto Departments) – "Did James Dean

Sculptor Kenneth Kendall puts finishing touches on his (what else?) larger-than-life bust of James Dean. Below: An early version of the same by James Dean, the ectoplasmic "Self."
LOEHR COLLECTION.

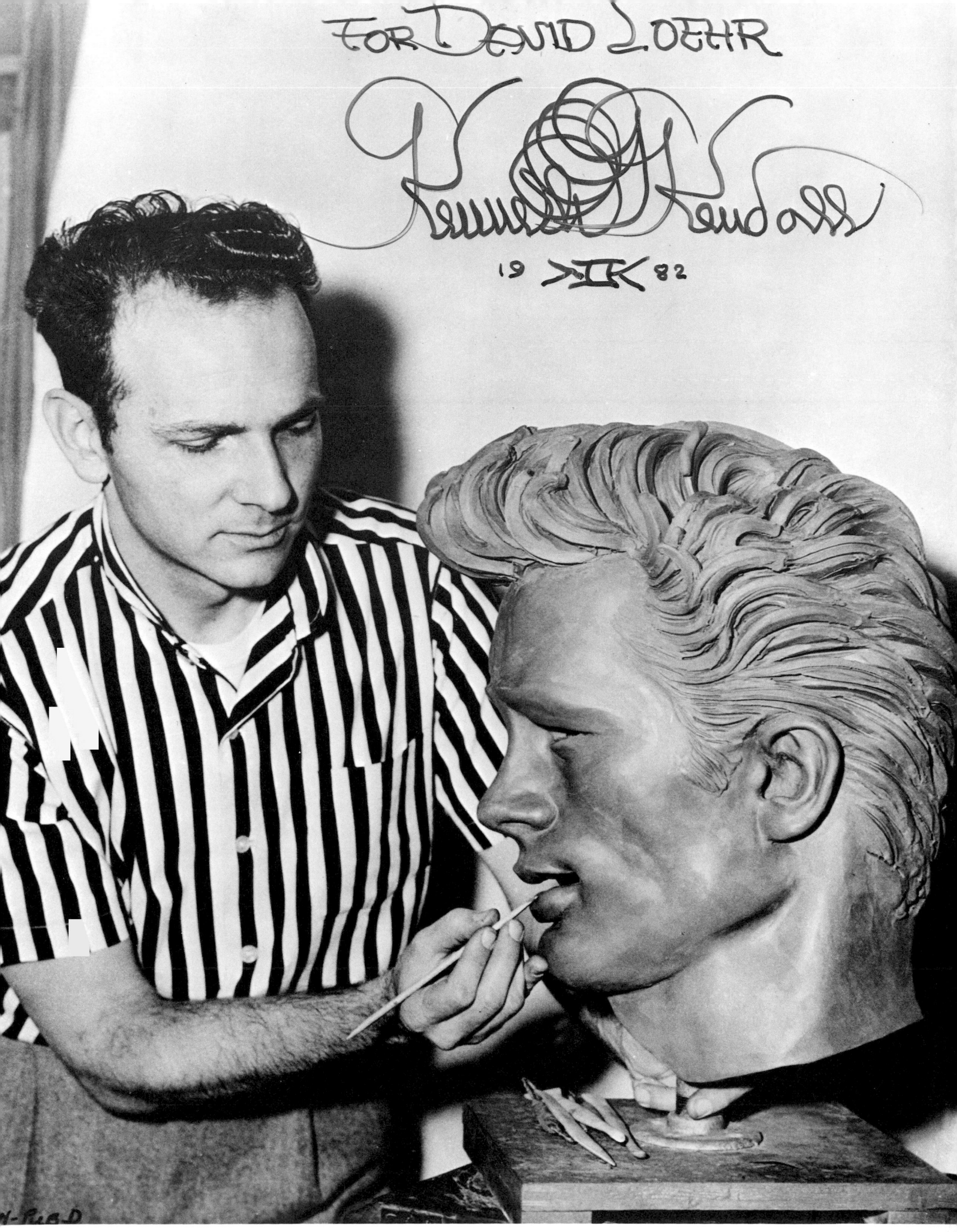

Commit Suicide?" (following rejections by Pier Angeli and Ursula Andress); "Can DEAN Stockwell Shake the Jimmy DEAN Jinx?" (Stockwell dents his Renault); "His Love Destroyed Him!" (cars); and "My Death Drive With James Dean," in which his mechanic, Rolf Wutherich, informs us that Jimmy "had good German steel in his hands."

"James Dean's Hidden Heartbreak" in *Hollywood LOVE & TRAGEDY* magazine gets into the real heavy stuff: "The crash that took his life made headlines but Jimmy alone knew the torment of the day he died — *inside.*"

Fiercely James Dean banged on the door leading from the doctor's office and wandered slowly down the stairs and onto the street.

Desperately, he tried to reconcile his mind to the outcome of those past 50 minutes under analysis.

If what the doctor said was true, then everything he had thought he had felt for the past fourteen years was a mass of confusion and lies.

He was deeply confused.

He had every right to be.

For in that office, on that hot summer day, Jimmy was being led to believe that he felt a true love for his father, Winton Dean, and that the motivations for his actions, his moods, and even his talent stemmed from the subconscious desire to have his father's love in return.

After all these ruminations about the "Cause or Causes Unknown" of Jimmy Dean's death, no one, I think, could have summed up the situation as well as Miss Emerson in the letters column of *Modern Screen:* "We feel Jimmy's death was not his own doing but something he was driven to."

Whole articles were devoted to the psychographology of James Dean's Significant Scribblings: "The Meaning of James Dean's Last Message": "Two babies in search for the world. Not everyman hears the same drum beat. I can't play your cadence, Mike,

Cult of the Living Dean takes over as artists add skin tone to MiracleFlesh masks.
©LIFE PICTURE SERVICE/ALLAN GRANT.

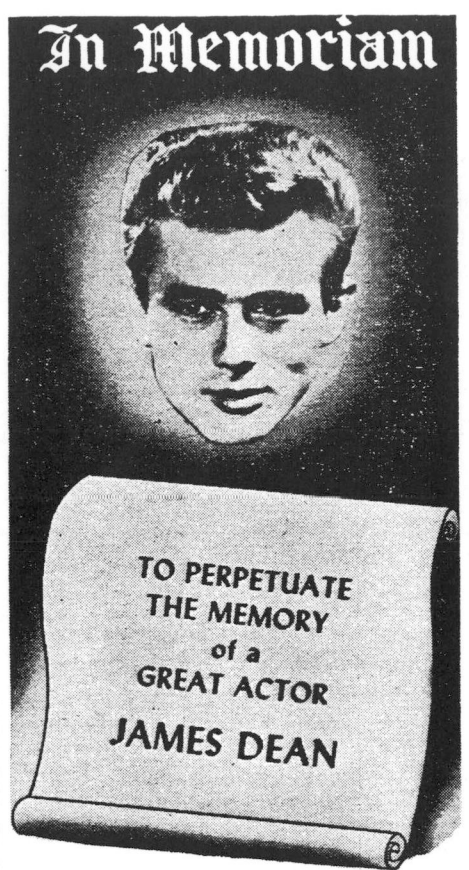

PHOTOPLAY NOV, 1956 107

JIMMY DEAN'S ALIVE!

Never, in the history of movies, has there been such a mass uproar as has been happening since the "death" of James Dean. Jimmy has served as an inspiration, to millions of teenagers. Here, for the first time is THE TRUE STORY OF JIMMY DEAN.

IS THIS JIMMY?

$50,000 REWARD

OFFERED TO FIND JIMMY DEAN!

THE DEEPENING MYSTERY OF JAMES DEAN

What are the questions fans still

ask? What are the hidden answers?

■ It has been eight long months since Jimmy Dean met sudden, tragic death in a highway accident. Jimmy himself has found peace in the quiet of a Quaker cemetery. But the friends who shared his too brief life and the fans who never met him are still tormented by the mystery that was Dean. To our offices has come a flood of letters asking questions, seeking help in understanding. As a part of our memorial, we are answering these questions here. To respect the writers' privacy, we are not including names or addresses, only the queries and answers. (*Continued on next page*)

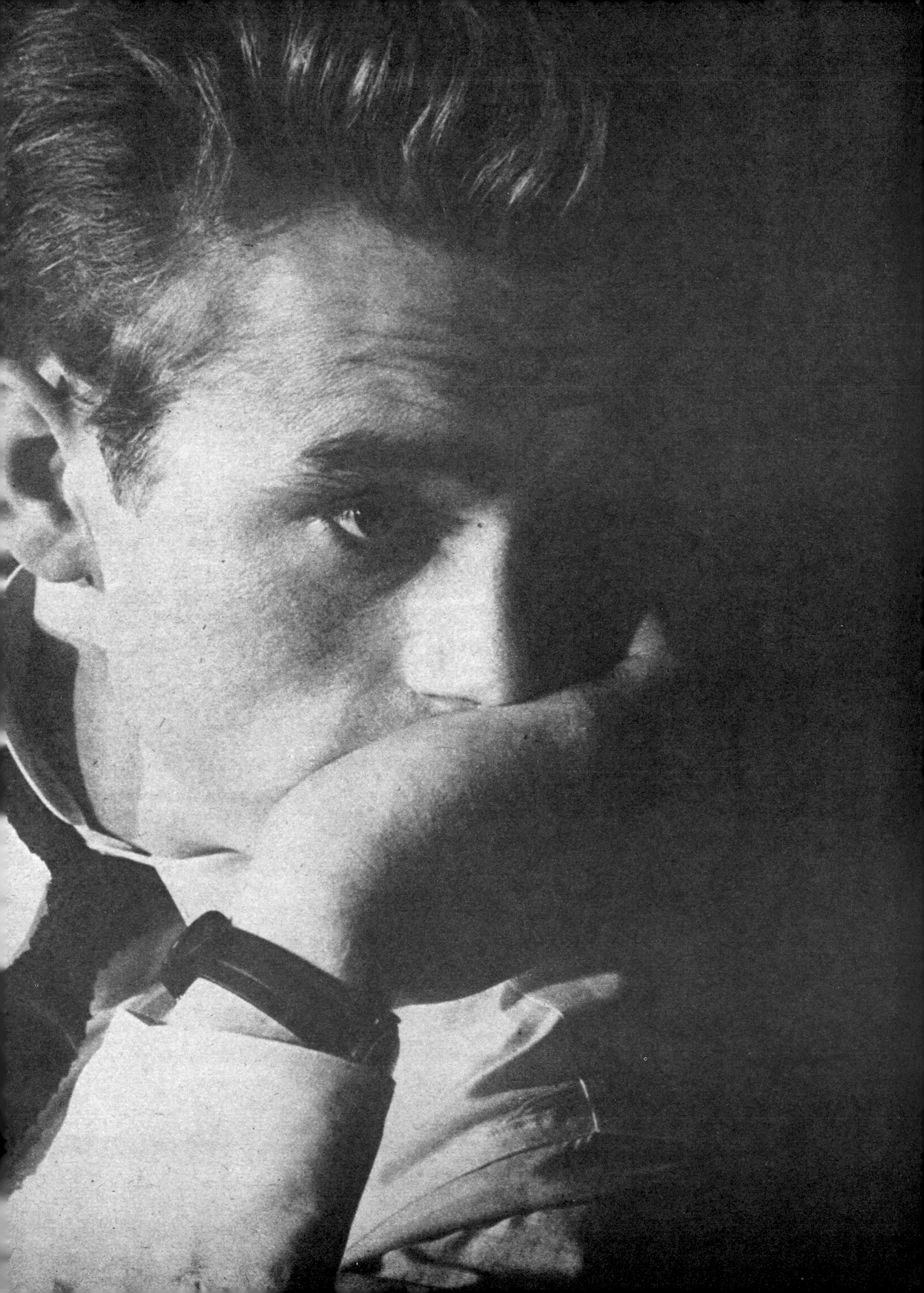

I Learned About LOVE From Jimmy Dean

The shapely photographer's model who was intimately acquainted with the late great idol reveals his romantic secrets

by Lynne Carter

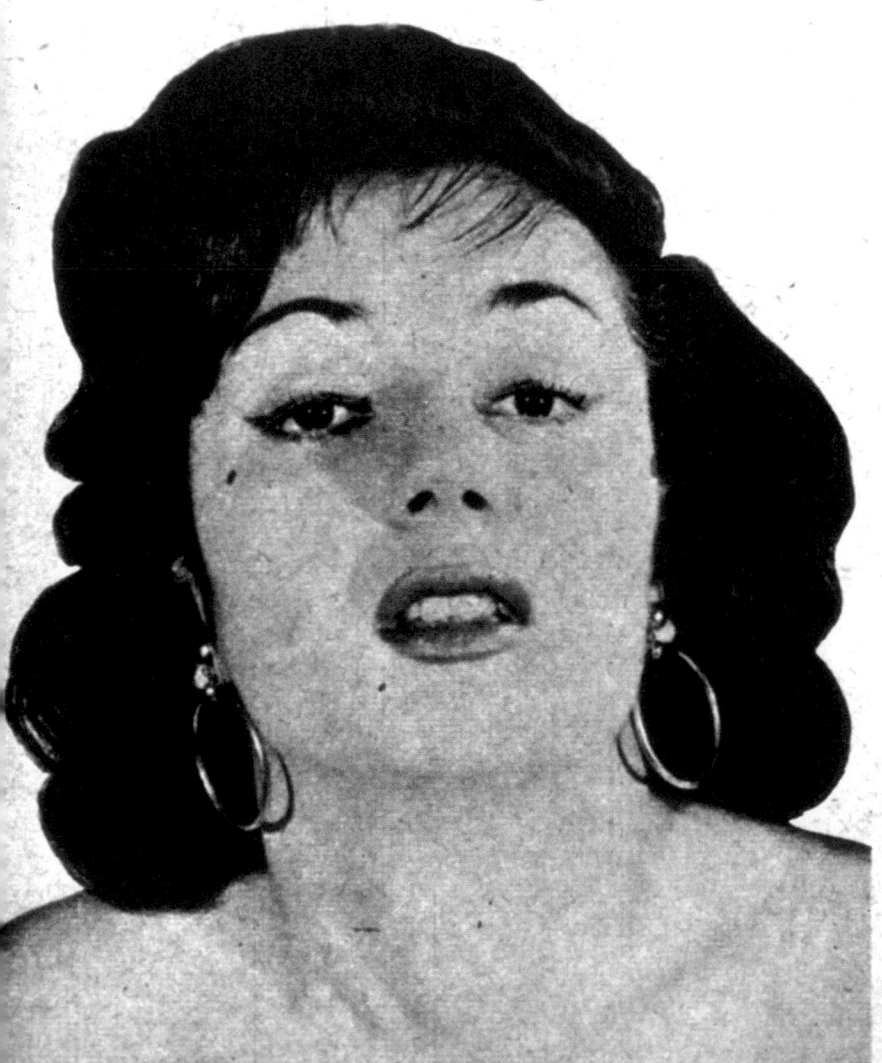

Sir:

I have known James Dean all my life and I think you are a — — to print anything about James Dean like you printed. . .

Camille Laverne Dean

2242 West Franklin, Chicago, Ill.

Dear Mr. Phillips:

The article that was printed in your January issue is an outrage. This girl, Lynne Carter, should try and do some work to earn her living instead of lying to get her money. Anyone who would say that about Jimmy is his enemy instead of his friend. . .

Maria J. Campo

2509 S. Lambert St., Philadelphia, Pa.

Dear Editor:

If I had been in this girl's place, even if I had no respect for myself, at least for Jimmy's sake I would have kept those things to myself . . . instead of publishing them to the whole world. There are times when silence is golden. . .

Viola Miller

Dayton, Ohio.

DEAR IRATE READERS:

The hundreds of letters you sent me attacking my article on James Dean in the January issue RAVE compels me to deliver an immediate answer

The lack of intelligence displayed in most of the letters is ludicrous. The ignorance and pettiness of M

PORTRAIT OF THE AUTHOR

She first met Jimmy in Philadelphia when he w shopping for a pair of boots. . . .

24

JIMMY & LYNNE
Many psychiatrists feel that the undying interest in Jimmy is a result of some form of self-identification. . . .

Dean's so-called "fans" is obvious. I could analyze your illiterate manners, but I'm sure it would accomplish nothing and the lead in my pencil is too valuable to waste on such advice.

When I decided to write an article about Mr. Dean, I did so with the idea of combating the morbid hysteria about Jimmy that has crept upon the American scene.

JIMMY LOVED LIFE

As I said in my article, I first met Jimmy during the winter of 1952 when *The Immoralist* was having its premiere in Philadelphia. He was shopping for a pair of boots at the time. His disdain for the conventionalities of life intrigued me. I had never met anyone like him.

Our first date was at the Russian Sun, a small restaurant in midtown Philadelphia frequented by theatrical people—and we later went to the Hickory House. This was also the scene of our second date, that same week. Jimmy ate a large meal and dis-

cussed acting. He never seemed to tire of the subject.

The next time I saw him was in his New York apartment at 19 West 68th Street, about three months later. Other dates consisted of impromptu phone calls, resulting in Forty-second Street movies, conversations lasting into the early morning, and listening to mambo records.

Jimmy loved to sit by candlelight. He seemed to find it relaxing. At our last meeting, when he

25

This, we believe is the only way to keep Jimmy's memory alive . . .

■ At this moment, James Dean is more famous than he ever dreamed possible while he was alive. He probably would have been hugely amused by the irony in this—that death at the age of 24 brought him the most favorable press of his career.

But there is tragedy in it, too. For there is no denying that, in addition to the truly sincere, heartfelt shock of millions of fans all over the world, a boy's death has been used as an excuse for one of the most selfish, vulgar, cold-hearted publicity exploitations in the history of show business.

Writers who never had a kind word for Jimmy while he lived have made a travesty of his death with their pseudo-mournful, dishonest eulogies, their ghoulish pictures of him as a spirit speaking from another world to chosen correspondents here among the living, their distorted versions of him as a kind of demi-god, to be worshipped by emotion-blinded followers. This is not the way to remember Jimmy. It is nothing but a crude sensationalism which threatens to crush the precious beginnings of what may be called the Jimmy Dean tradition.

There is another way—the *only* way—to keep his memory alive and vital. It is to remember the real Jimmy. To go back to the Jimmy of "East of Eden" and "Rebel Without a Cause." To rediscover the great actor as he really was, and as he must be remembered if he is to take his place among the ranks of film immortals. We all can, and must, do this if our affection for Jimmy is honest. The rest is up to his direct successors, the young actors and actresses who felt his impact and shared his dreams. They, and only they, can breathe life into the great, new Jimmy Dean tradition.

MORE ➤

James
A TRADITION

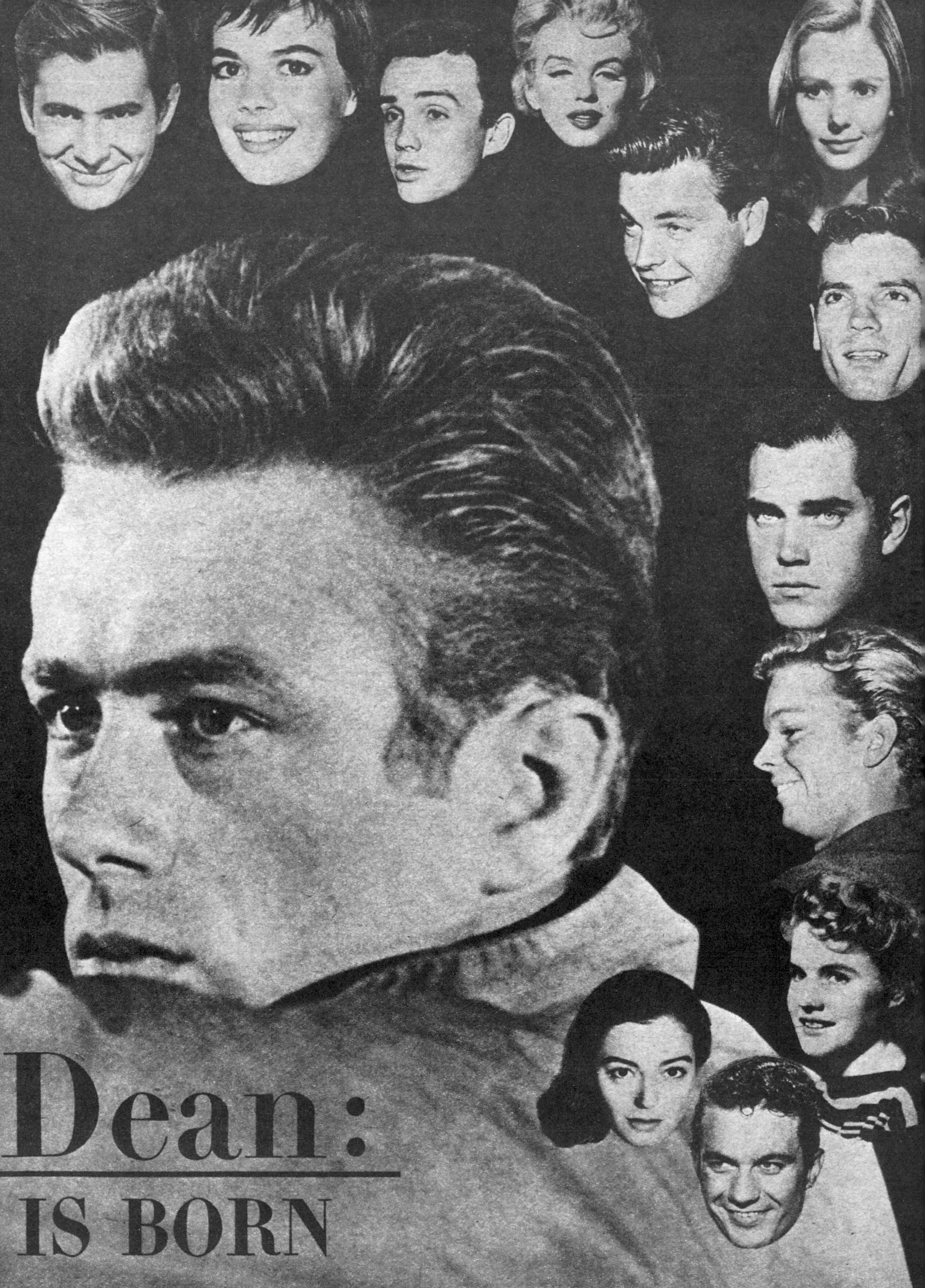

Dean:
IS BORN

Solitude in a crowded place

James Dean
A MOMENT IN HISTORY

THE THINGS HE DID — big things, little things, even foolish things are history now — history because Jimmy Dean flashed across the Hollywood sky like a meteor, but unlike its momentary blinding light, Jimmy stayed and was shown dazzling bright for all the world to see — until his untimely and sudden death. And so we feel that these pictures, showing the burning intensity he displayed in his work and at play, belong to you who loved him. His date was Ursula Andress (now Mrs. John Derek), and many believe that he had found in her the girl to take the vacant place left by Pier Angeli. No one knows. Perhaps even Jimmy didn't. But at this moment his wild spirit was captured by tender love, a moment of happiness before it took wings and flew blindly into death.

  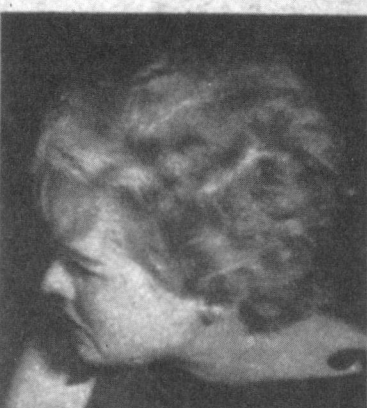

His thoughts were quicksilver, defying immediate expression, holding his confidante spellbound

 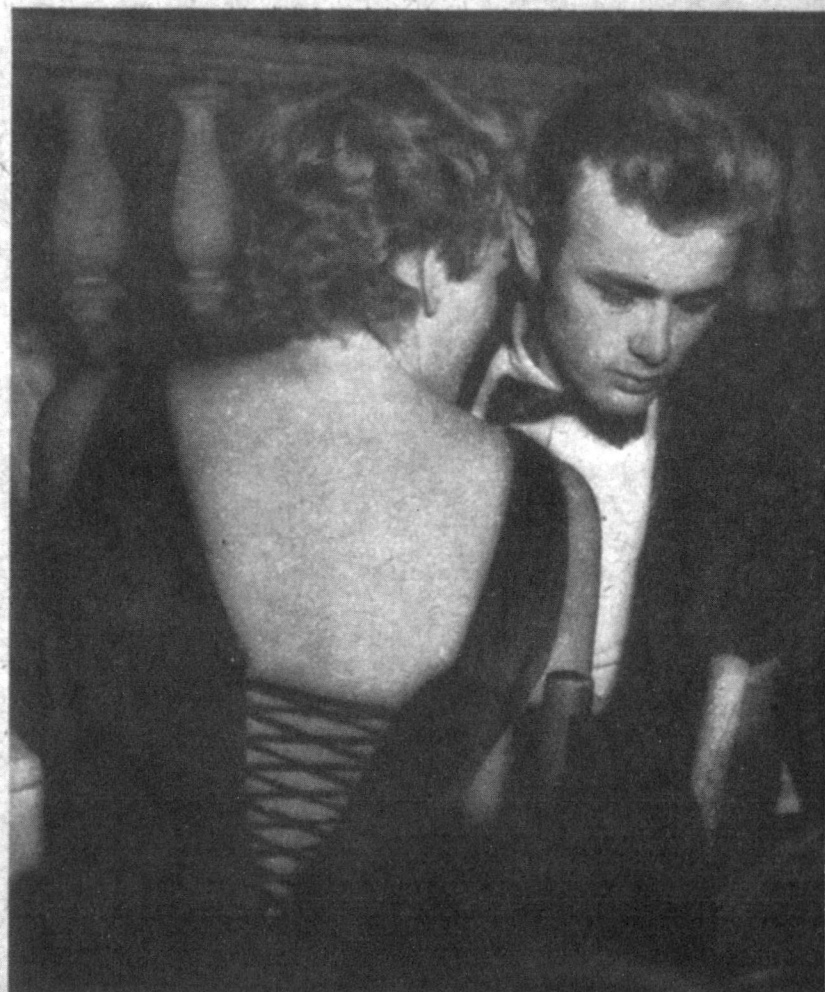

Small words, spoken softly and in confidence . . .   **. . . and eager attention to other words meant for him alone.**

His sensitivity and compassion responded perhaps too readily to moments that were meant to be fleeting

And when he was moved or touched, he exerted a magnetism few mortals possess, but none can deny

JIMMY TOLD ME:

"DON'T PRINT

A famous photographer unveils—for the first time—the picture Jimmy felt showed too much of his soul . . .

by Frank Worth

MY PHONE was ringing like crazy. I could see by the luminous dial on the clock by my bed that it was three in the morning.

"Frank," a low, familiar voice came to me, "what are you doing?"

"Sleeping, like any sane person," I told him, angry and relieved at the same time that the call was nothing serious. "God, Jimmy, what's the big idea of calling a guy at this hour?"

"I just thought maybe you'd like to have lunch with me at the studio tomorrow, that's all," he said calmly, as if this were the most natural thing in the world.

"Well, okay, I guess," I stammered. My first impulse was to tell him to go jump for waking me up but he always kind of fascinated me.

"Don't bring your camera," he added.

"That's like telling me not to bring my right arm," I told him.

You see, I'm a photographer. I don't move outside my apartment without my camera. I miss too many things that way.

"Okay, Frank," Jimmy said, apparently bored with the conversation by this time. "See you in the Green Room at Warner Brothers at one."

Once as a kid, I'd broken a thermometer and I'd watched the mercury spill and roll all over the place and break up into tiny pieces, then come together again in a million different shapes and forms. That was what Jimmy reminded me of. If you looked away for just one second, he might suddenly change into an entirely different mood or spirit, just like the mercury, then switch back again before you had a chance to ask him what was the matter.

Jimmy hated to have his picture taken. He was one of the few actors I've known who felt that way. Most of them go crazy when they see a camera.

"You've got to catch me moving, boy," he told me once, when I was trying to get him to pose for me. "I haven't got time for sitting still."

I've thought about that remark a thousand times since then. He was so right, and he didn't even know it at the time. At least, I don't think he did.

I first met Jimmy in 1952. There a restaurant in Hollywood called Googie's. It's right next door to Schwab's Drug Store on the Sunset Strip, where lots of movie stars hang out, so Googie's gets a lot of the motion picture trade.

One day I drove there in my new little Humber Haw. As I swung proudly into a parking place, I almost clipped a shiny motorcycle.

"Hey, watch it, fella," a voice called sharply. I looked around but saw no one. Then I noticed a dusty black boot sticking out on the other side of the motorcycle. I walked around and found a boy in a pair of old bluejeans and a leather jacket lying

Here's the picture—AT RIGHT—of which Jimmy said, "Don't print that!" But Photographer Frank Worth now feels Jimmy would like everyone to take a long, loving look at the REAL Jimmy it reveals.

THAT PHOTO!"

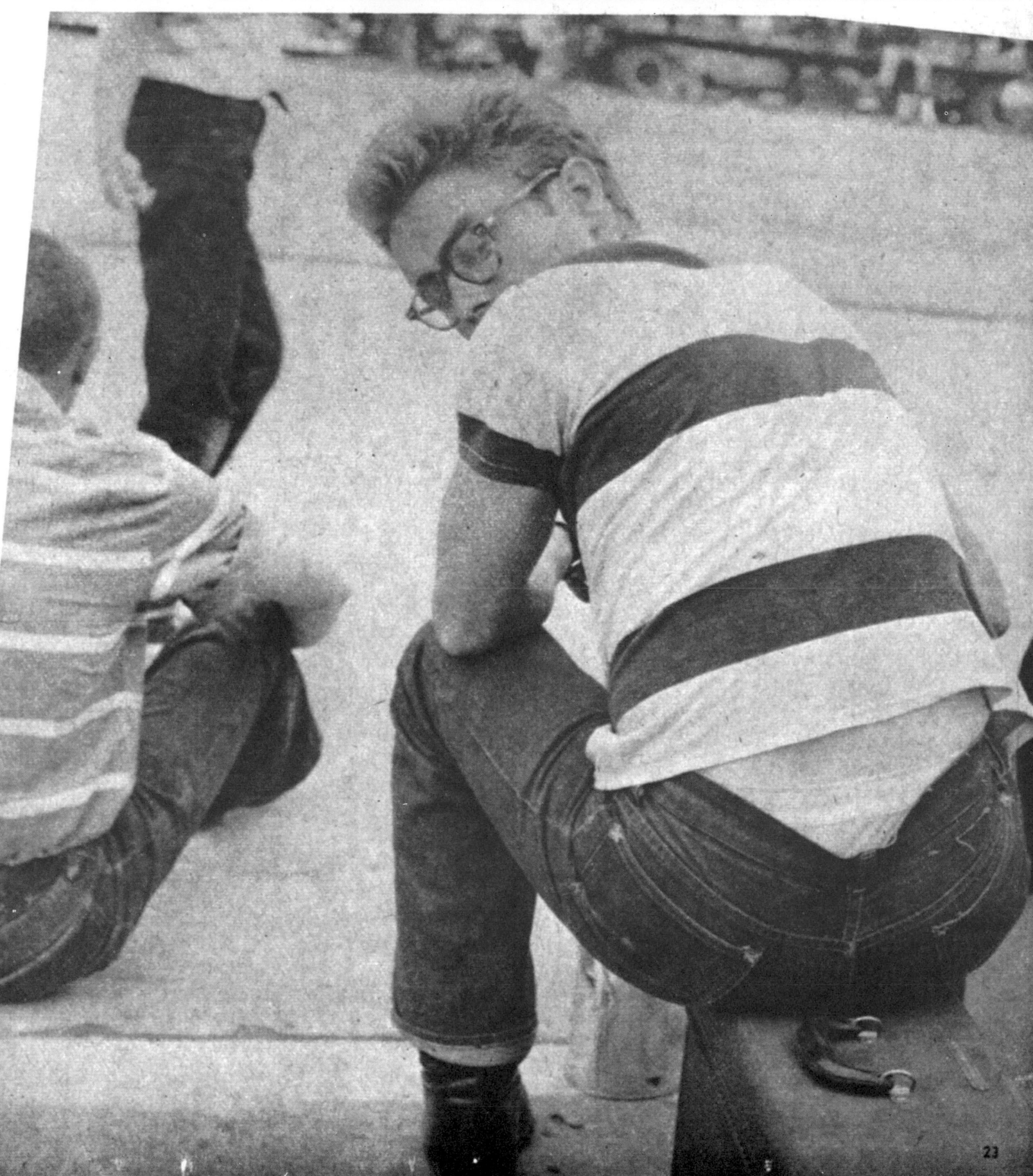

but I can offer you counterpoint." This inscribed on a photo of Jimmy and a toddler — drinking from milk bottles. Mysterioso, amigo.

In "A DATE WITH DEATH!", David Browne tells us that Jimmy's "most cherished book" was Hemingway's *Death In The Afternoon:*

On page 348, opposite a photograph of the matador Joselito lying dead in the bull ring infirmary, is this inscription, written by Dean: *"God gave James Dean so many gifts to share with the world, has he the right to throw them away in the bull ring?"*

On page 368, opposite a photograph of the matador Granero who also lies dead in the bull ring infirmary, Dean boldly inscribed four words, each in different colored crayon. The word "death" is written in red, "disability" in green, "disfigurement" in blue, and "degradation" in yellow. The colors are the key to the four violent categories in the book as Dean saw them.

On the second page of *Death in the Afternoon*, Hemingway observed that since the war had ended (World War I), the only place where violent death could be seen was in the bull ring. Dean underlined the words in red.

Yellow For Degradation

On page 60, where Hemingway writes of the disgrace that comes to a bullfighter who is gored because of a clumsy maneuver, the passage is underscored in yellow, for degradation.

On page 153, where the author writes of the horn wounds the bull fighter may suffer, the passage is underlined in green, Dean's color code for disability. And where Hemingway writes, on page 75, of an old matador's gnarled leg muscles, the passage is underlined in blue, for disfigurement.

The movie magazines that proliferated after his death were not only disseminators of the image of James Dean and purveyors of his secrets, they were the first in a long line of totemic objects associated with his cult. "I am not going to deny that I've cried every night since his death, seen his new pic twice, and go to sleep on sixteen mags containing articles about him," wrote P. Kneiss to *Modern Screen*.

While fan clubs form around living stars, cults form around the dead or divinized. A cult, even of a popular culture hero, could not exist without its sacrificial victim. James Dean's "tragic sacrifice on the road to Salinas" (as *LOVE & TRAGEDY* magazine put it) formed the necessary link between the mundane and the sacred that was essential to his canonization.

The James Dean cult, like any other, depends on artifacts, euphemistically called "memorabilia," to perpetuate its belief in the living spirit. These tangible symbols are felt to contain some of the hero's essence in physical form. They serve to unite members who otherwise would have nothing more in common than having seen his movies.

A catalogue raisonné of Dean memorabilia reveals the increasing stages of intimacy and magical appropriation associated with these artifacts.

ICONS (two-dimensional representations): photographs, post cards, posters, movie stills, lobby cards, placemats, postage stamps, seals, decals, bubblegum cards, jigsaw puzzles, stationery.

GOSPEL (books, articles about, and oeuvre): biographies, magazines, sheet music, this page, tribute 45s and LPs, soundtrack recordings, films and videocassettes.

TOTEMS (three-dimensional representations and objects bearing his image): busts in plaster, terra cotta, simulated stone, bronze and Miracleflesh, plaques, coffee mugs, drinking glasses, memorial plates, waterpipes, pencil boxes, pencil sharpeners and cigarette lighters.

TALISMANS (articles of clothing and fetish objects that imbue the wearer with his mystic substance): medallions, pins, buttons, sew-on patches, rubber masks, T-shirts, red windbreakers, silk scarves, wristwatches, switchblades ("The James Dean Special"), facsimile lariats, shopping bags.

RELICS (items touched by his life and death and objects of awe in themselves): fence posts from *Giant*, pieces of the Reata mansion, autographs, inscribed photos, books owned by or inscribed, letters from, telegrams from, drawings, paintings and sculpture by, speeding tickets, props from his movies (the toy monkey from *Rebel*, lariat from *Giant*), items

of clothing worn in the movies (Levis, red jacket, cowboy hat), items of clothing worn in life (motorcycle boots, leather jacket), fragments chipped from his headstone, his life mask, aluminum fragments from the Porsche, rings set with pieces of glass from the windshield, bloodstained lockets of his hair.

As presence fetishes the obsessional nature of these artifacts goes far beyond holiday souvenirs and collections of bottle caps. In the case of actual fetish objects, such as lockets of his hair, these sacred totems approach the idolatrous veneration of reliquaries in the Middle Ages. A memorabilium is nothing other than an object which has become invested with the divinity of the star, and through which fans are reunited with the object of their affection.

Anthropologists use the word *mana* to describe the supernatural force found in the sacred objects which symbolize the collective aspirations of a cult. *Mana* is really a primitive way of explaining a state of mind whose meaning is, paradoxically, defined by the individual's inclusion in the group soul. Objects invested with *mana* remind members of the cult of that "old familiar feeling" which brought them together in the name of the unknown.

The sympathetic magic attaching itself to James Dean depends for its power on the lines of alternating current that are the adolescent's ultimate resource. In this sense, James Dean's movies are seances through which his fans not only reassure themselves about what is happening to each of them, personally, but, through an ecstasy of identification, determine that something significant is taking place in the culture itself.

*Lobby cards and studio artwork
from* Giant.
©WARNER BROS. INC.

©Amy Arbus.

© Christina Yuin Cayen

Icons, totems, talisman, and relics of the Apostle of Adolescence. Buttons are among some 1,000 items of Deanabilia, sought by collectors, from pencil sharpeners bearing his image to rings made from the shattered winshield of his Porsche. David Loehr, the Dean of Deanabilia himself, surrounded by his awesome collection. Bottom: A street sign in Marion, Indiana, commemorates the site of his birthplace. Opposite: The memorial issue of The Fairmount News, entirely devoted to their native son, is printed up each year for fans who attend ceremonies marking the anniversary of Jimmy's death, September 30, 1955.

IN MEMORY OF JAMES DEAN

THE FAIRMOUNT NEWS

Volume LXXX | Fairmount, Grant County, Indiana | SPECIAL EDITION

Special

Because of the overwhelming demand for this week's issue of THE FAIRMOUNT NEWS, which contains exclusive material concerning the brief, briliant career of James Dean, we have sold all of our regular copies, even though we printed several hundred extras.

Consequently, we decided to publish this Special Edition to try and meet the public's demand.

We, as members of the staff, would like to take this opportunity of expressing our sympathy to the bereaved family of Jim Dean. Words can not begin to express emotions during periods of time such as this but Jim Dean and his influence on Fairmount will never be forgotten.

JAMES DEAN'S "EDEN" PROVES HIGH TALENT OF FAIRMOUNT ACTOR

Even if Jimmy Dean weren't a hometown boy, "East of Eden" would be one of the most powerful production ever released by Warner Brothers and it would well be worth the effort and money of anyone.

"Eden" opens Easter Sunday at Marion's Indiana Theatre and will continue through Thursday, according to John DeBoo, Manager.

However, homefolks will be going to see Dean. And, they won't be disappointed if they are looking to find a splendid performance and magnificient interpretation by Jimmy.

Fairmount's star has been compared to Marlon Brando and this writer can see some faint similarity between the two. But, Dean's is a warmer personality . . one that projects itself with a freedom of action that keeps movie-goers on the edge of their seats.

In "Eden" Jimmy plays the role of an unpredictable, love-starved youth who was reared with a brother by their father (Raymond Massey).

Plagued with an inferiority complex brought about chiefly because he thought his father prefered his brother to himself, Dean, as Cal, does everything in his power to "win" his father's love.

Three climatic scenes, each topping the former, are seen in the latter stages of the show and in each of them Dean seems to bare his very soul with his portrayal.

Written by John Steinbeck, "East of Eden" takes place in the Monterey-Salinas section of California, as is usual with Steinbeck. Elia Kazen, who produced and directed the picture, did an exceptional job; but, this is expected of Kazan, who is one of the nation's foremost producer-directors.

It has been said that there is a possibility Jimmy will be a candidate for an Academy Award in 1956 for his work in "Eden". This early in the year, though, it would be hard to forecast.

Packed houses have seen "East of Eden" every place it has played and in our opinion this will be true from Fairmount to Timbuctu.

Tuesday morning the Indiana Theatre gave a special performance of "Eden" for Mrs. Adeline Nall, Fairmount High School speech instructor, who started Dean on his way.

She, together with the senior class, school officials and several others, are enthusiastic with the picture as most people who see it will be.

(Reprinted from April 7, 1955 issue of THE FAIRMOUNT NEWS.)

Photo by Curtis Bernard, Santa Monica, Calif.

. . . a Student at U.C.L.A.

James Dean

A native son who startled the nation with a brilliant flash of genius was brought back home this week for last rites. His brief career was as bright as a meteor which flows like a golden tear down the dark cheeks of night.

By the law of averages, it was most unusual for a lad 24-years of age to leave a rural environment from an agarian community and go so far and fast in so short a time on Broadway and Hollywood. It is in the grass roots of Grant County from which he made his start that the body of this restless youth has been returned to rest.

He made his living at acting—by his own definition—"behavior of and for other people". For a little period of time he made the lives of many more entertaining, more interesting, and in some cases more bearable. Such a life is not suddenly wiped out in the wreckage of a car in California. Some of us have learned to distrust our senses and to know that as long as we remember, there will live on in our hearts the influence of others.

To be an actor requires a trained memory, the ability to be a severe critic of oneself, and to create moods and atmosphere for the development of that art. James Dean's path, to those of us who knew him best, was steep and rugged and was covered with sandpaper instead of velvet. As he said in a letter to a friend, "we are impaled on a crook of conditioning. A fish that is in the water has no choice that he is. Genius would have it that he swim in sand. We are fish and we drown. We remain in one world and wonder. The fortunate are taught to ask why. No one can answer."

Human life has been compared often to an automobile. Some get more mileage in 30 years than others do in 60. So even though we "weep for the dead, the doubly dead, in that he died so young", yet we feel that Jim who lived dangerously would have had the last act come as it did as last nights must come to all earthly things.

Perhaps he would recite for us, if he could, the lines of a lesser poet, John G. Neihardt who wrote,

"Let me live out my years in heat of blood!
Let me die drunken with the dreamer's wine!
Let me not see this soul-house built of mud
Go toppling to the dust—a vacant shrine!
Let me go quickly like a candle light
Snuffed out just at the heyday of its glow!
Give me high noon—and let it then be night!
Thus would I go.
And grant me, when I face the grisly Thing,
One haughty cry to pierce the gray Perhaps!
O let me be a tune-swept fiddlestring
That feels the Master Melody — and snaps."

JAD

$105,000 ESTATE LEFT BY ACTOR JIMMY DEAN

An estate valued at $105,000, according to court records, was left by James Dean, whose body will be buried in Park Cemetery Saturday afternoon.

Winton Dean, father of the young actor, is the only direct heir.

Attorney L. Dean Petty filed a petition for letters of administration to Dean's estate Wednesday in Hollywood. The attorney named Carl Coulter and William Gray as administrators requested by Dean's father.

James Dean Killed As Result Of California Car Accident

FAIRMOUNT IS STUNNED TO LEARN OF TRAGEDY WHICH CLAIMED NATIVE SON; HEADON COLLISION NEAR INTER[illegible]TION CAUSES FATALITY FRIDAY

Fairmount was stunned.

Saturday morning, which was the time most people learned of the violent tragedy that claimed the life of James Dean, the people who knew and loved him best could hardly conceive of the fact.

Death is always a hard thing to understand and especially when it strikes a young person, who apparently has much to give to the world and who is just beginning what could be a brilliant career.

That's how most people look at the accident which killed Jimmy (as he was known to homefolks).

Death came as result of a headon collision last Friday night near Paso Robles, California when the sports car he was driving was struck by another vehicle.

He died en route to the Paso Robles hospital after suffering multiple fractures of both arms and internal injuries.

Ralph Wueterich, 27, Hollywood, Dean's auto mechanic, was seriously injured. Donald Turnupseed, 23, Tulare, Calif., driver of the other car, escaped with minor injuries.

According to the California State Patrol, Tu[illegible]eed's car turned left from a road onto the highway where Jimmy was driving and the smash-up occured.

Warner Brothers, who owned his contract, had told Jimmy not to drive his sports car, a Porsche Spyder, while working on a picture. However, he had just finished "Giant" at its Texas location a few days beforehand.

Reportedly, he was traveling to an amateur car race.

Jimmy was born in Fairmount, the son of Mr. and Mrs. Winton Dean, on February 8, 1931. They lived here five years from that time when they moved to Santa Monica, Calif.

His mother, the former Mildred Wilson, died in 1940 when Jimmy was nine-years-old.

He then came to live with his uncle and aunt, Mr. and Mrs. Marcus Winslow, and graduated from Fairmount High School in 1949.

Following his high school graduation, Jimmy enrolled at the University of City of Los Angeles. Then he left college and went to New York City where he was cast in minor TV rolls on, "Studio One", "You Are There" and "Television Playhouse".

As result of his television acting, Jimmy was cast in the Broadway play, "The Immoralist", and ultimately won the David Blum award for the most promising stage newcomer.

Elia Knzan, famed Hollywood director, caught Jimmy's performance on Broadway and signed him to play Caleb in "East of Eden", based on John Steinbeck's novel.

Jimmy shot to stardom with almost unbelievable rapidity as result of his work in "Eden". Homefolks who saw the movie were heard to comment that many of the mannerisms Jimmy used were just like he did "at home".

Mrs. Adeline Nall, former Fairmount High School teacher, first started Jimmy on his road to success as she recognized his ability and tutored and encouraged him to develop it.

"That spontaneous laugh" Mrs. Nall said after seeing "East of Eden", "was so very natural. It was one of his traits I'd noticed throughout school."

James Bacon, Hollywood correspondent for the Associated Press, said, "Dean could well become Hollywood's first posthumous Academy Award winner for his role in "East of Eden".

Many critics have credited Jimmy's debut in the movie as the male Oscar performance to beat.

"Dean was the hottest property we had," a Warner Brothers official said. "We had great plans for him".

George Stevens, who directed "Giant", said Jimmy's death was "a great tragedy. He had extraordinary talent."

Comments like this could go on and on for it was generally conceeded that James Dean was "something special" . . . and he was "something special" to his home town, too, forgetting his achievements in movieland.

During high school days, Jimmy was extremely active in extra curricular work. His portrayal of "the monster" in a high school version of "Frankenstein" will be recalled by many.

. . . Basketball Star

Hockett Studio

Then too, he was a member of the ever-popular basketball team representing the Quakers from Fairmount High. During his senior year in the sectional tourney he shot a last-second field goal to beat Gas City 39-37.

In addition he was a member of the track and baseball teams and was awarded the school's top athlete medal his last year in high school at which time he was also given the art department medal.

Perhaps among the first signs of his dramatic talent came while he was a youngster and won silver and gold medals in WCTU speaking contests.

In 1949, his senior year in high school, Jimmy won first place for acting during the National Forensic League's state contest at Peru.

Outside of his school activities, many people will remember Jimmy ice skating on the Winslow pond just North of Fairmount. He was pretty good, too . . . could keep up with the older fellows.

Each time that he came home for a visit he would also visit the high school and talk to the student body. On one occasion he explained the art of bull fighting . . . which he had practiced somewhat.

On his last visit he arrived in time to attend a dance at the high school and during the evening he played the drums . . . mambo fashion.

Magazines galore have given valuable publicity space to the "Indiana farm boy" who had risen to a Hollywood star in such a short time. LIFE magazine even sent a photographer to Fairmount with Jimmy to get shots of him in his home surroundings.

(Copies of the magazine were sold before they arrived at the newsstands and are at a premium today.)

Just a few days before his death a Sunday supplement in one of the larger daily papers in this area carried an article dealing with the filming of "Giant" in Texas.

It went into detail explaining how the heat taxed the energy of all the actors. All of them, that is, except Jimmy Dean, who would go rabbit hunting in the evening.

Jimmy Dean contributed a lot in the 24 short years he lived. A great many people, who didn't understand him, called Jimmy eccentric. Perhaps he was. But then again, when a person becomes so wrapped up in something he forgets everything else but that one thing.

When he lets off steam it is apt to be outside the regular bounds of activity, according to the measure of society.

His homefolks understood him, though.

And they'll miss him.

Last Rites Will Be Held Here Saturday

Dr. James A. DeWeerd, Rev. Xen Harvey To Conduct

Funeral services for James Dean, 24, will be held at 2 o'clock Saturday afternoon at the Friends Church in Fairmount by Dr. James A. DeWeerd and the Rev. Xen Harvey, pastor of the church.

Dr. DeWeerd, who has a telecast at Cincinnati shortly before services begin at 2 o'clock, will be flown in the private plane of Buford Cadle to Marion Airport and is scheduled to arrive there at 1:45.

He will be met by a State Police Patrol car and be driven to the Friends Church.

Following the church service, burial will take place at Park Cemetery in Fairmount.

The Rev. Xen Harvey said Thursday night that his church will accomodate approximately 600 people by adding extra chairs. In addition to the amplifying system at the church, a public address installation will enable those outside to hear the rites.

Wilbur Hunt, director of Hunt Funeral Home which is handling arrangements, said he had received requests from Hollywood that seats be reserved.

Hunt said the requests were denied in view of the fact that this is to be a public funeral.

A Hunt Funeral Home ambulance met the plane returning young Dean's body from California at 10:17 Tuesday night at the Indianapolis airport.

The body was taken to Hunt's Funeral Home, where friends may call.

Survivors include the father, Winton Dean, Los Angeles; maternal grandfather, John Wilson, Marion; paternal grandparents, Mr. and Mrs. Charlie Dean, Fairmount; Charles Nolan Dean, uncle, Gas City; and Mr. and Mrs. Marcus Winslow, uncle and aunt, Fairmount.

DEATH OF JAMES DEAN, FAIRMOUNT HIGH ALUMNI CASTS A PALL OF SADNESS OVER STUDENT BODY

The shocking news of the death of James Dean has cast a spell of unbelievable saddness over Fairmount High School. The graduate of the class of '49 had soared to fame in his first picture "East of Eden" and had just completed two more pictures. The students, faculty, and townspeople have all been very proud of his great accomplishments in such a short time.

Jimmie's family had just spent a month with him in California and were on their way home when the fatal accident occured. The Winslows arrived home early Monday evening only then to learn of the tragic car accident which killed Jim just one week ago today.

The students feel they knew Jim well, because he spoke before them in convocations whenever he was home and visited many of the clasrooms especially speech classes. Because he was a Fairmount graduate the students felt especially proud when he came back to the school with his greatness never making them feel small or unimportant

Jim did everything with an intense desire to do it well. If he liked a certain thing, it seemed to be with everything he had. Racing, bull-fighting, and drums were things he loved with this intensity. They set him apart from others, made him an interesting person, not afraid to be different, but with a personality all his own.

Commentators from Hollywood have stated that Jim had a brilliant career ahead of him. In one picture he gained a popularity that usually takes young actors a long time to achieve.

Cards of sympathy have poured into the postoffice for the family from all over the United States. It is apparent that he has many, many friends. Actors and actresses he has worked with are expected to attend the funeral.

The final funeral rites will be held tomorrow in the Fairmount Friends Church.

Fairmount's Chamber of Commerce has made tentative plans for a James Dean plaque.

Complete details will be announced as soon as possible.

FAMOUS ARTISTS CORPORATION
AGENCY
CALIFORNIA BANK BUILDING
BEVERLY HILLS, CALIFORNIA

CABLE ADDRESS
FAC

TELEPHONE
CRESTVIEW 3222

Dearest Barbara

I don't like it here, I don't like people here. I like it home (n.y.) and I like you and I want to see you. Must I always be miserable? I try so hard to make people reject me. Why? I don't want to write this letter. It would be better to remain silent. "wow! am I fucked up"

Got here on a Thurs. went to the desert on Sat., week later to San Francisco. I DONT KNOW WHERE I AM. Rented a car for 2 weeks it cost me $130.⁰⁰. I WANT TO DIE. I have told ████████ and 5 other like to kiss my ass and what stench, spineless, stupid prostitutes they were. I HAVENT BEEN TO BED WITH NO BODY. and won't untill aiter the picture and I am home safe in N.Y.C. (snuggly little town that it is) sounds unbelievable but it's the truth I swear. So hold everything stop breathing, stop the town all of N.Y.C. untill (should have said everything here) Jan Dean returns.

wow! am I fucked up. I got no motorcycle
I got no girl. HONEY, shit writing
in capitols doesn't seem to help either
Haven't found a place to live yet, still
living with my folks — HONEY.
Kazan sent me out here to get a tan.
Haven't seen the sun yet. (fog + smog)
Wanted me healthy looking. I look like
a prune. Don't run away from
home at too early an age or you'll
half to take vitamins the rest of your
life. Wish you cooked. All be home
soon. write me please. I'm sad most
of the time. Awful lonely too isn't it (I
hope your dying) BECAUSE I AM.
                              Love.
                       Jim (Brando) Dean
                          (Cliff)

My address in (fathers that is) is
    1667 So. Bundy Drive
       L.A. 25, Calif.

CULT
OF THE
LIVING
DEAN

*I am from Beyond The Grave. Really.
And out of work.*
Illuminations, Rimbaud

As a consequence of the Canonization of James Dean at the Immaculate Conception of Teen, *Rebel Without a Cause* overthrew the notion that in order to grow up you must somehow *become* your parents. On the contrary, to accept yourself excluded any such compromise with conformity. Adolescence was no longer a frustrating phase on the way to the privileges of adulthood, but *the* desirable state, and James Dean's performances radiated the ironic defiance of the underdog. The Teen Dream was born, and Jimmy was speaking for all of us. This, compounded by the simultaneous rise of rock 'n' roll as anthem to itself, became the battle hymn to which the sixties, literally, would march.

His last visit to Fairmount, February 1955. Here with cousin "Markie" by the headstone of his grandfather, Cal Dean.
©DENNIS STOCK/MAGNUM.

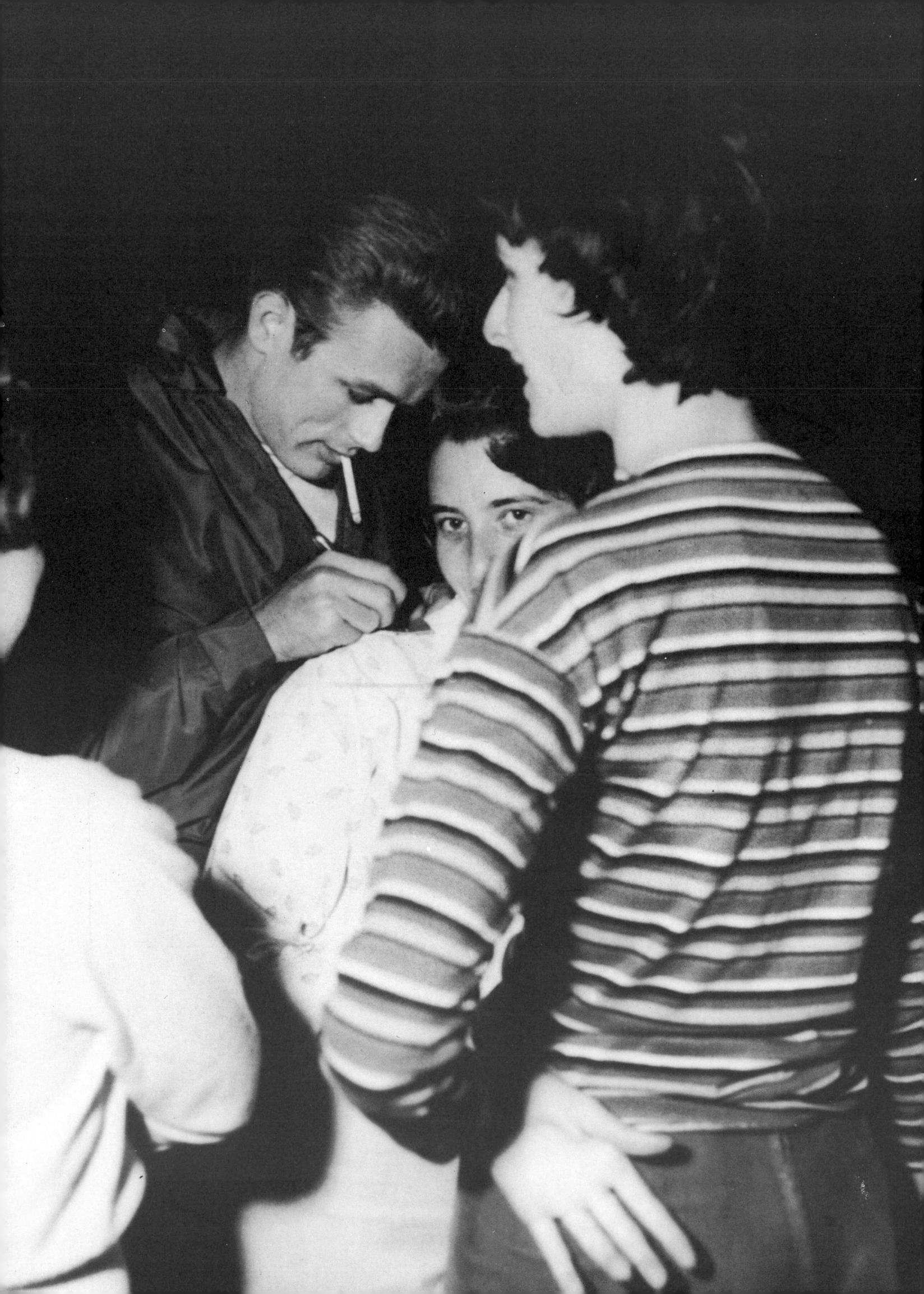

10-X194

*Preceding Page: With fans on Rebel's Griffith Park location, May
1955. By the time shooting finished, Jimmy's fan mail had
quadrupled—to some 1,200 letters a week. He was becoming a
tourist attraction on the set.*
©WARNER BROS. INC.

Teenage rebellion in the fifties took two forms: juvenile delinquency, characterized by gratuitous violence and vandalism, and the more "formal" gangs. Although the gang was supposed to be intimidating, its primary function was not random, lawless behavior, but a shared need for identity. Like college fraternities, these clubs had special insignia, jackets, code words, meeting places, ritual initiations and names.

John Steinbeck — who created the book that created the movie that created James Dean — could not resist pontificating on the matter. Perhaps he had a twinge of conscience about his part in all this. In any case, by the time he wrote *America and the Americans*, it was far too late to treat the patient: "I don't blame the youth; no one has ever told them that his tricks are obvious, his thoughts puerile, his goals uncooperative and selfish, and his art ridiculous. Psychoanalysts constantly remind their little patients that they must find the 'real me.' The real me inevitably turns out to be a savage, self-seeking little beast."

In other words, it's my adolescence and I'll die if I want to. James Dean looms monumentally at the beginning of it all: *the* rebel without a cause in the first a-causal rebellion. You could wear glasses and still be cool. Like James Dean. And would Buddy Holly or his clone, Elvis Costello, have had the temerity to perform in — imagine it! — *glasses*, if it hadn't been for Jimmy?

Rock 'n' roll was heir to the Mantle of Tormented Teen Fame. In Guy Peellaert's *Rock Dreams*, Jimmy's image on the billboard for *Rebel* appropriately dominates the background of the young Elvis slouching in a Memphis backstreet.

"When Elvis Presley arrived in Hollywood he had a marvelous opportunity to step into a vigorously swelling stream of cinematic energy, a genre and a tradition already well established," Albert Goldman wrote in his frictional biography of Elvis. "He was intensely aware of the opportunity created by the death of Jimmy Dean — at this time Elvis's favorite actor — and was nearly frantic with the desire to jump into Dean's shoes. The very first article on Elvis in

Fondling the Daniel Bloom Award he received for his performance in The Immoralist. LOEHR COLLECTION.

Photoplay, written by a reporter who interviewed Elvis on the first day of shooting for *Love Me Tender*, represents the rock star discussing earnestly with his producer, the young and much-admired David Weisbart (who had produced *Rebel*), the possibility of starring in a projected *Jimmy Dean Story*. Elvis is quoted as saying, 'I could do it easy. I want to play that more than anything else.' "

Just as John F. Kennedy's assassination is said to have set the stage for the Beatles, Jimmy's death in the first year of rock 'n' roll released the self-celebration of youth that is rock's primary impulse.

David Weisbart points out that, "So far as teenagers are concerned, Elvis is what I call a safety valve. By that I mean they scream, holler, articulate, and let go of their emotions when they see him perform. But when they watched Jimmy perform they bottled their emotions and were sort of sullen and brooding. Elvis is completely outgoing, whereas Jimmy was the direct opposite. Basically, Jimmy was a loner, whereas Elvis is gregarious."

Temperamentally the opposite of Jimmy, Elvis was ingratiating where Jimmy was aloof, gregarious in contrast to Jimmy's werewolvean exclusiveness, "a

200

natural" to Jimmy's calculated stage strategist, a charmer (then) in contrast to Jimmy's studiedly obnoxious behavior on the set.

"Elvis's great charm," Weisbart observed, "lies in his immaturity; but he is still a shrewd kid, with all Jimmy's knowledge and ability to use charm . . . Acting skill will probably ruin him because his greatest asset is his natural ability. That is what Jimmy appeared to have, and that is what made him a great actor."

In his twenty-nine feature-length movies, Elvis managed to pervert his facility into a farcical travesty, devolving from his endearing ingenuousness in *Love Me Tender* to the pathetically stock characters in his later films, a decline so precipitous that only a deity of his magnitude could have survived it. Even so, this mindless squandering of the mother lode of rock for the kingdom of kitsch often seemed on the verge of calling rock itself into question.

A more profound correspondence to James Dean in rock is Bob Dylan. Dylan, as persona and prophet, has more in common with Jimmy than motorcycles and a flagrant disregard for the highway code. And just as James Dean's mystery implied a longing for an undisclosed, hermetic Paradise, Dylan's fusion of Robert Johnson and Rimbaud articulated a Lost Key Theory of Civilization. The voice of the dead king echoes in Dylan's ventriloquil whine. James Dean's arrogant ambivalence paved the way for Dylan's contemptuous "something-is-happpening, but-you-don't-know-what-it-is" irony. Dylan transmuted James Dean's existential cowboy into a zen, motorpsycho, yazoo blues Isaiah as hieroglyphic and inscrutable as James Dean's presence; the enigmatic utterances of those in endless exile outside the Gates of Eden.

Dylan, just eighteen when Jimmy died, found in Dean the first and clearest model for his own future transformations from dust bowl drifter to seething amphetamine sibyl to Old Testament patriarch. Hikkala, the drummer in Dylan's first band, the Golden Chords, recalls: "We used to go to all the James Dean shows those couple of years after he died. We'd go down to the newsstand and get all the

Bohemian days in Greenwich Village, 1953. Right: Taking bongo lessons from Cyril Jackson, 1955.

magazines that had any articles at all on Dean. He was kind of our idol. This is one thing for sure, that Bob dug James Dean. We idolized him both as a person and an actor. We felt, including Bob, that his acting was actually himself. He wasn't just acting the roles he was in. The roles were him."

Jimmy liked to say, "In this hand I'm holding Marlon Brando saying, 'Fuck you!' and in the other, I'm holding Montgomery Clift saying, 'Please forgive me.'" Coyly converting Jimmy's two-headed philosophy of heroism into mawkish camp, Cliff Jahr (in a *Village Voice* cover story titillatingly titled, "James Dean was Dylan and Maybe Garbo Too") points out that: "Above all, Dean and Garbo shared some unconscious and unerring sense of timing, and left long before we wanted them too. After twenty-eight pictures, Marilyn was beginning to tire. Brando, at 250 pounds is playing a cowboy. What painful sights of Garbo and Dean have we been spared? Could she be doing shots on Carson, plugging a new horror film in which she softens people to death in a vat of cold cream? Could he be smiling Jimmy Dean, pitching

©Dennis Stock/Magnum.

James Dean

WARNER BROS

Rio Rancho Estates? No, better that younger people see Jimmy's incandescent performances on the Late Show and trust that, like every generation, we had our Dylan, too."

Nothing seems more essentially symbolic of the nature of the star in his projection and celluloid incarnation than the *Ka*. According to Egyptian mythology, the *Ka*, or celestial twin, is created in its immaculate state at the instant of birth, molded synchronistically on the potter's wheel of light by the god Khnum. Every star has one. Some have suggested that the death of his twin brother at birth was something Elvis was never able to overcome. Perhaps Mick and Keith (or John and Paul, or Dylan and any of his fissionable clones) are each other's *Ka* coordinates, their fates inexorably linked. The *Ka* is the double, and not even Warner Brothers central casting would have denied Jimmy one.

This *Ka*, or immortal self, is not only a shade, an image like that projected in the darkness of the theater, but is symbolic of the adolescent state itself: the adolescent at the height of his spiritual and sexual power preserved in the incorruptible *Ka* as essence, power, purity, and virility.

Raymond de Becker, in *The Other Face of Love*: "The *Ka* was sometimes shown as a mere black shadow, but the fact that it was more frequently represented by an adolescent proves that in real life the latter must have possessed the power of revelation and fascination which is attributed to the idea of the Double or the Shadow. Egyptian iconography shows us these adolescents bearing oriflammes and following the Pharaoh into the other world, and their conventional attitude in itself has a grace and tenderness."

The teen iconoclast had himself become an icon. And it's predictable, isn't it, that one of his former disciples should want to smash that enigmatic mask? (Very adolescent, too, come to think of it.) *Take This God and Bury It* by Tony Parsons (co-author of an equally hilarious and brilliant tract on punk aesthetics, *The Boy Looked at Johnny*) is a prime example of a heretical text. Just the sort of overamped rantings you'd expect from a lapsed idolator.

"That heady hybrid of drug-taking and style-making," writes Parsons, "this thing called counter culture. . . has a soft sentimental white underbelly. Wherein Jimmy Dean has lodged for a quarter of a century.

"The man who started it all! The first teenager! Part of our wonderful heritage! Martyred rock and roll Valentino!

"James Dean has been dead and buried for twenty-five years — happy anniversary, darling. . . . James Dean was a sex aid for social workers, rock culture's mooning love for James Dean is a hysterical, historical romance."

James Dean will continue to be a symbol of youth because he lived fast, died young, and has an *eternally* beautiful corpse. Sheltered and protected from subsequent failures, he is (mercifully!) preserved even from himself. The Eternal Teen, hence, inevitably, the semaphore for a culture of endless adoles-

Above: Warner Brothers promotional postcard stresses his eccentric life style. Opposite: A Chaplinesque Beat in midtown Manhattan, 1955.

bidity when the only death to be mourned is that of one's own childhood—like the "funeral" of Tom Sawyer and Huck Finn where the services are interrupted by the discovery of the "corpses" who are listening to the eulogies from the church gallery.

Jimmy, a morbid little devil himself, wallowed shamelessly in autonecrophiliac daydreams and was given to doomy, portentious pronouncements: "Death is the only thing I respect." And then there was the business of posing in a coffin (flashing a "V" sign!) for Dennis Stock at Hunt's General Store. Supposedly, this was Jimmy's re-creation of a well-known incident in Rimbaud mythology. It is said that Mme. Rimbaud used to make her children get into coffins and have them lowered into open graves in order to demonstrate the vanity of human existence, although some scholars now believe this to have been fabricated by Rimbaud. Jimmy, like Tom Sawyer, was always trying to turn his friends into the inconsolable Aunt Polly mourning the demise of her nephew. Beverly Long, the silent gang member in *Rebel*, turned down Jimmy's offer of a ride around the Griffith Observatory parking lot in his new Porsche Spyder, the car in which he was to die: "For a minute we sat there talking, and finally I got scared and told him I wouldn't go. 'You drive too fast, Jimmy!' I said. 'I got to,' he said. 'I'm not going to be around very long.'"

As undertaker and chief valedictorian he surpassed even Tom Sawyer, composing his own funeral orations and eulogies on his Webbcore tape recorder! Photographer Frank Worth, who visited Dean at his San Fernando home during the last week of September 1955, listened to some of the tapes: "They gave me the creeps. They were all about death and dying, poems and things he just made up! They were his ideas on what it might be like to die, how it would feel to be in the grave and all that."

The fusion of his own death in a sort of trinity with *Rebel*'s other teen angels, Buzz and Plato, cast a pubescent pall over the movie and haunted Jimmy's mourners.

"*Rebel*'s appeal was obvious," wrote Joy Williamson in *Esquire*, "if unmentionable in healthy circles.

cence for which he is martyr, model, and Point Omega.

William Zavatsky, at age twelve, no less, dwelt on the delicious, wistful transience of life and James Dean as a sort of classic comics' version of Hamlet, that adolescent Prince of Doom: "At the bottom of all these whirling questions was the great one," says Zavatsky, "because Dean, standing on that edge, reminded me of Hamlet facing the nothingness of the sea below the crags of Elsinore. 'Y'know something?' he says to Judy. 'I woke up this morning, you know — and the sun was shining, and it was nice, and all that type of stuff. And the first thing — I saw you. And, uh, I said: 'Now, boy, this is gonna be a terrific day, so you better live it up, 'cause tomorrow you'll be nothing. See? And I almost was.'

"All my teenage years I moved under that cloud; I would never make it to twenty-one. 'And I almost was *nothing*.' You could end it all in one minute, if you wanted to."

"O death, where is thy sting?" has always been the stuff of teenage reveries, an indulgence in mor-

Being And Nothingness in Times Square; and attending Lee Strasberg's class, at the Actors Studio, with Ben Gazzara and Kevin McCarthy, New York, 1955.
©DENNIS STOCK/MAGNUM.

We were watching the intense, doomed performance of a dead youth, a myth, the myth of those who would wish to see themselves dead without dying. Dean was dead, pre-dead, dead upon our discovery of him. His vivid presence projected a fathomless absence. It was thrilling."

Ghouls, graveyards, and eerie creatures with flesh dripping off their bones. Very E.C. Comics. Very Edgar Allan Poe. *Tales of the Grotesque and Arabesque.* Jimmy would've relished some of the macabre rites performed in his name.

Death is just another teen *frisson*, a fascination with something vaguely unspeakable and obscene lurking in adolescent bosoms along with sex and bodily functions. Zavatsky, contemplating the magazine racks in his local drugstore, found it intriguing:

"NEW STORIES. 175 PICTURES! JIMMY'S LIFE LOVES DEATH. THE STRANGE MYSTERY THAT LIVES ON."

"I wasn't immune to the strange poetry of how anyone's life could 'love' death," confessed Zavatasky. "Though it had never occurred to me that anyone could actually be in love with death. The thought sent a weird tingle through me."

Photographer Dennis Stock told me he saw in Jimmy's life the inevitable progression of death's closure: "Cradle, cocoon, tractor, car, coffin." Faced with an insupportable present sealed in an inexorable past that could only predicate an inevitable future, Jimmy was poised between two tenses as his personality exhausted its nuances. Drained, he

With Eartha Kitt in Katherine Dunham's
dance class, New York, 1955.
©DENNIS STOCK/MAGNUM.

entered the last state that can be named and to which he gave his name. While searching for the absolute, he ran into it head on.

"The mythological hero confronts more and more touchingly the world he desires to seize in its entirety," wrote Edgar Morin in his account of Hollywood's cosmology, *The Stars*. "James Dean's destiny became increasingly breathless. He was obsessed with speed, the modern ersatz absolute. . . . The automobile is escape at last: Rimbaud's sandals of the wind are replaced by James Dean's racing Porsche."

James Dean as actor and person was approaching an impasse from which there seemed to be no way out, or so the turgid dramaturgy of his death (a particularly morbid manifestation of teen mystique) would have us believe. A current T-shirt in sepulchral yellows and greens carries the logo: "HE'S DEAD. HE'S BACK AND BIGGER THAN EVER."

James Dean must be one of the few idols whose *death* is celebrated each year (like the flooding of the Nile), as a matter of course. The date even provided the title of Jim Bridges' film, *9/30/55*, in which Bridges and friends reenact the Oedipal agonies they supposedly suffered following Jimmy's death.

Pazooka (the biker who leads the annual procession to the Fairmount cemetery with a wreath of flowers on the bars of his Harley) has the date on his license plate!

"He liked death – he liked the idea of death," wrote John Gilmore in *The Real James Dean*, "not dying by it. He took it as a game. He considered it a game that he should play with the studio. He told me one evening on the telephone: 'The studio says I'm gonna kill myself, can you figure that? What do you think? I think it's great . . . doing this article in *Photoplay* and it's got a picture with me sitting on a Speedster and it says, "The studio says this crazy kid's gonna kill himself."'"

In their gleeful morbidity fans often resemble children, and Jimmy, too, had the exaggerated morbidity of one who has let death "play" on his mind since childhood.

Sal Mineo, when interviewed by Peter Lawford, agreed that Jimmy's was not a death wish: "Sure, he liked speed, thrills, excitement, being in control of your life. He used to drive Natalie and me to location at incredible speeds 'till the studio stopped it. They stopped *us*. But they couldn't stop Jimmy – he didn't fear death the way people normally do. He really believed in personal immortality."

One of the torments of the adolescent is the intoxicating conviction that everything is happening for the first time, every act a matter of Life and Death. Like adolescents, actors thrive on breathtaking suspensions of ego and belief, injecting the same sense of urgency and risk into every moment.

We don't worship Janis Joplin, Jimi Hendrix, Otis Redding or Buddy Holly *only* because they are dead. But those who die young do leave us with an immaculate legacy. After all, Clift, Brando, Tennessee Williams, Elvis, and Dylan all had more *time* to fail. As Kenneth Kendall cynically remarked in *The First American Teenager*, "One wonderful thing about dead movie stars – they can't disappoint you. And that's about *all* the live ones ever are capable of doing."

Jimmy's obsession with bullfighting was both pathological and choreographic. Warner Brothers Backlot, 1955. LOEHR COLLECTION.

Proof, in his own handwriting, that...

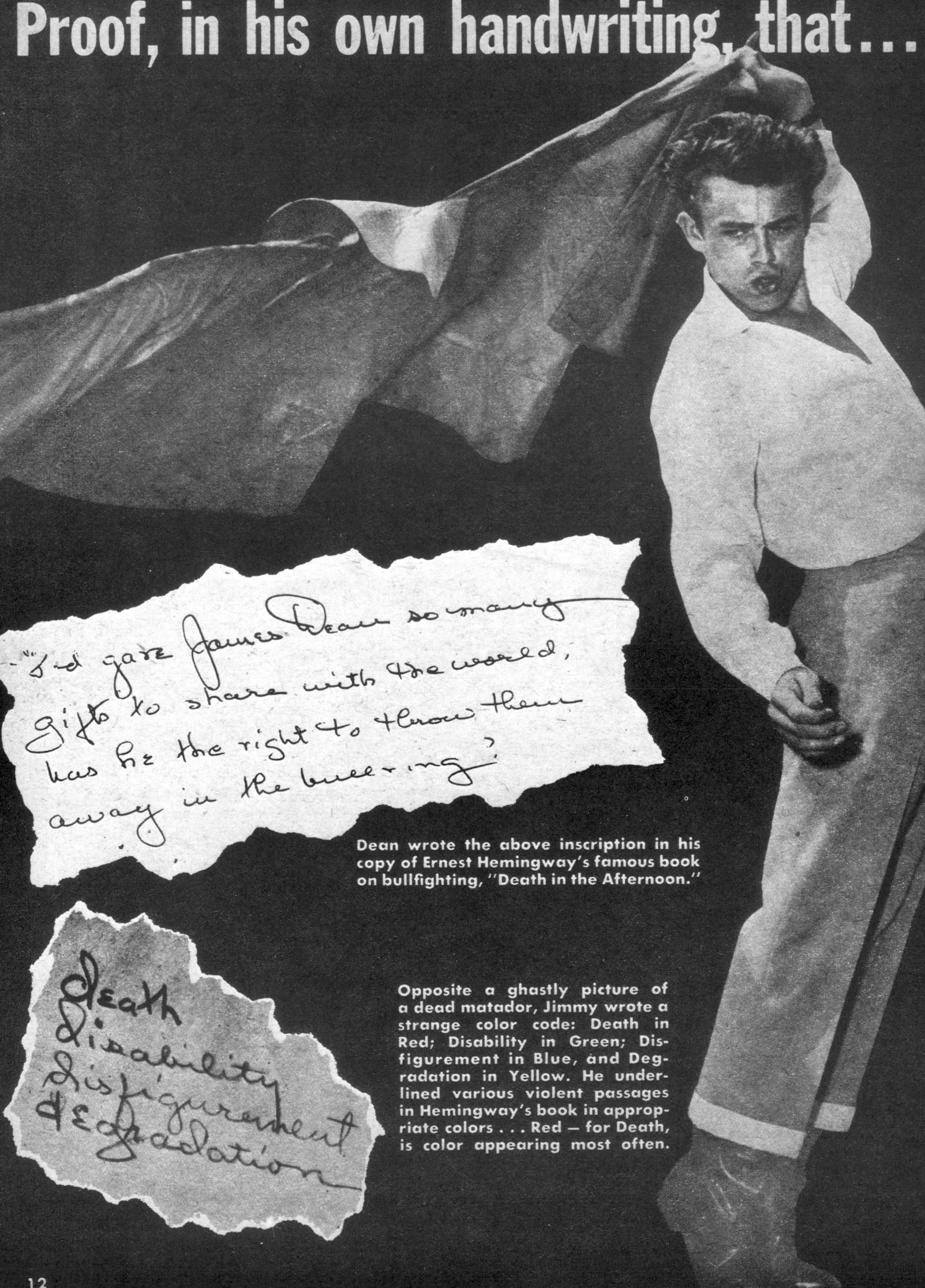

"I'd gave James Dean so many gifts to share with the world, has he the right to throw them away in the bullring?"

Dean wrote the above inscription in his copy of Ernest Hemingway's famous book on bullfighting, "Death in the Afternoon."

*Death
Disability
Disfigurement
& Degradation*

Opposite a ghastly picture of a dead matador, Jimmy wrote a strange color code: Death in Red; Disability in Green; Disfigurement in Blue, and Degradation in Yellow. He underlined various violent passages in Hemingway's book in appropriate colors . . . Red — for Death, is color appearing most often.

Knew He Had

A DATE WITH DEATH!

Jimmy's fans thought they knew all about him, but they never knew—till now—that he had a premonition of a violent end . . .

By DAVID BROWNE

REAMS UPON REAMS of copy have been written about the intense life and untimely death of James Dean, brilliant young Hollywood film star whose meteoric career came to a violent end two years ago. Although his remains lie peacefully in a little shaded cemetery in Indiana, his fans refuse to let him die, and the silly rumor persists that he still lives in some secret seclusion because he was maimed beyond recognition.

The Facts Speak for Themselves

There have been rumors, too, that Dean knew he had a rendezvous with death and left cryptic messages with his friends that fatal day he drove off. None of these has ever turned up. But in the last month, solid, documentary evidence—the only concrete evidence of James Dean's preoccupation with death—has come to light.

This new evidence will probably send his fanatic followers into a whole new phase of analyzing Dean's premonitions and subconscious, but we will not attempt to offer any conclusions. The facts, written in James Dean's own hand, speak for themselves.

It was 5:59 in the afternoon in Bakersfield, California when Dean was crushed to death in the tangled steel of his racing car. Perhaps it was macabre coincidence, perhaps it was destiny that Dean's most cherished book was titled *Death in the Afternoon*, Ernest Hemingway's famous tome on bullfighting. The star had loaned the book to a close friend some weeks before the fatal accident.

Toyed with Idea of Becoming a Matador

Bullfighting, like auto racing, fascinated Dean, and it is no small coincidence that man seems to be extremely expendable in both of these sports.

The smell of death in the bull ring excited Dean and obviously he toyed with the idea of becoming a matador. He became a keen student of the sport and often practised passes at an imaginary bull in his apartment. The Hemingway epic became more than a book to him—it became Dean's conscience.

On page 348, opposite a photograph of the matador Joselito lying dead in the bull ring infirmary, is this inscription, written by Dean: *"God gave James Dean so many gifts to share with the world, has he the right to throw them away in the bull ring?"*

On page 368, opposite a photograph of the matador Granero who also lies dead (Continued on page 46)

"Cradle, cocoon, tractor, car, coffin," as Dennis Stock put it. Above:
With Porsche Speedster. Right: His Porsche Spyder after fatal crash.
LOEHR COLLECTION.

DID JAMES DEAN COMMIT SUICIDE?

BY MIKE GOTRAM

ON a sunny California afternoon, September 30, 1955, a sloe-eyed Swiss miss with tumbling blonde hair and a pouting red mouth turned down a date that few females would have refused.

Over and over again in her husky-voiced accent Ursula Andress wearily said "no" to the persistent baritone on the other end of the wire.

For the man pleading with her that afternoon was James Dean, the Indiana farm boy who skyrocketed across the Hollywood skies to stardom and even in death has become

SEE NEXT PAGE ➤

13

The week before he died, Jimmy traded in his first Porsche for a racing model, the Spyder 550, and had Kustom Kar artist, George Barris, paint his racing number and name ("Little Bastard") on it. Forbidden, by contract, to race during *Giant*, he'd entered himself in the races at Paso Robles, the weekend after filming ended. Above & opposite (top): At competition Motors in L.A. Opposite (bottom): High noon, the day of the crash, September 30, 1955. ©SANFORD ROTH.

Mike Wilmington, in *High Times*: "They saw in Dean an image of themselves: purified, idealized, and spread triumphantly across a Technicolor CinemaScope screen. But there was something more, too. Who would have predicted that their loyalty to this tyro actor in blue jeans would so far outstrip and survive his death? Would survive their youth, too — and the times that engendered them — and would, in turn, grip the next wave of youth, and the wave after that, nettle them, get under their skin, give them a touchstone, an idol and, in the end, make James Dean something he always sought — in his confused, inchoate, murderously determined way — to be a symbol. Immortal. The Man Who Could Cheat Death."

There is a recurring feeling that Jimmy, like a schoolboy involved in some feat of derring-do, simply "got caught." The line between winning and losing is so infinitesimal. It would have taken less than a second — slower *or* faster — for Jimmy and Donald Turnupseed to have missed each other.

John Gilmore: "A few times he'd talk about 'Fatima' and say, 'I gotta be faithful to her.' Grinning, he'd mention 'fates,' that things were predestined, that 'I'm going to make it like Marlon did,' that 'I'm going to be a gigantic movie star.' It was to me, a little younger than Jimmy, as if a child had spoken."

"Some men bet on horses, or dogs, I gamble on myself," said Jimmy in a typical piece of *ex cathedra* self-commentary. And no one ever seemed more determined to fulfill his fate than Jimmy. It's a rather bizarre idea — to sacrifice yourself *for* yourself. Jimmy thought of himself as the Divine Victim, as if sooner or later his life might be demanded of him. As Norman Mailer said of John Kennedy: "[Kennedy]

has the wisdom of a man who senses death within himself and gambles that he can cure it by gambling his life." Remember that Jimmy's last words were: "That guy's got to stop. He'll see us."

At the time of his death Jimmy was literally invisible. In a gray Porsche on a gray road at twilight, and with Jett Rink's receding gray hair, he wasn't there at all. Just a gray ghost, the last shade of a color that can be seen. Jimmy was already gone. Donald Turnupseed "never saw him."

Jimmy called his last car "Little Bastard." That little bastard was Jimmy: "Why should I be loved? I'm a bastard, a nothing, a no good." He could never forget he was an orphan, nor was he about to let us forget it either. In all his films, Jimmy played orphans — either metaphorical or actual. The foundling adopted by uncomprehending human parents, the heroic orphan of mythology.

There is a sense in which celebrities are already dead. As remote from us as the dead, their death merely seals the bargain. They are suspended in life, creatures whose insubstantiality is the stuff of which their star is made. Gossip is "News from the Invisible World," but these "legends in their own time," embalmed in gossip columns while still alive, live on after death — only more so.

Sal Mineo, in the *Enquirer,* contributed to his own public ridicule with his "confessions" about his talks with Jimmy in the Beyond. Tabloids have taken over the function of the Egyptian priesthood as the Weekly Message Centers of the Great Departed, and communications with the dead through psychics and

6:00 p.m., September 30, 1955. Site of the fatal crash near Chalame, California. Mechanic and co-driver, Rolf Wutherich, thrown clear on impact, lies on the ground on the near side of the car.

rd Roth.

seances were a personal obsession with Sal: "Knowing Dean changed my life completely. At moments of doubt or insecurity, he's a source of tremendous strength to me. After he died, I became obsessed with him, trying to make contact with him. I feel his presence and I hear his voice. . .in my own realm. I know it's him, because he called me Plato, the same name as in the film."

A large body of folklore of the order of King Tut's curse has grown up about the rather substantial number of Jimmy's friends who have died in somewhat bizarre ways: Pier Angeli, of an overdose of barbiturates; Sal Mineo, brutally murdered; Natalie Wood, in a freak drowning accident; Nick Adams, also of an overdose; and Rolf Wutherich—who survived *Jimmy's* fatal crash with only a few scratches—in a car crash.

Cathy Damian, who dated Jimmy briefly, said of their hair-raising drives: "He wants to die, and he's too chicken to do it himself so he's going to take someone with him."

Perhaps he just got lonely up there. The Geography of the Beyond, from descriptions we have of it, is even less inhabited than Marfa, Texas. According to C. S. Lewis, Napoleon lived 15,000 years from the nearest settlement, and when he got there had nothing but recriminations for past wives and generals. Like the Little Prince arriving at his own constellation or planet, Jimmy may have doubted that he was dead. It is the deceptive reassurance of meeting in eternity. The population of the hereafter is of such a magnitude that Egyptians had to provide maps— otherwise, it would take an eternity to find *anyone*. All those trees with white crosses on them. Space madness! Infinity sickness!

Apparitions of Jimmy periodically reveal themselves to his old friends and lovers. The most chilling re-creation being the dream sequence at the beginning of Bill Bast's TV movie, *James Dean: Portrait of a Friend.* Some are just unnerving incorporations, like The Kid Who Looked Like James Dean who haunted Zavatsky's adolescence: "Suddenly, to my left, there was a hush in the crowd as heads turned and fingers pointed . . . . He moved slowly down the bleachers, wearing blue jeans and that red windbreaker over his white T-shirt, looking as if he had just stepped off the screen. His physical resemblance to Dean was uncanny—the same head of blond hair, the sunken eyes, the cigarette dangling from his pouty lip. Every so often he would show up at a football game or concert, lending credence to the growing legend that Jimmy, mutilated and out of his mind after his car wreck, is still alive in a mental ward somewhere in southern California or Indiana."

Jimmy's "live-fast-die-young-have-a-beautiful-corpse," philosophy set a trap for future teen idols, especially for rock 'n' roll. Never trust anyone over thirty soon took on the meaning, when translated to rock stars, of not trusting anyone who *lives* past thirty. Adolescents don't like their heroes to get out of their world alive. To do so is a betrayal, and anyone who has the nerve to flaunt this commandment—has the bad manners to actually *want* to go on living—has had to suffer the humiliating consequences. James Dean baptized the fatality of youth cults. Henceforth, only those who have the decency to sacrifice themselves before they're actually *asked* to leave can even be considered eligible to enter the pantheon. Who *will* be invited to Jimmy's thirtieth anniversary in heaven?

Julie Burchill and Tony Parsons in *The Boy Looked at Johnny:* "Bob Dylan broke his neck— close, but no cigar. Sealed integrity is reserved for the feted self-immolated. Choking on their own idolized vomit allowed a fistful of White Youth Culture luminaries—Brian Jones, Jimi Hendrix, Janis Joplin, Jim Morrison—to escape the fate of life-sucking godhead, as did their fifties antecedents."

A child of the Bomb Culture, James Dean bequeathed to us the fifties urgency of pending doom, the ticking of the cosmic clock. The hour is getting late was a sensibility that infected the apocalyptic atmosphere of the late sixties, an almost spiteful imprecation that the world would end when our vision of a new heaven and a new earth did not come to pass. What was about to end, however, was not the world, but the adolescence of a counterculture which worshipped itself in the image of its youthful idols.

Movie magazine recreation of the day of the crash.
COURTESY JERRY FAGNANI

This is Grapevine where Jimmy got a speeding ticket 2 hours before his crash Sept. 30, '55.

In this little cafe he had his last meal, a sandwich and coke, 33 miles from accident.

jimmy
dean's
last
miles

Jimmy's last mile, looking west on highway 466; where picture ends, his Porsche crashed.

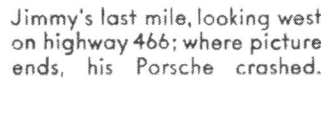

This is the tragic intersection; a car traveling toward jimmy suddenly turned to the left.

This is the photo record of that tragic day; this is the path Jimmy took to death.

Where these girls stand, Jim's car came to rest virtually demolished after the impact.

From shed at right of this garage came the ambulance that took Jim to hospital.

Here he was pronounced dead; he'd sustained a broken neck, been killed instantly.

From hospital body was taken to Kuehl mortuary in Paso Robles to remain for 3 days.

Then after the inquest this hearse took Jimmy to airport for his final journey home.

The only
Eye-witness
account

James Dean's Last Passenger Recovers— Tells Complete Story of Fateful...

DEATH DRIVE

by Rolf Wütherich

*In memorium—this second year since Jimmy Dean's death—*MODERN SCREEN *prints this story by the man who was with him at the end . . .*

When Dean, on September 30, 1955, raced to his death in his Porsche car, he was not alone. His mechanic, Rolf Wütherich, was in the seat beside him. Miraculously, Wütherich survived. He had to spend many months in the hospital. Here, for the first time, he tells the story of what really happened on that fateful day when his friend Jimmy Dean was killed . . .

■ I don't think I shall ever forget that day in September, two years ago. That was the day I rode with Jimmy Dean to his death.

I was a service mechanic for Porsche cars, and I was a very busy man indeed—film stars like fast cars, and I was experienced as a racing car mechanic in major European motor races.

That's how it happened that I was James Dean's last passenger, on that awful day when he rode to his death.

When I first met Jimmy Dean, he owned a Porsche *Speedster*, a somewhat smaller sportscar than the Porsche *Spyder* he crashed in. The *Speedster* had carried him to victory at Bakersfield, Santa Barbara and other races. It was at one of these races that I first met Jimmy. I was looking over the Porsche cars— that was my big job as a mechanic—and Jimmy and I got to talking.

I had seen him driving in another race—he hadn't been racing long, but he was a good driver: he had that essential feel for fast cars and dangerous roads. He had that sixth sense a racing driver can't do without. We talked about his car for a couple of minutes, and then he took off—for a win.

Two weeks later, I was walking along Hollywood Boulevard when I saw Jimmy Dean coming toward me. *(Continued on page 76)*

3

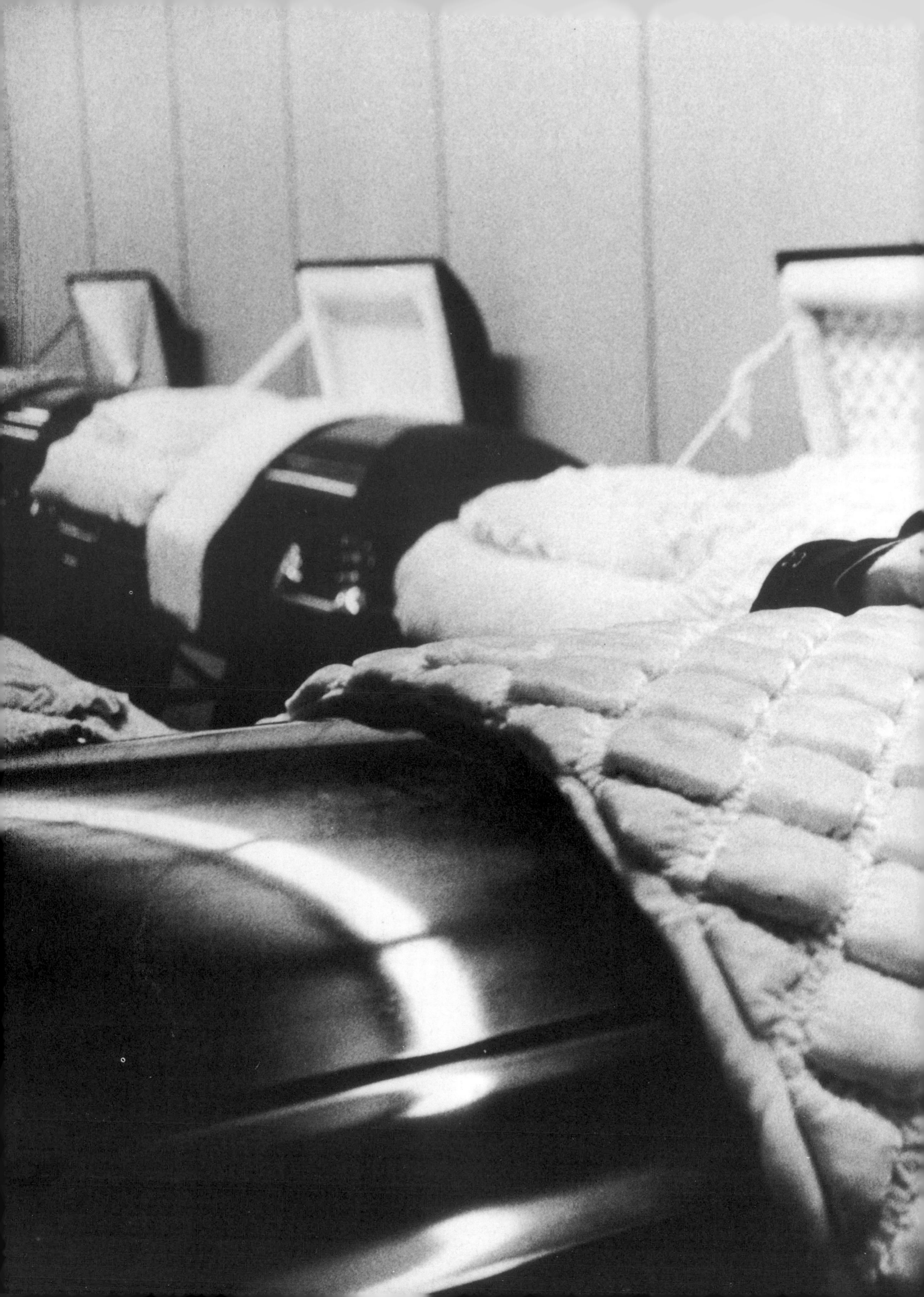

"Moody New Star" posing (for Life magazine) in coffin at Hunt's Funeral Home, where his body would be taken seven months later. Fairmount, Indiana, February 1955. ©DENNIS STOCK/MAGNUM.

STAR STATE

Most of all I like to mold and create things.
My Case Study, James Dean

Picture into Picture. We've taken his art for his life and vice versa. Even the private "lives" of stars are a movie, extracted as they are from movies. These images tantalize us, as do the artifacts-of-the-life-of, but they remain a sealed, self-mirroring mystery. We will never again get Cal Trask, Jim Stark or Jett Rink out of Jimmy. Few who read this book will ever have known James Dean personally. There is no yardstick to measure it all against. Perhaps we should accept the shells he constructed so methodically, his serial enigma, *as* his essence.

"Ripping Off Layers to Find Roots," was the title Jimmy gave to the scene he wrote with Christine White for their Actors Studio audition. But if he revealed fragments of himself while looking for Cal Trask, Jim Stark, and Jett Rink, these fragments only reinforce the eerie feeling that behind that wolfish head lies a deep abyss, a bottomless pit, and that we are asking questions of a phantom now eclipsed by myth.

Back lot at Warner Brothers,
with his new Porsche speedster.
LOEHR COLLECTION.

Portfolio headshots from his first year in New York (aged 21). One can see the features and the future Pentecostal wave of hair begin to be molded into the matrix of the Archetype of Adolescence.
JOSEPH ABELES COLLECTION

*Above: With Mildred Natwick in an
early TV drama, New York, 1952.*
LOEHR COLLECTION.

The "I" of James Dean, his greatest performance of all, was assumed. His roles are "moles," doubles, roles within roles. Secret sharers.

"I don't know who I am, but it really doesn't matter, " was the way Jimmy put it as a seventeen-year-old high school senior. "I don't mind telling, you, Mr DuBois," he wrote in *My Case Study*, "this is the hardest subject to write about considering the information one knows of himself, I ever attempted."

The shapeless sculpture that Jimmy molded that same year, a lumpy ectomorphic shroud titled "Self," was only the first in a number of selfless reflections. In the end, others would better define Jimmy than himself: Cal Trask, Jim Stark and, finally, Jett Rink, whose *identity* has been stolen from him by his own vengeful dreams. After all these incarnations, Jimmy's death following the completion of *Giant* seems almost a case of mislaid identity.

In photographs of his last days on the set of *Giant*, Jimmy looks haggard and Warner-weary. "The last time I saw him," an actor recalled, "he looked so awful, I mean really shockingly bad, so bad I couldn't look at his face. This was, I guess, a week before he died. I didn't realize until afterwards what it was. He was doing *Giant*. The make-up department had given him a receding hairline and bleached his hair and *that* combined with the way he lived...he'd just *aged*, taken on the look — it seemed to me at that time — of a very old man, 40, 42. I thought...after his death, my god, James Dean died physically a middle-aged man."

Perhaps Jimmy's gift as an actor was perhaps his solution to the perplexing questions of individual identity. Jimmy quite deliberately invented James Dean, but, unlike Baron Frankenstein, made his creature out of his *own* body parts, with a little help from his friends. And, like any chameleon, Jimmy observed his prey with infinite patience.

According to his roommate, Bill Bast, "Jimmy was always calculating what he could appropriate from whomever he met. He sapped the minds of his friends as a blood-sucker saps the strength of an un-suspecting man. Almost fanatically, he approached each person he met, whether prominent or obscure, with the same attitude: 'I will draw from him all he knows and everything he is.' It was an irresistible

challenge to him, to get them 'down.' He'd size people up; he'd say to himself 'I can do that. I can be you, too.' "

An uncanny mimic, Jimmy's impersonations were so larcenous that when friends and fellow actors saw him doing *them*, they sometimes felt oddly violated. As one friend said of him, "There goes my personality!"

With an Indiana habit of tinkering, Jimmy craftily put himself together, revamping his hair, realigning his facial expressions and contours, coordinating the taxonomy of gestures and attitudes he had collected in the form of a pre-conceived inner image. Trying on torsos, mannerisms, and inflections, Jimmy came up with the distilled essence of adolescence, a classic image and pose that would prove endlessly durable as each successive generation put him on.

On a purely physical level, James Dean was a ready-made, a model so well designed that it never went out of style, a *prêt à porter* personality. The pre-shrunk sheath of his persona fit his body so precisely that who he appeared to be became indistinguishable from who he was. And the pattern was so easy to duplicate because it had been molded, modeled, and pre-tested by Jimmy. He soaked up adolescent styles: the ingenuousness of the farm boy, the calculated nonchalance of the bohemian, the custom hair and self-conscious slouch of the city slicker.

James Dean is, then, a collective portrait, a composite image of teenage America in the mid-fifties. He orchestrated his poses into *attitude*, institutionalizing a vocabulary of random gesture into a language that would be decipherable to adolescents. Jimmy gathered together the assets of his being in those critical instances when all one's spiritual and physical forces are challenged, and, with this fused strength, kicked open the door of the future.

To participate in the cult of James Dean is to involve ourselves in a fantasy of which he is (and this is his supreme invention) much more the crystallizer than the true object. His invention was flexible enough to be infinitely adaptable, and as amorphous

In his West 68th Street apartment.
Note the paperback of Edna Ferber's
Giant *on lower far right bookshelf.*
New York, 1955.
©DENNIS STOCK/MAGNUM

as adolescence itself: a buzzing, ambivalent form identified only by its oscillating boundaries.

Neither ordinary nor "the natural" he was assumed to be as an actor, his secret was the same laborious magic of all performers — conjurers, athletes, and actors — who make almost superhuman feats seem effortless extensions of themselves.

Through a subtle, tactical act of will and imagination, Jimmy became the personification of the American teen, an instantly recognizable type that his fans would see as the "real me" latent in their tormented teen souls. It's a sort of standard-issue subversiveness — that oxymoronic entity, the all-American delinquent. It is particularly ironic that Jimmy, a genuine outsider with a pathetic sense of dislocation, should become *the* teen icon and role model for American youth. It was as if the only way he could become one of them was to make them one of him; if he couldn't get into their club, they would have to join his!

William Zavatsky describes the way in which he performed this ritual as a teenager in the late fifties: "On one page of the special issue *James Dean Album* I found a gallery of portraits — 'Jimmy's Moods' the editors called it. It furnished me with a catalog of facial expressions I worked on for the next five years. Dean became my secret poser, the mask I wore because I lacked one of my own. For hours I would stand before my mirror, with my bedroom door closed, trying to look 'pensive,' 'amused,' 'attentive,' 'quizzical,' 'bored,' 'wary,' 'withdrawn' or 'angered.' Of this anthology of possibilities, my best grades were in 'quizzical' (the crinkled brow and puzzled look carried me through high school Latin), 'wary' (I didn't need much practice; my last big crush had dropped me for an older Brando-style kid) and 'withdrawn' (I was a natural).

"For the next few years, I rehearsed James Dean relentlessly. I let my hair grow out and started brushing it back and I hunted for the red windbreaker. It was the only piece of clothing Dean wore in the film that you could really latch on to; I carried Jimmy Dean's image inside me until I didn't need it anymore, until I could shed it like a skin, the way Jim Stark had to shed the part of him that was Plato, the part of him that never wanted to grow up.'"

Few were immune. Even the contumacious Tony

Opposite: Screen test with Paul Newman for East of Eden. *Brando and Clift were also considered for the roles of the two brothers. Above: As Bachir in André Gide's* The Immoralist, *February, 1954.* COURTESY BARBARA MALAREK.

Opposite and above: From the TV drama,
"The Unlighted Road" with co-star, Pat
Hardy. May 1955.
©WARNER BROS. INC.

Right: In See The Jaguar, his first
Broadway role, with Arthur Kennedy,
October 1952.
©FRED FEHL.

In General Electric Theater's *"The
Dark, Dark Hours,"* Ronald Reagan plays
*a doctor whose sleep is disturbed by the
appearance of a "hep cat" killer played
by James Dean.*
©DENNIS STOCK/MAGNUM.

*Overleaf: Impromptu street theater,
midtown New York, 1955.*
©DENNIS STOCK/MAGNUM.

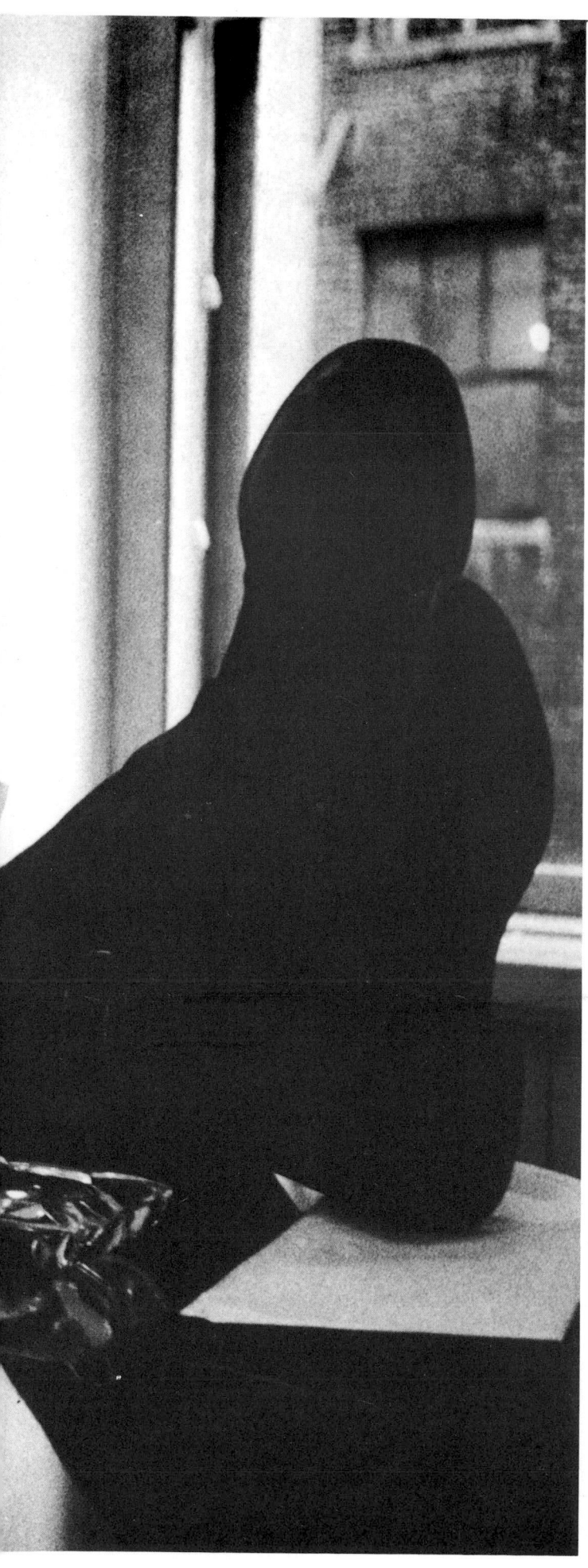

Parsons consorted with this phantom: "Me too—I was ten years old when I first saw James Dean and he made a massive impression on me, real instant satori stuff. I wanted to weep all over his headstone and see him when I went to the bathroom, I grew up acting as though he were looking over my shoulder at all times, taking notes."

Ultimately, Jimmy came to symbolize a collective identity characterized by uniqueness, a group whose philosophy sprang from an individual who was himself a collection of identities. It was the first clear outline of what came to be known as the counterculture. In his comprehensive singularity, Dean suggests a collapsing or imploding of types into the typical, which expresses itself as much through the rejection as through the assertion of the self.

The attraction of James Dean seems to be based on a species of Coleridgean "Negative Capability," an insatiable, obsessive absence. That blankness of identity which, offering no resistance, allowed him to magnetize himself to all his characters was the same force that made him so irresistible. Like an anti-matter star, his core was a vacuum that sucked in everything indiscriminately and converted it into his image. This image, in turn, exerted a gravitational pull of equal magnitude on his generation. Jimmy had a power known as valency, a capacity to both attract and unite things and to make them interact at random.

The lives of stars are instructions for individual and group behavior, and, in Jimmy's case, the signals emitted are those of the mutant in a stage of transition from the old to the new. After being tested in isolation, the star returns to the normal cycle of life only after he has been transformed—like the saint or sport of nature. Stars live on as mental maps and models, transmitting psychic signals on which we clone ourselves.

James Dean was the shapeshifter and matrix of adolescence, literally its *master*-piece, in the original sense of the master mold or form from which statues are cast. After Jimmy, adolescence began to seem an end in itself, the that-beyond-which nothing would,

The price of success. In his agent Jane Dacey's office, New York, 1955.
©DENNIS STOCK/MAGNUM.

even if possible, be desirable. By determining that we would never have to "grow up," he made what had heretofore been seen as a "passing phase" into a phenomenon.

He proved that growing up was impossible. It just couldn't be done. It was a state, in the case of Jett Rink, of something literally not-to-be-believed, just as Jimmy's own aging is unimaginable to us. It was, at best, a cosmetic condition. But the unformed, embryonic character James Dean left behind condemned his followers to a provisional life, and the culture he prefigured would be undermined more by an absence of foreseeable future than by rebellion.

"America has known many rebellions — but never one like this: millions of teenage rebels heading for nowhere," is the way the *Picture Post* described the first wave of the Dean Cult a year after his death. "Some in 'hot rod' cars, others to the blare of rock 'n' roll music, some with guns in their hands. And at their head, a dead leader." If his emerging age/class had not yet defined the causes of Jimmy's discontent, the sixties would do so soon enough.

Since the forties, Hollywood had been developing aberrant types in the so-called *film-noir*. These new characters, with their ambivalent motives and anti-social behavior, were known, collectively as anti-

heroes.

The *film-noir* proposed that it is only the outsider whose alienated point of view (even if disturbed and psychologically unstable) is capable of exposing the corrupt society that has alienated him. His violence and manic outbursts seem thereby redeemed by a righteous indignation at an injustice whose sources are no longer traceable.

John Garfield, Montgomery Clift, Marlon Brando and James Dean succeeded in casting a glamorous aura on the psychopathic, criminal and delinquent types they played. Convincingly playing the outsider in all of his films, Jimmy formed a bond with hostility,

With Dennis Stock (far left and far right) and Gjon Mili, back lot, Guys and Dolls, *1955.*
©PHIL STERN.

his intrusion into the action bringing latent tension to a head. In his television roles, especially in the *Danger* series, Jimmy lent a real edge of menace to the crazy-mixed-up-kid killed by unfeeling cops who'd never read Freud. The implied threat came not from the violence these roles generally demanded but from Jimmy's truly unnerving portrayals of schizoid mood swings.

These new stars had enough personal quirks in their own makeup to make them dangerously attractive. Offstage, the new star was expected to be a psychoerotic replicant of the personality portrayed on the screen. This tendency was fatal to someone like Marilyn Monroe, who was irrevocably sealed into a malleable living doll, a vehicle for American fantasies. To the general public, Brando became indistinguishable from Johnny, the biker in *The Wild One*, or Stanley Kowalski in *A Streetcar Named Desire*. He found it almost impossible to disassociate himself from his early roles, and it would be years before he was allowed to hang up his biker colors.

But the prototype for the new adolescent had to be far more pliable and ambivalent than the static stances that made Brando's proletarian lout or Marilyn's blond bombshell believable. Teenagers were not looking for another monolithic stereotype that fitted neatly into conventional roles endorsed by the society it was looking to overthrow. Jimmy's personas would have to include a set of contradictory, half-formed qualities with enough differential to be believable to an age/class that needed a *new* model for its new society.

Songwriter Antonia describes the source of Jimmy's magnetism from an adolescent's point of view: "Things I couldn't even speak to my mother, my priest, my best friend, well, this person was saying right up there on the screen—in front of strangers! I worshipped Jimmy, he spoke for me. He just got out there and did it in front of God and the world. It wasn't so much the rebelliousness. *We* could rebel. It was the vulnerability which we couldn't show, which we didn't dare to show because we were fighting it so hard. We were afraid to let *them* see any weakness. And here's James Dean, just blubbering right out on the movie screen. And asking his folks to help him! We knew how hard that was for him to do because we were in the same situation,

Jimmy only got drafted in the movies. Opposite: His first movie role (in Father Peyton's TV Theatre production, "Hill Number One") was as a G.I. St. John, and won him his first converts: The Immaculate Heart James Dean Appreciation Society. LOEHR COLLECTION.

Overleaf: ©DENNIS STOCK/MAGNUM.

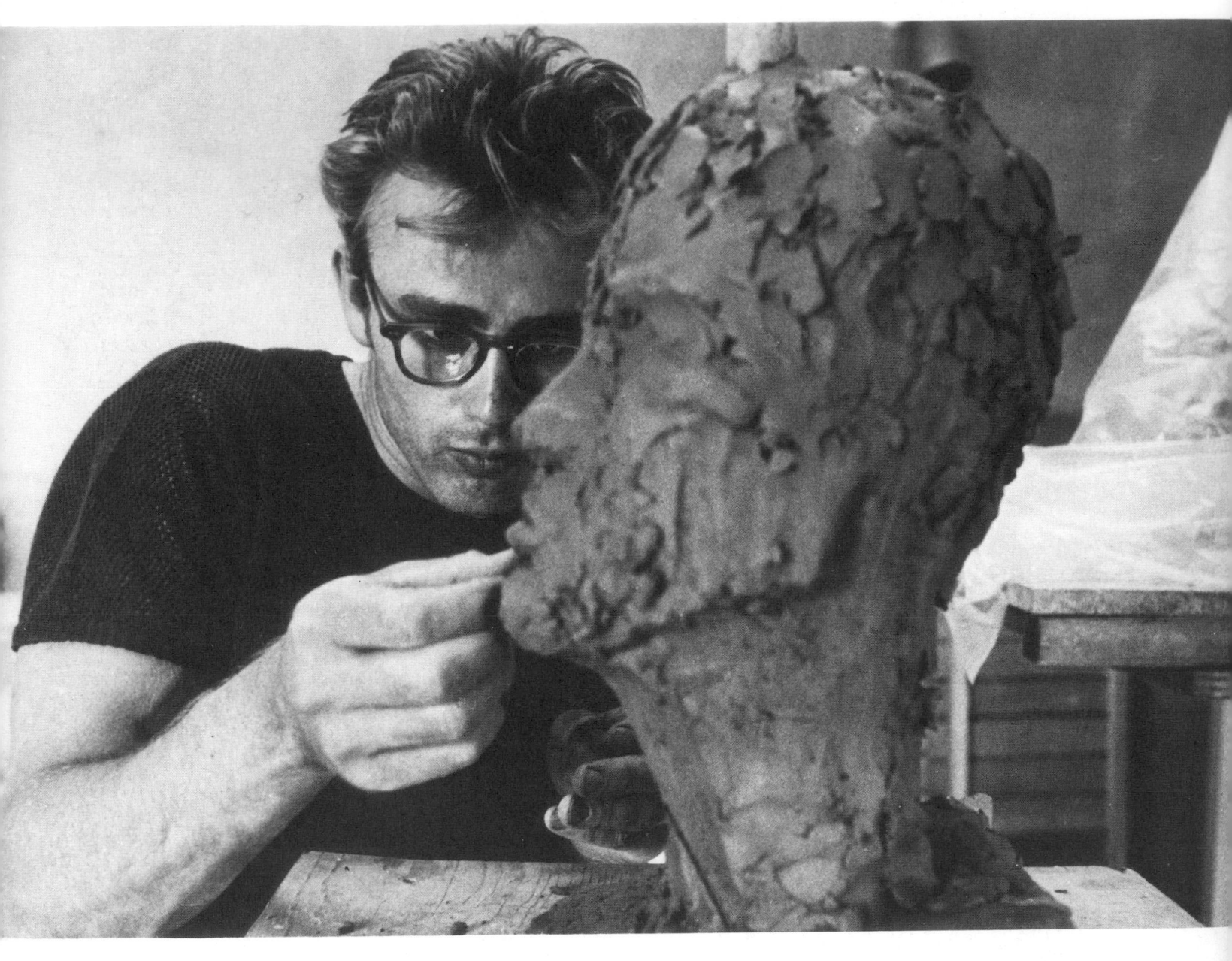

"I like to mold and create things,"
Jimmy wrote in his high school
composition, My Case Study. *His best*
subject, as here in a self portrait now in
the Fairmount Historical Museum, was
also his most ingenious invention, James
Dean.
©SANFORD ROTH.

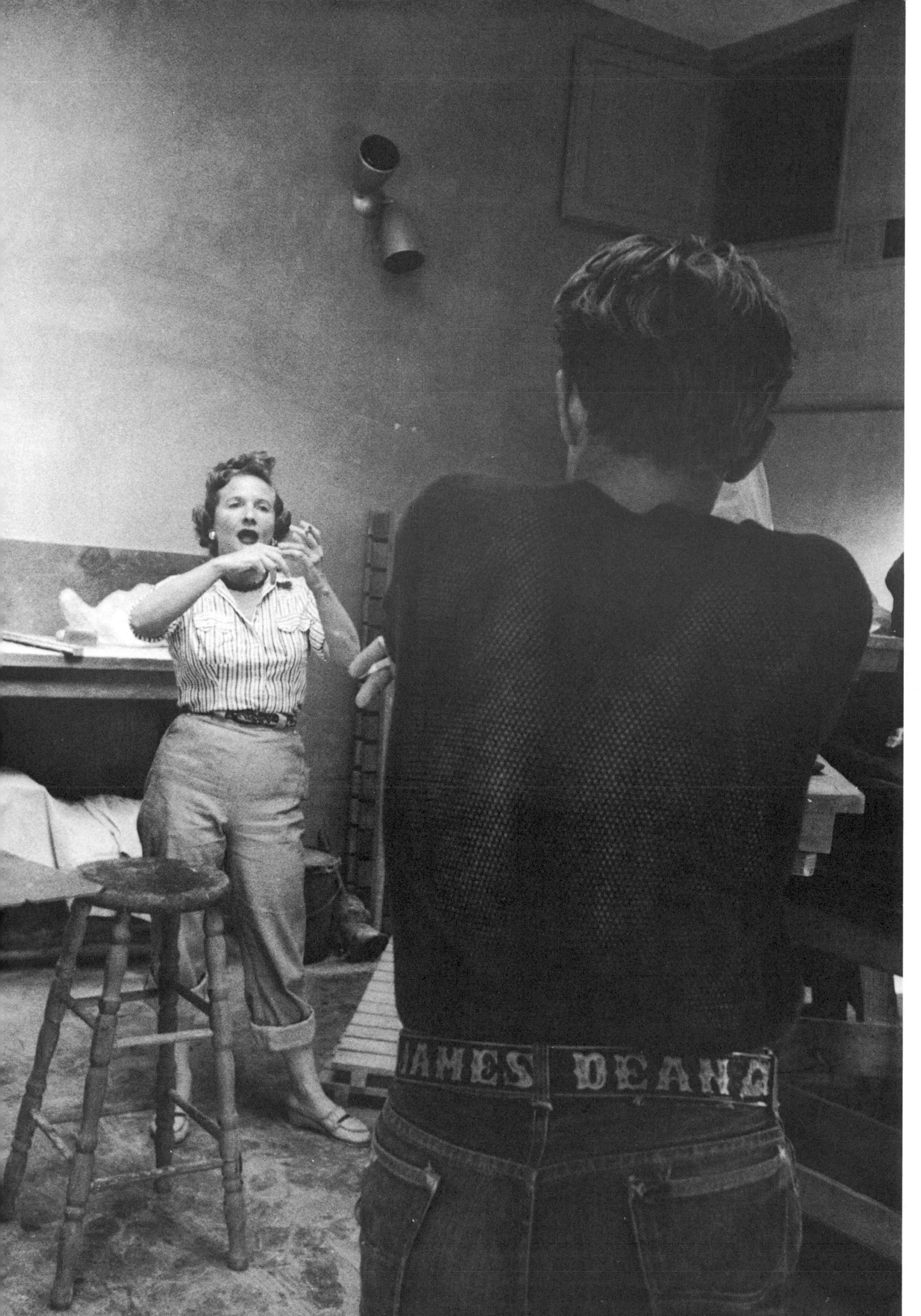

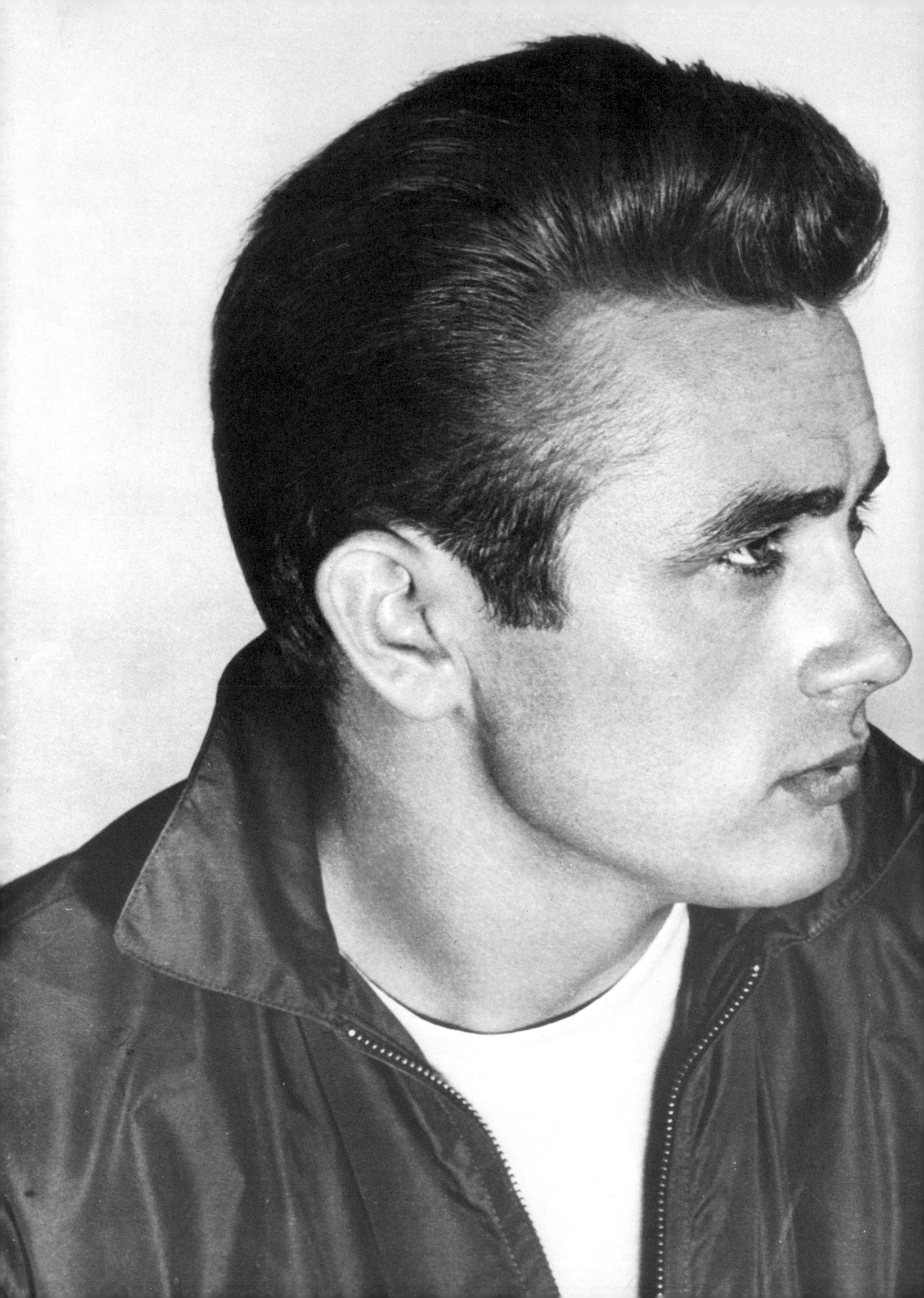

and our parents were the last people we'd go to for help. But in *Rebel Without a Cause* Jim Stark finally gets to the point of asking his father for help —'Dad, say something!' — and that is precisely the dividing line between child and adult. When you're a child you can't ask your parents for help unless its life or death. But as an adult you lose the importance of *not* asking."

A master of making the most of his own shortcomings, Jimmy's nervous twitch, erotic slouch, and menacing prowl combined with a chronic headhanging to become part of our history. But far from being an aberration, this now represented a new American value.

James Dean slipped in at the core of fifties America, piping its essence. He put his reservoir of values under sufficient pressure to yield up his essence in a repertoire of gestures that in themselves form a permanent portrait of an era as it passed through his nervous system. The history of all images involves communication with phantoms, forms that have reached their fulfillment and are ready to dissolve. In the twentieth century, these mirages are often movies, the form in which the codes of the star are most transmittable.

Everything about James Dean is ambiguous: his image *floats* in suspension between child and adult, androgynous and macho, actor and person. There's something fixed about the images of Gary Cooper, Jimmy Stewart, and John Wayne. Uncomplicated. But Jimmy has a multitude of differing images. Each one isolated would have had a static quality, but in combination, simultaneously moving towards you and withdrawing, they create James Dean's indefinable aura. A fugitive presence that suggests something distinct *only* when in motion, his genius was in blurring the lines.

In shattering the corrupt and obsolete stereotypes of American myth, Jimmy created even more powerful ones to replace them. He is an American icon, almost as remote as Washington or Lincoln. James Dean has become what he represents, the incarnation of the Dean Age values coined for him.

The classic Dean in the red windbreaker.
Still from Rebel Without a Cause.
LOEHR COLLECTION.

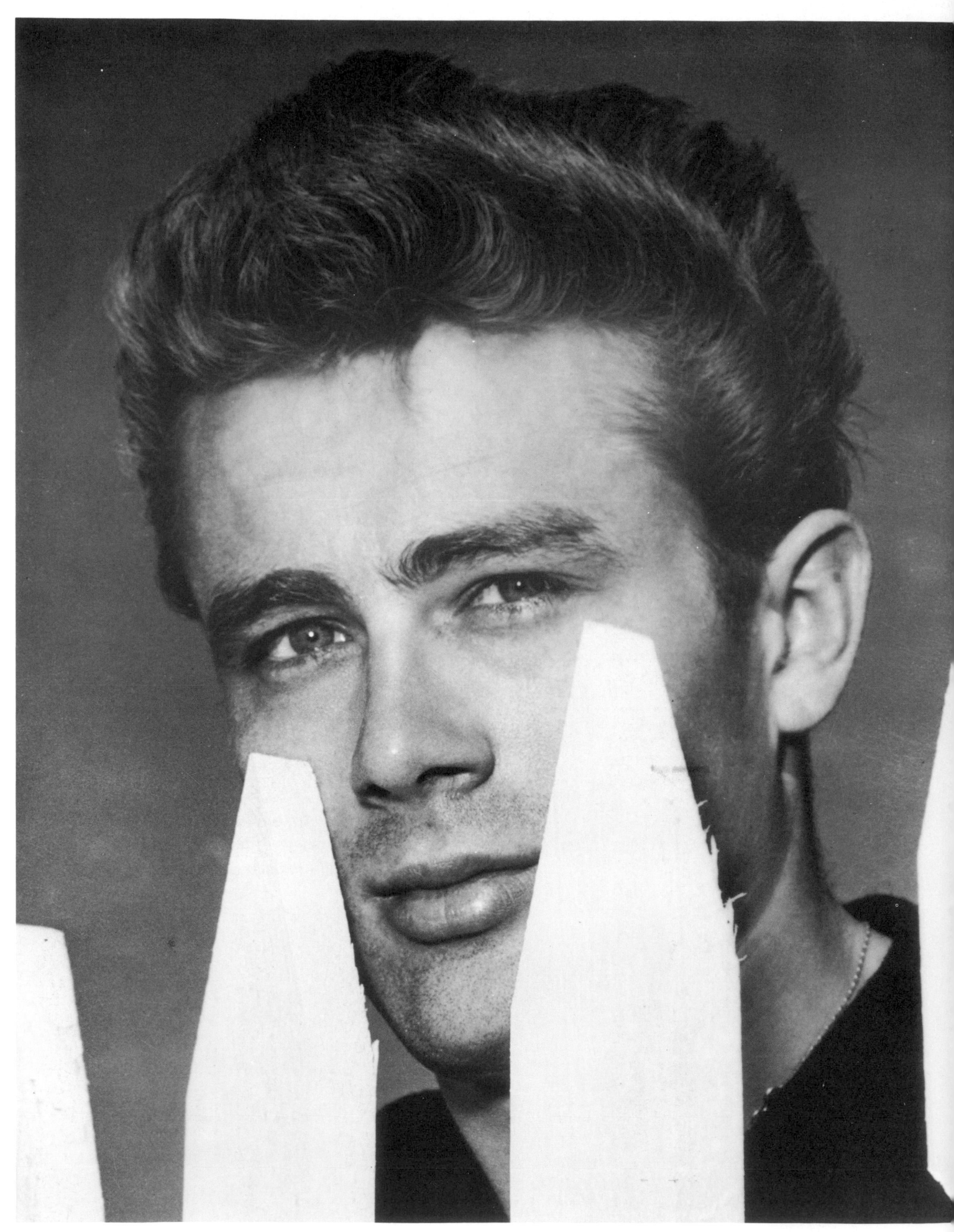

*A Hollywood Huck Finn on Warner Brothers' Anytown, U.S.A. set.
These photos show a brief attempt to make even the Teenage
Werewolf conform to standards.*

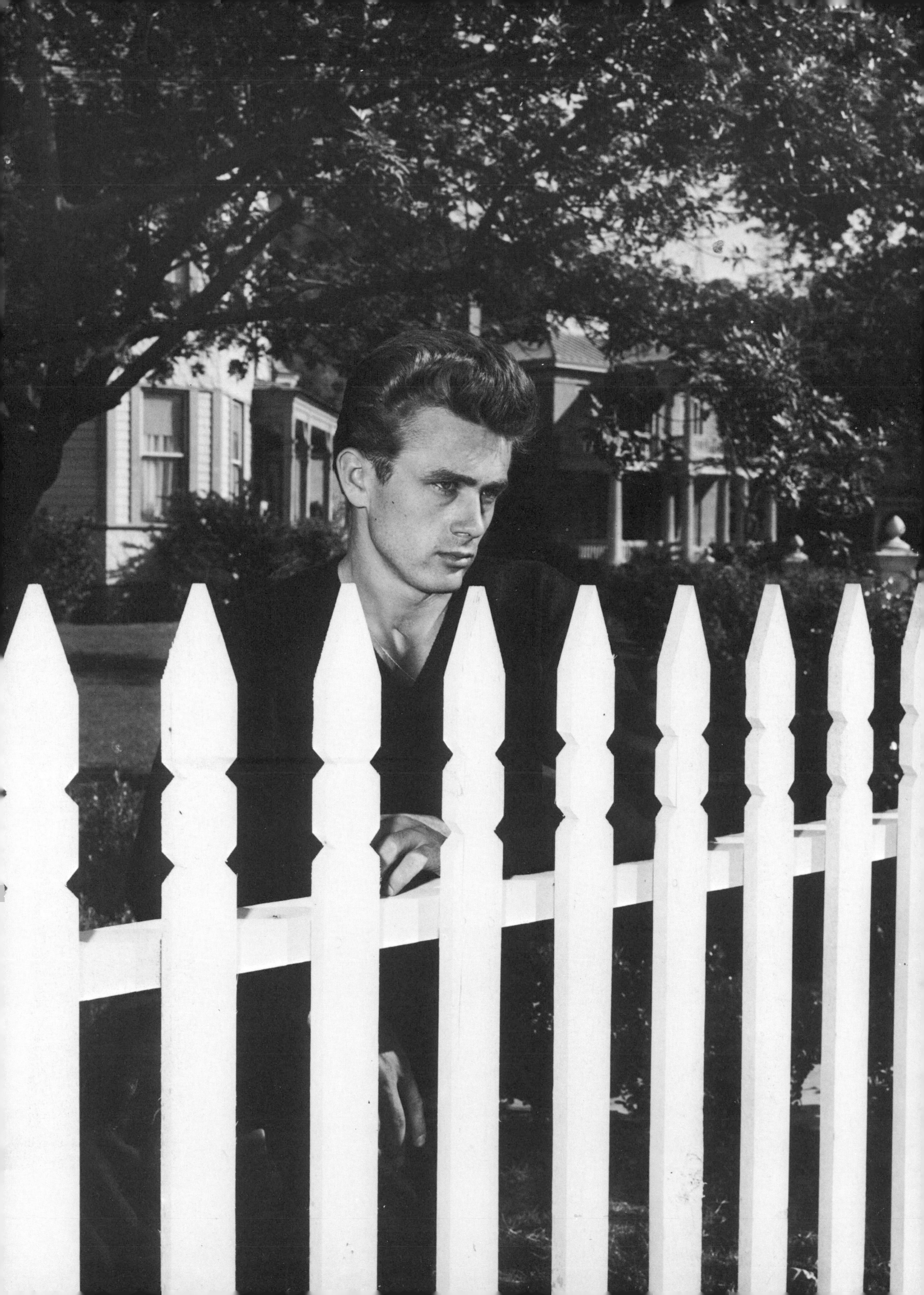

Opposite: "JAMES DEAN'S NEW HEART-THROB: THE FEMALE MARLON BRANDO!!" Confidential *magazine torridly announced when he showed up with Ursula Andress at the 1955 Academy Awards.*

Above: "Dates" arranged by the studio's publicity department, even when beyond belief, provided fodder for the fan mags and gossip mills; this unlikely soirée features the vivacious Terry Moore and a bristling Jimmy Dean. Hollywood, 1955. LOEHR COLLECTION.

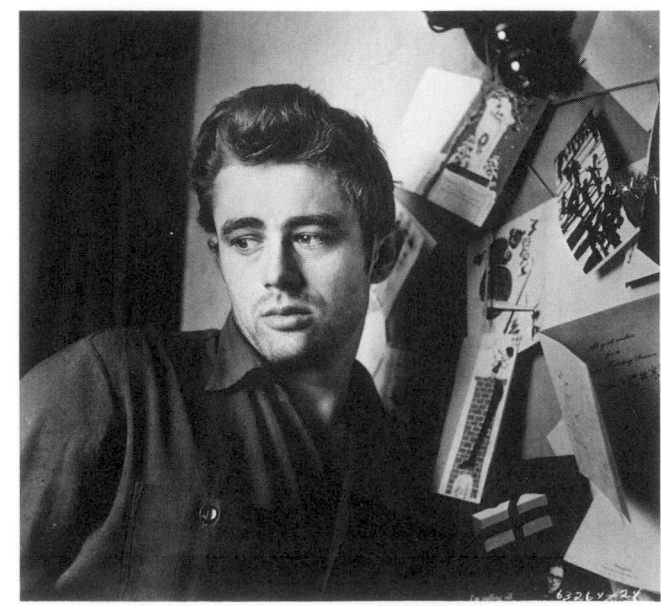

*Preceding Page: Backyard Ping Pong at
Sanford Roth's House.*
©SANFORD ROTH.

©Sanford Roth.

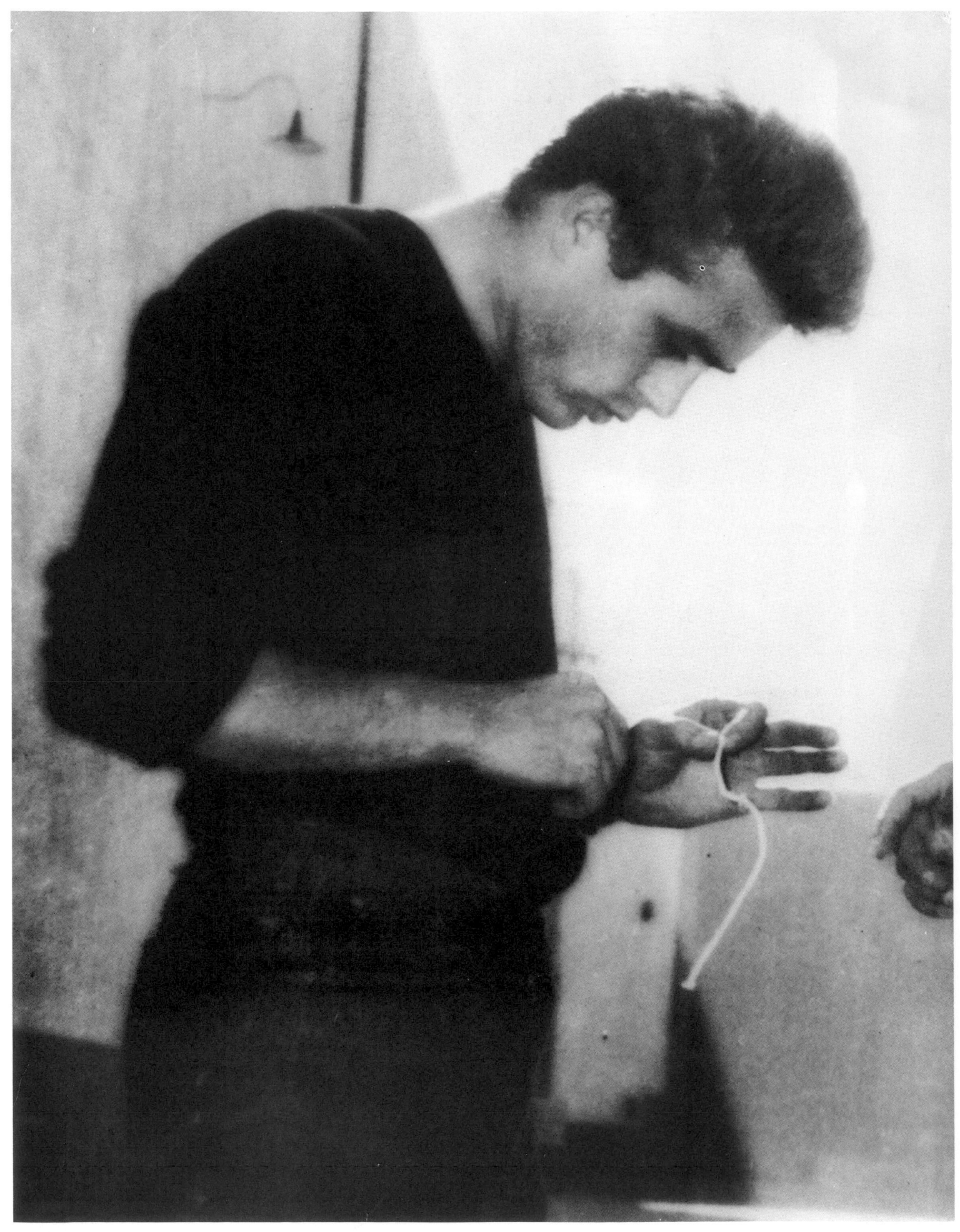

270

In their cosmic narcissism, stars tend to become transparent through each other. "The young Gary Cooper looked in the mirror and saw Greta Garbo. Greta Garbo looked in the mirror and saw James Dean," said Jackie Curtis. First headshots for his portfolio, Hollywood, 1951.

A CHRONOLOGY

*How much happier that man is who believes his native town to be
the world, than he who aspires to become greater than his nature
will allow...Farewell, Walton! Seek happiness in tranquility
and avoid ambition, even if it be only the apparently innocent
one of distinguishing yourself...*
Frankenstein, Mary Shelley

1931

February 8th, 2 a.m.   James Byron Dean born to
Winton and Mildred Dean, at home, Seven Gables
Apartments, 320 East Fourth Street, Marion, Indiana.
Given first name of attending physician, James
Emmick, and middle name, it is said, for poet, Lord
Byron.

1933

July 5th   Deans move from Marion to nearby farm-
ing community of Fairmount, Indiana.

1935

June 7th   Winton transferred to Sawtelle Veterans'
Hospital in Santa Monica; Deans move to California.

1940

April 14th   Mildred dies of cancer in Los Angeles.

63246-13

*James Dean's genius as an actor was to
be able to track himself through the
mind's eye and transform it into the "I"
of the audience. On location, Marfa,
Texas, August 1955.*
LOEHR COLLECTION.

April 20th Jimmy accompanies mother's body by train to Fairmount. Goes to live with aunt and uncle, Ortense and Marcus Winslow and their young son, Markie, on Winslows' farm just outside Fairmount.

August 18th Adeline Nall—a major influence in Jimmy's decision to become an actor—arrives in Fairmount to teach Spanish, French, Speech and Dramatic Arts.

1947

March 28th Plays part of John Mugford in Fairmount High School sophomore production of *Mooncalf Medford*. During this year, also plays part of Herbert White in *The Monkey's Paw*, and leading role in *An Apple from Coles County.*

1948

August 30th Fairmount High baseball team, the Quakers, trounces St. Paul, 7-0, in season's final game.

October 8th Dr. George Davis of Purdue University gives first of his rousing recitations of stories and poems by Hoosier poet laureate, James Whitcomb Riley, leaving profound impression on 17-year-old, Jimmy.

October 29th At Halloween Carnival, plays Frankenstein monster in Fairmount High production of *Goon With the Wind.*

November 2nd Fairmount High basketball team, the Quakers, over Jefferson Township Yeoman, 44-39, in first game of season.

November 16th Quakers over Middletown, 39-30.

November 19th Quakers over Windfall, 59-31.

December 10th Quakers over Jefferson Township, 40-27.

December 23rd Featured in Fairmount High Thespians' production of two one-act-plays for Christmas program.

1949

February 4th Quakers over St. Paul, 41-39.

February 8th Jimmy's 18th birthday; registers for the draft. Quakers over Alexandria Tigers, 41-39.

February 13th With Barbara Leach, represents Fairmount on Grant County Voice of Youth, WBAT radio. Together they subsequently win debate: "The United States President Should Be Elected by a Direct Voice of the People."

February 16th Fairmount High senior class trip to Indianapolis.

February 24th Quakers over Van Buren Aces, 41-38.

February 26th Quakers over Mississenewa Indians, 39-37; Jimmy scores winning points at the buzzer.

March 19th Fairmount High senior class holds "penny supper" to raise funds for trip to Washington, D.C.

April 7th Senior class play, *You Can't Take It with You*, opens with Jimmy in the role of Grandpa Vanderhof.

April 9th First place honors in National Forensic League's state contest, Peru, Indiana, with recitation of "The Madman"—from *The Pickwick Papers* by Charles Dickens.

April 22nd Fairmount High School Senior Prom.

April 29th & 30th Accompanied by Adeline Nall, competes in National Forensic League's national contest, Longmont, Colorado. Sixth place in Dramatic Declamation competition.

May 7th & 8th Senior class trip to Washington, D.C.

May 16th Graduation Day.

June 14th "JAMES DEAN HONORED AT FARE-WELL PARTY MONDAY NIGHT"
(Headline in *The Fairmount News)*

June 15th Leaves by bus for California.

1950

January 18th Begins freshman year at Santa Monica City College.

October 10th Lands role in UCLA Theatre production of *Macbeth*: as "the world's worst" Malcolm.

December 13th First professional acting job: Receives $30 for Pepsi-Cola commercial in which a group of teenagers (including Nick Adams) dance around a jukebox singing "Pepsi-Cola hits the spot..."

1951

January Withdraws from college. Begins attending drama workshop organized by James Whitmore.

April 9th Job at CBS radio.

April 1st John the Apostle in *Father Peyton's TV Theatre*—"Hill Number One." Airs Easter Sunday. Girls at local parochial school form the Immaculate Heart James Dean Appreciation Society.

July 22nd First bit part in movie, *Fixed Bayonets*, directed by Sam Fuller. His one line, "it's a rear guard coming back," is later cut. This summer he also gets bit part in the Dean Martin, Jerry Lewis comedy, *Sailor Beware*; works as an extra in *Trouble Along the Way* with John Wayne; and, in *Has Anybody Seen My Gal?* with Rock Hudson, gets to deliver this immortal line to Charles Coburn: "Hey, Gramps, I'll have a choc malt, heavy on the choc, plenty of milk, four spoons of malt, two scoops of vanilla ice cream, one mixed and one floating...."

September 1st On advice of drama coach, James Whitmore, leaves for New York to look for work in the theater.

November Gets job as stunt tester on TV game show, "Beat the Clock."

1952

February 20th Appears in TV drama, "The Web."

May 11th NBC's *U.S. Steel Hour:* "Prologue to Glory."

August Dramatic reading of Franz Kafka's "The Metamorphosis" at the Village Theatre, New York.

October Lands first leading role on Broadway (in

See the Jaguar). Plays a sixteen-year-old boy who has been locked in an ice house all his life by a demented mother.

November 12th With Christine White auditions for Actors Studio in scene they have written themselves: "Ripping Off Layers to Find Roots." Dean and White among the seven selected.

November 30th Home to Fairmount for Thanksgiving.

December 3rd *See the Jaguar* opens at New York's Cort Theater. Closes three days later.

1953

January 15th NBC's *Kate Smith Hour:* "Hound of Heaven."

January 29th NBC's *Treasury Men in Action:* "The Case of the Watchful Dog."

February 8th TV drama, *You Are There!:* "The Capture of Jesse James."

March 14th CBS's *Danger* series: "No Room."

March 16th Featured role in *The Scarecrow* at the Theatre DeLys.

June 16th NBC's *Treasury Men in Action:* "The Case of the Sawed-Off Shotgun."

July 17th NBC's *Campbell Sound Stage:* "Something for an Empty Briefcase."

August 17th CBS's *Studio One Summer Theatre:* "Sentence of Death."

August 25th "Death Is My Neighbor" on CBS.

September 11th "The Big Story" on NBC.

October 4th "Omnibus" on NBC, with Alistair Cooke, Hume Cronyn, Jessica Tandy and Carol Channing.

October 14th NBC's *Kraft TV Theatre:* "Keep Our Honor Bright" and "Long Time Till Dawn," written by Rod Serling.

October 16th NBC's *Campbell Sound Stage:* "Life Sentence."

November 11th NBC's *Kraft TV Theatre:* "Long Time Till Dawn," written by Rod Serling.

November 17th NBC's *Armstrong Circle Theatre:* "The Bells of Cockaigne."

November 23rd NBC's *Johnson's Wax Program:* "Robert Montgomery Presents: Harvest," with Dorothy Gish.

December Drives Triumph 500 motorcycle to Fairmount.

1954

February 8th On Broadway as Bakir in *The Immoralist*, with Louis Jordan, Geraldine Page. "I am now a colorful, thieving, blackmailing Arab boy played by James Dean." Hands in two weeks notice.

February 12th Rehearses *Women of Trachis*, Ezra Pound's translation of Sophocles, at Cherry Lane Theatre—with Eli Wallach and Julie Harris.

March 6th *The New York Times:* "*Immoralist* Star Signed By Kazan for *Eden.*"

March 8th First flight—to Hollywood with Elia Kazan. Clothes in a brown paper bag.

April 7th Signs contract with Warner Brothers for role of Cal Trask in *East of Eden*. Advance of $700.

May Buys first sportscar, a used MG TA.

May 27th *Eden* begins shooting in Mendocino, California.

June 4th *Eden* shoots in Salinas for a week. Returns to Warner Brothers for indoor scenes.

July 6th Gets California driver's license.

August 13th *Eden* filming ends.

September 5th NBC's *Philco TV Playhouse:* "Run Like a Thief."

September 27th Director Nicholas Ray moves into office at Warner Brothers to start work on script for *Rebel Without a Cause*.

October 7th Warner Brothers exercises right to extend Jimmy's contract.

November 9th CBS's *Danger* series, "Padlocks," with Mildred Dunnock.

November 24th Former girlfriend, Pier Angeli, marries Vic Damone at the Westwood Church; Jimmy guns motorcycle from across the street.

December Plays a "hep-cat" killer subdued by a country doctor, Ronald Reagan, in CBS's *General Electric Theatre:* "The Dark, Dark Hours."

December 17th Appears in *General Electric's* "I Am a Fool," with Natalie Wood and Eddie Albert.

1955

January 4th Warner Brothers announces James Dean to play role of Jim Stark in *Rebel Without a Cause*. ABC's *U.S. Steel Hour,* "The Thief," co-starring Mary Astor.

January 18th Returns to Hollywood. Begins pre-production meetings with director, Nick Ray.

February Ray holds juvenile delinquency "classes" for actors playing gang members. Warners' wardrobe department soils and launders more than 400 pairs of Levis for stars and extras in the movie.

February 14th With Dennis Stock attends "Sweetheart Ball" at Fairmount High School. Sits in on bongos.

With Nick Adams on the set of Giant.
©WARNER BROS. INC.
Overleaf: ©SANFORD ROTH.

March 1st   Buys 1500cc Porsche Super Speedster. Wins races at Pacific Pallisades and Pasadena. Enters prestigious two-day meet at Palm Springs.

March 7th   Dennis Stock's photo essay, "Moody New Star," appears in *Life* magazine.

March 8th   Jimmy returns to Hollywood.

March 9th   Celebrity preview of *Eden* at New York's Astor Theater. Marilyn Monroe hands out programs. Jimmy does not attend.

March 10th   *Eden* opens at the Astor.

March 13th   Interview by Howard Thomson, "Another Dean Hits the Big League," appears in *The New York Times*.

March 14th   NBC's *Lever Brothers Lux Video Theatre*, "Life of Emile Zola." Interview with Jimmy follows broadcast.

March 21st   Rave review of Jimmy's performance in *Eden* appears in *Time* magazine.

March 27th   Hedda Hopper, reversing previous opinion, praises Jimmy's performance in *Eden*.

March 28th   *Rebel* begins shooting. In opening sequence, Natalie Wood's five-minute crying scene beats Bette Davis's all-time record set in *Winter Meeting* (1948).

April 2nd   Warner Brothers again extends Jimmy's contract. Slated to play Jett Rink in movie version of Edna Ferber's *Giant*.

April 4th   Screenwriters Fred Guiol and Evan Moffat finalize script for *Giant*.

April 10th   *Eden* opens nationwide.

April 14th   Warner Brothers announces: "Dean to play Grazziano role in *Somebody Up There Likes Me.*"

May 1st   Night shooting begins at Griffith Park Planetarium. Switchboards of downtown Los Angeles papers flooded with callers (who've spotted glare of arc and spot lights) reporting raging forest fire.

May 6th   CBS's *Schlitz Playhouse*, "The Unlighted Road," with Pat Hardy.

May 21st   *Giant* begins shooting.

May 25th   *Rebel* filming ends. Jimmy and Ray are last to leave set.

May 28th & 29th   Races car in Santa Barbara, California.

June 3rd   Joins *Giant* filming in progress.

July 8th   *Giant* cast and crew leave for Marfa, Texas.

August 1st   Takes one year lease on house in Sherman Oaks.

August 12th   The *Hollywood Reporter*: "Jimmy Dean is studying German so that he can fight with Ursula Andress in two languages."

September 16th   Press release: "James Dean plans to go on racing kick when *Giant* ends."

September 17th Makes 30–second commercial for National Highway Committee with Gig Young. Signs off with: "And, remember. . .drive safely. . . because the life you save may be. . .*mine*"

September 21st Trades in Porsche Speedster for Porsche Spyder 550. Custom car artist, George Barris, paints "130" and "Little Bastard" on it.

September 22nd Finishes "Last Supper" scene in *Giant*.

September 29th Visits friend, Jeannette Mille, and gives her his Siamese cat, Marcus, a gift from Elizabeth Taylor. Attends party in Malibu.

September 30th a.m. 8:00 a.m.: arrives at Competition Motors to check out Porsche with mechanic, Rolf Wutherich. 10:00 a.m.: Jimmy's father, Winton, and uncle, Charlie Nolan Dean, pay him a visit. Together they have an early lunch at Farmer's Market.

September 30th p.m. 1:30 p.m.: Jimmy and Rolf Wutherich, pick up Sanford Roth and Bill Hickman. Group departs for Salinas in two cars. 3:30 p.m.: outside Bakersfield, Jimmy, in Porsche, receives ticket for speeding. 5:45 p.m.: at intersection of routes 466 and 41, near Chalame, Porsche collides with Ford sedan driven by Donald Turnupseed. Wutherich is thrown free; Jimmy dies within seconds.

October 26th *Rebel Without a Cause* opens in New York.

1956

November 10th *Giant* opens in New York.

Compiled by David Loehr

ACKNOWLEDGMENTS

*Sight is bent to lick
your heart;
A liquid mouth dilutes
my thought.
Souls knit a nebula mat
We live here in every world
Secret loft in azure habitat.*
Untitled poem by James Dean

Of ALL THOSE WHO CONTRIBUTED so generously to this book, we would especially like to thank: Adeline Nall for her recollections; Martin Sheen for kindly allowing us to use his words as the introduction; Jerry Fagnani for his insights and generous loan of his collections; Antonia for giving us our bearings; Bob Miller, our editor at St. Martin's Press, without whose astonishing foresight and special pleading this book would not have come into existence and, by dint of whose Argus-eyed persistence, it materialized; our agent, Carol Mann, whose diplomacy kept the lines clear; Dana Ohlmeyer for perspicacious persistence; Linn Varney for attention to detail above and beyond the call of duty; Frank Cafiero, Jerry Cimbol and Black Ink Typographers for their care in setting the type for this book; and last, but not least, Susann Dalton, Terrence and Katy.

We would also like to acknowledge the following people whose help and cooperation have been invaluable in the creation of this book: Archives of Performing Arts at the University of Southern California, John Abrams, Sid Avery, Peter Beard, Sylvia Bongionvanni, Nick Callaway, Hugh Caughell, John Coplans, Jackie Curtis, George Dudley, Lynne Edelson, Larry and Sandy Engle, Michael Flanagan, Richard Gearin, Mark Glabman, Lester Glassner, Larry Goldman, Suzanne Goldstein, Howard Greenberg, Bob Guccione, Marie Guisti, Ron Ianitello, Marvin Israel, Sara Jones, Wayne Jones, Wilbur Justus, Bhupendra Karia, Robert Knutson, John Kobal, H. Kwan Lau, Dorothy Loehr, Thomas A. Miller, Neal Peters, Phillip Pocock, Ivan Powell, Sylvia Price, Lenny Prussack, Robert Pulley, Paul Quatrochi, Robert W. Richards, Bob Rodriguez, Beulah Roth, Karen Sandt, Richard Sassin, Stuart Shaw, Irwin Sirota, David Smith, Rubert Smith, Matt Stampalia, Phil Stern, John Stevens, Dennis Stock, Rhinehart Straub, Phillip Swenson, Richard Taddei, Allen and Florence Terhune, John Tompkins, Regina Trapp, Vincent Vallarino, Warner Communications, Harry and Ann Warr, Lyman Wickwire, Marlin Wilson, Marcus and Marylou Winslow, Daniel Wolf, Christina Yuin, George Zeno and 380 Gallery.

THE CLIP JOINT
AMERICA'S SMARTEST
POODLE SALON
CR. 1-0092
420
POOD
PUPP
For S